GBC

GOVERNMENT BEYOND THE CENTRE

SERIES EDITOR: GERRY STOKER

The world of sub-central government and administration – including local authorities, quasi-governmental bodies and the agencies of public–private partnerships – has seen massive changes in recent years and is at the heart of the current restructuring of government in the United Kingdom and other Western democracies.

The intention of the *Government Beyond the Centre* series is to bring the study of this often-neglected world into the mainstream of social science research, applying the spotlight of critical analysis to what has traditionally been the preserve of institutional public administration approaches.

Its focus is on the agenda of change currently being faced by sub-central government, the economic, political and ideological forces that underlie it, and the structures of power and influence that are emerging. Its objective is to provide up-to-date and informative accounts of the new forms of government, management and administration that are emerging.

The series will be of interest to students and practitioners of politics, public and social administration, and all those interested in the reshaping of the governmental institutions which have a daily and major impact on our lives.

GOVERNMENT BEYOND THE CENTRE

SERIES EDITOR: GERRY STOKER

Local Democracy and Local Government

Edited by

Lawrence Pratchett

and

David Wilson

in association with
CLD Ltd

First published 1996 by
MACMILLAN PRESS LTD
Houndmills, Basingstoke, Hampshire RG21 6XS
and London
Companies and representatives
throughout the world

ISBN 0–333–66432–9 hardcover
ISBN 0–333–66433–7 paperback

A catalogue record for this book is available
from the British Library.

10   9   8   7   6   5   4   3   2   1
05   04   03   02   01   00   99   98   97   96

Copy-edited and typeset by Povey–Edmondson
Okehampton and Rochdale, England

Printed in Hong Kong

Series Standing Order

If you would like to receive future titles in this series as they are published, you
can make use of our standing order facility. To place a standing order please
contact your bookseller or, in case of difficulty, write to us at the address
below with your name and address and the name of the series. Please state with
which title you wish to begin your standing order. (If you live outside the UK
we may not have the rights for your area, in which case we will forward your
order to the publisher concerned.)

Standing Order Service, Macmillan Distribution Ltd,
Houndmills, Basingstoke, Hampshire, RG21 6XS, England

Contents

v

List of Tables and Figures

Tables

Figures

Notes on the Contributors

Chris Game is Senior Lecturer in Local Government at the Institute of Local Government Studies (INLOGOV), University of Birmingham.

Alan Greer is Senior Lecturer in Politics, University of the West of England, Bristol.

Paul Hoggett is Professor and Associate Director, Centre for Social and Economic Research, University of the West of England, Bristol.

George Jones is Professor of Government at the London School of Economics and Political Science.

Hilary Kitchin is an Information Officer at the Local Government Information Unit.

Steve Leach is Professor of Local Government at De Montfort University, Leicester.

Martin Loughlin is Professor of Planning and Environmental Law, University of Manchester.

Anne Phillips is Professor of Politics, London Guildhall University.

Lawrence Pratchett is Senior Research Fellow in Local Government in the Department of Public Policy and Managerial Studies, De Montfort University, Leicester.

Colin Rallings is Director of the *Local Government Chronicle's* Election Centre at Plymouth University.

John Stewart is Professor of Local Government and Administration at the Institute of Local Government Studies (INLOGOV), University of Birmingham.

Gerry Stoker is Professor of Politics, University of Strathclyde, and co-ordinator of the five-year ESRC Local Governance Research Project.

Michael Temple is Senior Lecturer in Politics at Staffordshire University.

Michael Thrasher is Director of the *Local Government Chronicle's* Election Centre at Plymouth University.

Tony Travers is Director of Research, Greater London Group, London School of Economics and Political Science.

David Wilson is Professor of Public Administration and Head of the Department of Public Policy and Managerial Studies, De Montfort University, Leicester.

Melvin Wingfield is a Research Student in the Department of Public Policy and Managerial Studies, De Montfort University, Leicester.

Foreword

This book is an important addition to the work of the Commission for Local Democracy (CLD). It provides specially prepared versions of ten of the Commission's original research reports, as well as additional analysis of the Commission's findings and recommendations. Being rooted in the research of the CLD, this volume both complements its work and adds new dimensions to the debate which the Commission has begun.

The CLD was launched on 10 November 1993 to enquire into the state of local democracy in England and Wales and to consider its future. As an independent body our remit was not constrained by existing political or institutional concerns, nor directed by a particular ideological agenda. The Commissioners included former leaders of all three major parties in local government, as well as academics and former public servants. Our terms of reference gave us scope to investigate the definition and purpose of local democracy and its present institutional structure, to analyse the contribution made by other bodies involved in local administration, to draw upon the lessons to be learnt from the practice of local democracy in other countries, and to identify new forms of democratic participation. Consequently, we were able to consider the theory and practice of local democracy and to make recommendations on how democracy might be enhanced, both within the institutions of local government and beyond.

The Commission was created at a time of widespread fear on the part of many democrats that a vital element of the constitutional mix – the local element – has withered and is in danger of disappearing altogether. The centralisation of many services, the circumvention of local government and the diminution of local politics have all compounded to foster a democracy that increasingly ignores and belittles all things local and which gives excessive emphasis to national politics. The persistently low turn-out at local elections and the tendency for them to be used as indicators of national party preferences are symptomatic of this trend. The practice and habits of democracy at local level, which remains the foundation of our national democratic culture, are in retreat. We were concerned that, in recent years, democracy has become interpreted through the citizen as a consumer rather than an active participant in the political process. Against this background we set out to examine the challenges facing local democracy and to make recommendations about how its institutions might be modified.

The Commission was not alone in its concern. During our deliberations we were aware of other major research programmes being conducted by the Economic and Social Research Council, the Joseph Rowntree Foundation, the Local Government Management Board and the Department of the Environment. All touched on local democracy as part of their activities. Consequently, we saw part of our task as bringing together material from this research. Early in the Commission's life we established a sub-committee consisting of the late Kieron Walsh, Gerry Stoker, David Clark and Roger Jeffries which oversaw the Commission's research programme. Researchers were commissioned to produce their reports to tight deadlines within specific terms of reference. In total the CLD sponsored sixteen separate reports which it published between May 1994 and November 1995 and which covered a broad cross-section of political research. Much, though not all, is covered in this book. Copies of all of the Commission's research reports, as well as its final report *Taking Charge: The Rebirth of Democracy*, can be obtained from the Commission for Local Democracy, University of Greenwich, Churchill House, Wellington Street, London SE18 6PF.

In bringing the Commission's research together and providing fresh analysis of its findings, this book makes a valuable contribution to the debate on local democracy. Nothing but radical change can halt the drain of local democratic activity from British politics. This book develops the themes that were closest to our deliberations and which underpin the radical recommendations which we have made for the rebirth of local democracy.

SIMON JENKINS
Chair of the Commission for Local Democracy

Preface

The Commission for Local Democracy was launched in November 1993 to inquire into the nature of local democracy in England and Wales and to consider its future development. Between then and the publication of its final report in June 1995, the Commission produced sixteen reports which guided its thinking and informed its final recommendations. This collection of essays incorporates ten specially commissioned versions of those reports, as well as two chapters contributed by the editors. This volume, therefore, both complements and develops the work of the Commission.

The co-operation of all the authors (especially those who had to fillet their original papers) was exemplary. The publishing deadlines were necessarily tight to retain topicality and without their cheerful co-operation this project would have run into the sand. We wish to thank all of them for making our task as editors considerably easier than it might have been.

A number of others also deserve acknowledgement for their support and assistance. David Clark, until recently Director of the Commission for Local Democracy, was an enthusiastic initiator of this project. Gerry Stoker provided careful guidance throughout, especially over the difficult decision of what papers to include and what to leave out. Our publisher, Steven Kennedy, was his usual enthusiastic self, offering encouragement from the outset and keeping the deadline in the forefront of our minds throughout. Our respective families have put up with much while we pressed on with the task in hand. Finally, we gratefully acknowledge the generous co-operation of CLD Ltd, and especially that of its chairperson, Dennis Reed, in allowing copyright material to be published for a wider readership in book form. We hope all involved will regard the end product as worthwhile.

LAWRENCE PRATCHETT
DAVID WILSON

1 Local Government unა Siege

Lawrence Pratchett and David Wilson

Setting the scene

The establishment of the Commission for Local Democracy (CLD) in November 1993 reflected widespread concern not only about elected local government but about all forms of democratic activity at sub-national level. In a nutshell there was a fear that the 'local' element in our democratic mix had withered and was in danger of extinction. British politics had 'become too exclusively national'[1] with too much power concentrated in London. The centralist tendencies of post-war governments had, the CLD's final report argued, become excessive.[2] In order to examine these claims this book incorporates specially commissioned versions of ten of the sixteen CLD research papers. Additionally, the editors provide a critical analysis of both the diagnosis and prescriptions offered by the Commission.

The relationship between local government and local democracy and, indeed, the traditional interdependence of the two, is central to this book. This is not to suggest that the relationship has ever been unproblematic; idealistic pictures about a supposedly previous 'golden age' of elected local government need to be treated with caution. Indeed, for academics such as Jim Bulpitt it is difficult 'to equate, automatically, local democracy and local authorities', and he is not sure that 'local democracy, in that sense, is a necessary component of democracy in late twentieth century Britain'. Commentators who 'argued that local government was all good' have, Bulpitt maintains, an uncritically idealistic view of the institution.[3] Advocates of reform need to pay attention to critics of elected local government who do not see it as a haven of democracy but rather as a sector in which producer interests are dominant. This collection of essays provides a solid research base for an informed analysis of local government and local democracy in contemporary Britain not simply as an end in itself but as a means to an end, namely offering prescriptions for securing the future health of sub-national democracy.

1

The CLD's final report argued:

> We do not believe that the present state of local government in Britain can be improved merely by tinkering with the relationship between the centre and localities. This relationship is deeply flawed, its flaws contributing to the emasculation of local democracy since the war.[4]

The Commission's recommendations are most radical when considering the internal structure of local government, the relationship between localities and the centre and the nature of citizenship at local level. For the CLD these areas provide the key to a revival of local democracy. A central question for this book, therefore, is whether the CLD's proposals really do offer a way forward for local democracy. Indeed, is contemporary local democracy really in crisis? In 1966, for example, William Robson wrote *Local Government in Crisis*,[5] lamenting the possible demise of elected local government, and this was itself an update of earlier texts written in 1926 and 1947! This book examines what is distinctive about the current so-called crisis.

This introductory chapter has three major aims:

1. To set the context of local government and local democracy in contemporary Britain, especially by reference to recent changes and events which give rise to a sense of crisis in the institutions and practice of local democracy.
2. To emphasise the fundamental importance of local democracy, and debates about its form and practice, in relation to local government.
3. To introduce the other chapters in the book by identifying key themes, issues and concerns.

It will undertake the first two of these tasks by considering the various changes that have led to the apparent crisis in local government before going on to explain how the remainder of the book will address the issues in more detail.

Local governance

Elected local government is but one element of what has become known as 'local governance', a term which seeks to capture the shift away from a system in which local authorities were the key actors in their localities to one where decision-making authority and service provision is *shared* among a range of agencies. Local authorities are increasingly working alongside other public, private and voluntary sector organisations in providing services for a locality. Cochrane, for example, argues that 'into the 1990s . . . it will be no longer possible to equate local politics with the politics of local government, since many of the most important decisions will be taken in quite different forums'.[6] The system has become increasingly differentiated and fragmented. Elected local government, he predicted, could become increasingly marginalised as an element of local governance. Most notably, the 'democratic' element in local service provision seems set to become increasingly blurred.

New Right theory[7] provides a sophisticated rationale for combining fragmentation and democracy. The government's own rationale for reduced direct service provision by elected local government is set out most clearly in the 1991 White Paper *Competing for Quality*:

> The Government's model for local government in the 1990s and into the 21st century is that of the enabling authority. Here the task of local authorities lies in identifying requirements, setting priorities, determining standards of service and finding the best way to meet these standards and ensuring they are met. This implies a move away from the traditional model of local authorities providing virtually all services directly and a greater separation of the functions of service delivery from strategic responsibilities.[8]

The concept of 'enabling' has occupied a central place in Conservative central government thinking in the 1980s and 1990s. It is, however, an 'infinitely elastic' concept with many different meanings. At one extreme is the position taken by Nicholas Ridley[9] in his pamphlet *The Local Right: Enabling Not Providing*. The task of the enabling authority was to find a range of other organisations to provide services and carry out its responsibilities. The role of the local authority would no longer be that of the universal provider. But it would continue to have a key role in ensuring that there is adequate provision to meet needs, in encouraging the various providers to develop and maintain the necessary services, and where necessary, in providing grant support or other assistance to get projects started and to ensure that services are provided and affordable for the clients concerned. A very different model[10] is based on enabling communities to resolve their problems and meet their needs in the most effective way. The second approach differs from the first in avoiding any assumption that the authority will not provide services itself. The test to be applied is: which is the most effective way? In practice, as Leach *et al.* remind us,[11] 'enabling' has come to mean all things to all people.

Directly elected local authorities have, in recent years, lost service provision to single-purpose bodies. These agencies include: urban development corporations (UDCs); training and enterprise councils (TECs – in England and Wales); London Regional Transport (LRT); housing action trusts (HATs); grant maintained schools and the Funding Agency for Schools; further education colleges; and registered housing associations. In addition, from April 1995, the establishment of new free-standing police authorities has meant the further demise of local authority responsibilities.

As Stoker[12] notes, there is a division of opinion about whether such local institutional diversification represents a problem or an opportunity:

> From a traditional view the lessening of the role of local authorities is seen as a weakening of local democracy. As the only agencies subject to local electoral control the relative reduction in the dominance of local authorities might be seen as a loss for local democracy and more broadly for effective local government because of the increased fragmentation and complexity of the emerging system. On the other hand the forms of direct participation offered through some of the new agencies of local governance and the capacity of these agencies to work together to tackle a range of social and economic needs in localities might be seen as a gain for local democracy and government.

John Stewart (see Chapter 9) laments the growth of what he calls a 'new magistracy', non-elected, largely central government appointed personnel, controlling an increasing proportion of service provision at local level. Stewart's major concern is the ability, or rather the lack of ability, of local people to hold such bodies to account. William Waldegrave,[13] however, adopts a very different perspective arguing that the Government has 'broken crucial new ground in strengthening accountability' by its reforms. Answering John Stewart's 'new magistracy' claims Waldegrave observes:

> We have to ask who is likely to be able actually to run a school more efficiently, effectively and with a greater sense of responsi-

bility to pupils and parents; its own headmaster and governors, or officials within the local council structure? Let us not forget, in the midst of all this talk about a 'democratic deficit', that there was very little democratic about the culture of 'the man in Whitehall' – or, in this case, Townhall – 'knows best'.

The emerging world of local governance presents both potential drawbacks and opportunities. Those concerned with the future of local democracy need to develop their ideas in the context of the complexity of local governance.

Compulsory competitive tendering

Alongside the above developments an increasing number of local authority functions have been subjected to the process of compulsory competitive tendering (CCT). The 1988 Local Government Act was particularly important in specifying a range of activities which were to be subjected to competitive tender. Subsequent legislation (1992) incorporated provision for compulsory tendering of a number of so-called 'white-collar' services on a rolling programme by the end of the 1990s. Interestingly, the private sector did not sweep in and take over services wholesale as many had predicted. As Table 1.1 shows, local authority direct service organisations (DSOs) have retained the bulk of contracts.

The share of business by *value* in England and Wales provided by local authorities in 1994 was 75.9 per cent – so six years after the

TABLE 1.1 **DSO success by % number of contracts, June 1994–June 1995: England and Wales (Scotland in brackets)**

	June 1995	*Dec 1994*	*June 1994*
Building cleaning	42.5 (87.6)	40.8	40.5
Refuse collection	61.4 (88.7)	64.4	67.6
Other cleaning	62.3 (100)	63.7	66.3
Vehicle maintenance	76.7 (86.5)	74.9	75.1
School catering	75.0 (90.2)	75.1	86.0
Other catering	61.9 (N/A)	67.8	69.8
Grounds maintenance	56.3 (76.7)	57.8	58.9
Leisure management	85.9 (99)	84.8	85.8
Average	**59.7**	**58.8**	**61.8**

Source: LGMB Surveys, June, Dec 1994, June 1995.

1988 Act and the advent of CCT, DSOs still retain three-quarters of the business. In Scotland the proportion is even higher. The greatest impact of CCT on local government has, however, been *organisational* rather than financial. Local authorities have been obliged to differentiate between purchaser and provider units. New patterns of management have mushroomed as DSOs challenged to win contracts. Fragmentation *within* individual local authorities has become the norm. As Leach *et al.*[14] have observed, 'one of the most powerful organisational effects of the Government's post-1987 programme of legislation has been to fragment – or differentiate – the activities of a local authority into their component parts'. The ethos of service provision has, in many local authorities, changed beyond recognition. Rao and Young[15] have shown that although CCT would not have been established without being imposed, it is now sufficiently entrenched in practice to make a return to non-competitive ways of working unlikely, even if the elements of competition were removed. Tendering is part of local governance; prescriptions for the future need to recognise this.

Fragmentation and finance

Fragmentation and differentiation characterise service provision at local level. As noted earlier, the advent of local governance has meant that elected local government is now but one part of a complex mosaic. Public/private partnerships have become increasingly widespread; greater reliance on the private and voluntary sectors for service provision is, albeit in a non-uniform manner, becoming the norm. Elected local authorities are no longer in a monopoly situation. Prescriptions which hark back idealistically to bygone eras fail to recognise the deeply rooted cultural change which has developed since the early 1980s. Blueprints for the future need to take account of contemporary realities and not build upon a largely illusory golden era. As we enter a period of alternative service delivery the respective strengths and weaknesses of local authority, voluntary sector, quango and private sector provision must be high on any reform agenda.

Central to vibrant local democracy is a system of local taxation which enables local authorities to shape their own destinies. No such system exists. Loughlin provides a detailed account of the financial powers acquired by central government under the Rates Act, 1984 and other legislative enactments. The net result of this legislation was a substantial weakening of the financial autonomy of local authorities. Local authorities had, in effect, become for the government, administrative agencies which provided certain services. Issues of *local* democratic control were perceived as secondary. In the mid-1980s, 60 per cent of local expenditure was covered by locally determined taxes. Today that figure has declined to under 20 per cent. Local spending patterns are, to a considerable extent, being determined by central government SSAs – Standard Spending Assessments (central government's calculation of what local authorities ought to be spending, given the character of their population and geography). As Loughlin[16] observes, local council budgets now tend to cluster around their SSAs – thereby leading to a system 'in which local authorities assume a degree of formal responsibility out of all proportion to their ability actually to control services'. The undermining of local democracy stemmed from central government wanting to control local spending and taxing; flourishing local democracy needs underpinning by an appropriate financial system as earlier reformers such as Layfield (1976) have recognised.[17]

Electoral demise?

In Chapter 4 Rallings *et al.* paint a picture of a local polity which, while not devoid of activity and achievement, nevertheless faces a number of severe difficulties. Less than half the electorate (38 per cent in 1995, comprising 40.3 per cent in the English shire districts and 32.6 per cent in the metropolitan boroughs) bothers to take the opportunity to vote in local elections; councillors are drawn from a relatively narrow cross-section of the public and significant numbers of them do not bother to seek re-election. National rather than local issues are often seen to predominate at local council elections. To quote a *Local Government Chronicle* editorial:[18]

> Labour's landslide in last week's [May 1995] elections was bad for local government. Nothing could have been more insulting than to have virtually every voter treat the local elections as a referendum on central government.

Referring to the same (May 1995) elections Jones and Stewart observed:[19]

> Anyone concerned for the welfare of local government should be worried about the recent elections. The low turn-out (38 per cent)

undermines those seeking strong local democracy. It weakens the position of local authorities in dealing with central government which can claim a wider electoral base.

The *Local Government Chronicle* editorial must be treated with caution. When, as with the 1995 results, there is a large national swing local variations are harder to detect but they are nevertheless present. As Jones and Stewart[20] show, compared with 1991 the decline in the Conservative vote was only 1 per cent in Norwich and 3 per cent in Bristol, yet in Rochester it was 19 per cent and in Southampton 15 per cent. The Liberal Democrat vote increased by 15 per cent in Sheffield but fell by 9 per cent in Plymouth. The Labour vote dropped by 3 per cent in Sheffield but increased by 22 per cent in the Wirral. Jones and Stewart conclude:

> Those who see only national trends do not look at actual results. Let them ponder Epsom and Ewell, Elsbridge and Stroud whose councils contain – as well as Labour, Conservatives and Liberal Democrats – Ratepayers, Independents and Greens. It is wrong to regard local elections as just an opinion poll on the way people will vote at a general election.

As Wilson and Game[21] show, local elections are not simply national elections writ small. Local issues and local personalities are far from irrelevant in council elections although their salience clearly varies from locality to locality.

A major concern is that the constant demeaning of local politics and its relegation to a place far below national politics is inexorably eroding the fundamental strengths of local democratic institutions. There is, therefore, a desperate need, articulated in the CLD's prescriptions, to raise the level of interest and turnout in local elections. Technical changes could be useful in this context. In summer 1995, for example, Derby City Council asked the Home Secretary for permission to hold local elections at weekends. As an attempt to try and improve turnout this should be welcomed. What is certain is that no democratic institution can be considered strong and secure with the current low levels of electoral participation.

Accountability

Much of the debate about recent developments in local government has lamented the shift away from public accountability mechanisms such as elected local government and its replacement by 'the very different and much weaker conception of accountability through the market satisfaction of consumers and through contract compliance, an accountability in the hands of accountants'.[22] The danger, however, is to fall back on existing patterns of political accountability as though they were unproblematic whereas, as Hirst argues, they themselves need supplementing in ways that will give greater power to citizens. There is an overwhelming tendency to react to the rise of local quangos, CCT and the like with an uncritical acceptance of the virtues of past and present patterns of local democracy.

The nature of public accountability has invariably been at the heart of debate about local democracy. Too often the non-elected element has been dismissed out of hand. As Ken Young argues,[23] the actual activities, priorities and motivations of non-elected bodies need to be examined before dismissing them (simply because they are not directly elected) as being inherently inferior to, or less desirable than, elected local government. 'Being caught up as I am in the public/private/voluntary/community partnerships in regeneration persuades me that accountability has not withered, nor is it in crisis. It has simply begun to develop along lines which complement the elective mechanisms.' Young emphasises that it is important to move debate on and to recognise the subtle complexity of accountability in the context of both elected and non-elected bodies. 'What we are presented with in many of the arguments about accountability is a false dichotomy. Accountability is not an "either/or" question; it is a "how much and in what ways?" question.' Zeal for elected local government should not lead to a cursory dismissal as 'non-accountable' of all non-elected agencies operating at local level.

Recent research shows the population as having relatively little knowledge about existing patterns of local democracy. The Widdicombe Report (1986)[24] found that less than one-third of respondents could name any of their councillors and barely a half could correctly identify their county or regional council. A study for the Department of the Environment (1992)[25] found that 'respondents exhibited quite a broad knowledge of which services the council provided (but that) interest in local politics was not high'. Allegations of corruption (e.g. Lambeth, West Wiltshire, Copeland, Sunderland) have done little to enhance local government's image. To again echo Hirst, the existing patterns of political accountability are not unproblematic.

Any reform strategy needs to face up to contemporary realities. Indeed councils themselves have recognised the need to develop more consumer oriented cultures. Many local authorities have established a wide range of initiatives to improve the quality of their services and get 'closer to their customers': from corporate logos to neighbourhood offices, from front-line staff training to public attitude surveys, from council newspapers to the systematic monitoring of public complaints. Some have also pioneered customer contracts and guarantees: the publicised specification of quality standards, backed by guarantees of action and compensation in the event of those standards not being met. Edinburgh City Council, for example, guarantees that all council housing emergency repairs will be carried out within three hours – and the guarantee is monitored by a Tenants' Federation.

The National Consumer Council report, *Consumer Concerns 1995*, provides some evidence that the efforts local authorities have made to get 'closer to their public' are bearing fruit.[26] To find out what people thought about their local services MORI was commissioned to ask a number of questions to a cross-section of the public and to compare the responses with those given four years earlier in 1991. Consumer satisfaction with services individually and services provision as a whole has increased. A clear majority (61 per cent) of respondents agreed that the quality of local council services was good, an increase of 10 points over the 1991 survey. Customers were also asked about specific services. Nine in ten people were satisfied with refuse collection (91 per cent), again an increase of 10 points since 1991. Although council tenants were more satisfied with council services generally there was no change in satisfaction (62 per cent) with council housing, and the level of dissatisfaction (24 per cent) was also unchanged. The majority of people who contacted the council in the period 1993–5 found staff friendly (80 per cent) and helpful (76 per cent). An increasing number of councils are seeking the views of their consumers through consultation exercises; the majority of consumers polled (52 per cent) thought that councils kept them fully or fairly well informed – an increase of 17 per cent on 1991. There is, of course, always room for more information to be made available and for complaints procedures to be improved, but the 1995 survey was overwhelmingly positive in tone.

Getting to be more responsive in service delivery is part of the challenge facing local government. The other element in the challenge is in securing wider community involvement in local decision-making. One means of community involvement – the referendum – is rarely used. At national level referenda have been used over European and devolution decisions; at local level a small number of authorities have conducted informal polls. Most notable was the Strathclyde referendum in 1994 on the government's proposal for the future of the water industry. A 71.5 per cent turnout was achieved – a figure which contrasts sharply with voter turnouts in local elections. Coventry likewise held a referendum on increasing its annual rate in 1981. Perhaps referenda offer a way forward – indeed, they are relatively common elsewhere in Europe. In Germany a number of Länder have, or are introducing, the right to hold referenda in local government. Italian communes use them as does Danish local government. Referenda can be instituted by either the council or its citizens. They might precede certain decisions; be taken between decisions and implementation in effect to ratify or endorse; or be taken at any time. As the CLD's final report notes[27] the subject matter could either be limited or open-ended. Despite the risks associated with reducing complex issues to simple questions, local referenda 'do give citizens direct participation in decisions and open debate on questions of possible long term importance to communities wider than the forum of the council'.[28] As part of a strategy designed to draw citizens into local decision-making, referenda merit consideration.

Councillors

At the core of traditional electoral democracy lies the local councillor. Only 25 per cent are women, nearly 80 per cent are over 45 years of age, and a third are retired.[29] Such aggregate data, though interesting, have their pitfalls. They can all too easily prompt misleading generalisations. 'They may obscure real and significant contrasts among councillors in different parts of the country, on different types of councils, and from different parties. They can also be seen as implying that "representative government" is more about trying to produce, like President Clinton's 'Mirror on America' Cabinet, a socio-economic cross-section or statistical reflection of the electorate, rather than a representation of ideas and ideals'.[30] Aggregate data must always be treated with caution. For example in Birmingham (1992) there were 17 ethnic minority members on the 117-seat City Council:

This 15 per cent might seem like a not unreasonable representation of the city's approximately 20 per cent ethnic minority
population – until you consider the sheer diversity of the population: the Afro-Caribbeans; the Kashmiri restaurant owners, taxi
drivers and textile industry outworkers; the Punjabi Sikhs, with
their prominent role in the local economy; the small business-
owning Gujuratis from both India and East Africa; the smaller
Chinese and Vietnamese communities. Several of these groups are
bound to regard themselves as *un*represented – not merely under-
represented – on the City Council in any direct racial, religious or
cultural sense, and if this is true in Birmingham, it is even more so
in most other towns and cities.[31]

The social representativeness of councillors (or lack of it) is not
the only problem. Their workload, considering their part-time
status, is excessive. Widdicombe (1986) (see note 23) found that
the average time spent by members of all types of authority on their
council work was estimated at 74 hours per 'typical' month. Alice
Bloch's 1991 survey of ex-councillors found an average reported
time of 82 hours per month.[32] One effect of CCT has been to
enhance the power of officers at the expense of councillors. Indeed
'enabling councils' have become more 'hands off' organisations than
in the past which has made them less appealing for some councillors.
One in four councillors today has less than three years' experience.
There is considerable turnover at each election with the number
voluntarily standing down greatly exceeding the number defeated in
elections. The turnover in London boroughs (1978–90) is 50 per
cent; 40 per cent in English counties (1981–93); and in shire districts
(1986–91) 40–47 per cent. Councillors, with all their diversity, remain
an essential democratic ingredient in our local government system.
There is, as Rao[33] stresses, urgent need to address the role of
councillors in the light of their expectations, motivation and potential contribution. Their new role with the advent of enabling
authorities requires careful attention if an essential ingredient of
local democracy is not to be marginalised.

Democratic deficit

The current restructuring of local government in England, Scotland
and Wales means a significant reduction in the number of elected
local authorities. The position in England is least clear given the
creation of a second Local Government Commission in 1995 under

Sir David Cooksey to look at possible unitary status for a further 21 authorities. This new Commission proposed eight new unitary authorities based on nine existing districts in England. If their proposals are accepted this will mean a total of 46 new unitaries in England following the 1992–5 reviews. There are, by 1997, likely to be some 425 local authorities in England and Wales compared to the 1725 which existed thirty years earlier. Looking at Wales and Scotland in greater detail (given that the final position is known here) there has been a dramatic decline in the number of primary units over little more than 20 years:

> As a result of the two reorganisations in 1974–75 and 1996, the number of local government units will have fallen by 159 in Wales and 398 in Scotland. The forthcoming reorganisation itself cuts the number of separate units by 51% in Wales and 51% in Scotland, thereby confirming the long-term decline in the number of local authorities in the UK.[34]

Yet *before* this recent reorganisation the average size of English and Welsh local authorities was ten times or more the size of authorities in the rest of Europe (see Table 1.2).

Fewer authorities means fewer councillors. In Wales, 22 new unitary authorities will replace the existing 45 councils with effect from 1 April 1996. The number of elected councillors will be reduced from 1977 to 1286, a 38 per cent reduction. In Scotland, 32 single-tier authorities are set to replace the existing 65 from 1 April 1996. The three all-purpose island authorities have remained and 29 new unitary authorities will subsume the existing regional and district councils. Some 1695 district, regional and island councillors will be reduced to 1245. Their workload, however, remains substantial as it does in England, where some reduction in councillor numbers is also likely following the deliberations of the Local Government Commission.

TABLE 1.2 Average population size of local authorities, 1994

England and Wales	122 740	Italy	6 717
Sweden	29 527	West Germany	2 694
Norway	8 891	France	1 320
Denmark	17 963		

Note: The England and Wales figures include only principal authorities, i.e. *not* parish, town and community councils which are not universal and are mostly very small with very limited service responsibilities.

The 'democratic deficit' associated with the reduction of numbers of locally elected councillors is part of a broader debate about the changing nature of public accountability at local level.[35] Clearly, the role of councillors has been affected by the increased use of single purpose non-elected bodies operating locally. The dominant role of local authorities in direct service provision has been challenged and elected local government is now only part of a complex mosaic of local governance. As Leach *et al.*[36] observe, much of the 'new legislation implies (or requires) a hands-off approach from councillors in relation to the detailed management of services, a broad change in emphasis from the organisational role to the representational role'. In the context of a diverse and fragmented pattern of local governance in which elected members have a less direct operational role is it in fact unreasonable for there to be fewer councillors? Is not a more pressing priority to search for new forms of accountability for those non-elected bodies which are delivering services at local level rather than simply lamenting the demise of an often idealised directly elected element?[37] Are more councillors necessarily the answer if, once in office, they have relatively little influence on policy initiation and implementation? True, their community representational role remains but is this in itself (in an era of 'customer charters' and performance 'league tables') sufficient reason to clamour for yet more elected members? Jones and Stewart[38] have no doubts:

> Local government is enhanced as local democracy by the closeness of council members to those they represent. A greater number of members embeds local government into the grass roots. They make local government more responsive to the local community and understanding of its wishes and needs.

Fragmentation of agencies has not helped elected local authorities to articulate a common agenda for a locality, but no other body can easily assume this role, particularly in relation to crucial issues which cross agency responsibilities like the environment, community safety and health. This offers a challenge to elected local government. Nevertheless, the reform debate must squarely face up to the shift from local government to governance and the associated need to manage local political, economic and social networks – the management of influence.

Renewing democracy requires a new framework for the local polity, a framework for the management of influence. It has been argued by Stoker[39] that a system of local governance needs a capacity for openness, deliberation and integrated action. Any strategy to breathe new life into local democracy needs to take these elements on board. Openness is at the heart of good local governance. While citizens might decide not to avail themselves of the opportunities to participate because they believe that their interests are already being protected, the value of openness does not automatically mean large-scale, ongoing direct participation:

> It rests its case on the richness of democratic practice and the options for extending participation that are available. These options should operate without making overwhelming time demands and in a way that enhances the broad social representativeness of those involved.[40]

Good local governance also requires opportunities for deliberation. Alternatives and possibilities need to be widely discussed. 'Indeed it is difficult to imagine how some of the more complex social and economic challenges we face can be comprehended, let alone tackled, without access to opportunities for deliberation'.[41] A system of local governance also needs to be judged by its capacity to provide an integrated approach to social and economic issues. Crucially, it requires the capacity to act. Governance recognises the interdependence of organisations. Indeed, the essence of governance is the interactive relationship between and within governmental and non-governmental forces. Recognition of these realities must shape the reform agenda.

Organisation of the book

The remaining chapters discuss in more detail the issues outlined above, and the ways in which they affect the relationship between local democracy and local government. They move from a general discussion of the theoretical and empirical context of local government and the institutions of local democracy, through a focus on the changing perceptions of the various actors involved in local democratic processes, to an analysis of the opportunities and prospects for local democracy and local government in the future.

In Chapter 2, Anne Phillips argues not only that democracy matters but, more specifically, that local democracy has much to commend it. Local democracy is particularly attractive because it decentralises power and provides opportunities for citizen participation in government. In the context of a widely perceived crisis in local government and democracy Martin Loughlin analyses the removal of discretion from local government and the near collapse of the conventions which have traditionally given it an important place in the British constitution. Hence Chapters 2 and 3 concentrate, in turn, on the theoretical foundations of local democracy, and the constitutional status of its institutional home, local government.

The following five chapters build upon this foundation. Colin Rallings, Michael Temple and Michael Thrasher (Chapter 4) delineate the nature of political participation at local level. Despite the current level of activity there are some very real problems. Less than half the population typically vote in local elections; the workload of councillors is excessive and they are increasingly drawn from the ranks of the retired, self-employed or unemployed. Recruitment of people to stand for council elections is becoming increasingly problematic and their reliance upon professional officers is on occasions too great. Rallings *et al.* delineate the many positive aspects of local political participation but emphasise that it is becoming increasingly difficult to sustain existing levels of interest.

George Jones and Tony Travers (Chapter 5) examine what ministers and civil servants think about local democracy and local government. Clearly, the attitude of senior civil servants and their political bosses towards local government is critical to local democracy's future. They show that civil servants have a more disparaging view of their local government counterparts than ministers and that there is a significant gap of understanding between civil servants and local government officers. The routine nature of many local government services appears to encourage some civil servants to believe that they possess 'Rolls Royce minds and local government officers . . . motor cyclists' minds'.

Pratchett and Wingfield (Chapter 6) argue that the underlying value systems and culture of public servants makes bureaucracies highly resistant to change and ensures a degree of stability and continuity in administrative processes and outcomes, despite extensive attempts at managerial reform. Based on detailed study of a number of local authorities they suggest that the public service ethos, as a political institution, has been able to mediate and obstruct the reform process, capturing and moderating transformation initiatives (many of which emanate from central government), and creating a 'sanitised' version of new public management that is more acceptable to the permanent officials.

Moving from the world of professional officers to that of political parties, Chris Game and Steve Leach (Chapter 7) examine the intensification of party domination of local government in the last decade. The more the current two-tier system is replaced by unitary authorities, the greater is likely to be the reduction of Independent councillors in both absolute and proportionate terms. This chapter is essentially a balance sheet of the pros and cons of party politics in local government. The increasingly prevalent 'balanced' authorities are examined in the context of their contribution to the development of local democracy.

The chapters by Alan Greer and Paul Hoggett (Chapter 8) and John Stewart (Chapter 9) focus on 'the quango debate': the rise of non-elected single purpose bodies operating at local level. This is one of the issues examined by the Nolan Committee on Standards in Public Life. Greer and Hoggett delineate the wide range of quangos which run local public services while Stewart suggests ways of making quangos more accountable. Quangos are central to any debate about local governance and local democracy; their direct accountability to the public is often non-existent. These chapters present ideas about 'democratising' local quangos and providing greater accountability to the local population.

John Stewart's piece plus the final three chapters offer prescriptions for revitalising local democracy and local government. In Chapter 10 Gerry Stoker further develops a number of the ideas put forward by Anne Phillips. He argues that local government must be seen as much more than simply a service provider; a wider vision of the virtues of *politics* within local public life needs to be engendered. 'Empowering' the citizen is central to Stoker's vision. The strategic role of local authorities in the fragmented world of local governance provides opportunities for shaping community interests. Experimentation (for example, different systems of voting; referenda; neighbourhood forums) is advocated with the aim of stimulating greater interest in local politics and local democracy.

Unlike many other European countries British local authorities have no 'power of general competence'. In, for example, France, Germany and Sweden local authorities have a general right to undertake any activities which they believe to be in the interests of their citizens unless such activities are specifically assigned to other bodies. They can, in other words, do anything they are not expressly forbidden by the law to undertake. In Chapter 11 Hilary Kitchin explores this power of general competence and sets it against the prevailing restrictive concept of *ultra vires*. If nothing else, the adoption of a power of general competence in the UK would have enormous symbolic value as a statement about the importance of local government.

In its final report, *Taking Charge: The Rebirth of Local Democracy*, the CLD argues that nothing but radical change can halt the drain of democratic activity from British local government. Among the CLD's 43 separate recommendations (see appendix for details) are proposals to have directly elected salaried council mayors/leaders who can serve a maximum of two consecutive terms. The report also advocates that councils should be elected by proportional representation and that there should be regular use of referenda. In short, a comprehensive reform of local democracy is proposed. The concluding chapter of this book evaluates the CLD's proposals for change and in the light of the empirical and normative analyses which these chapters offer asks to what extent they really do provide a prescription for the rebirth of local democracy.

Notes and references

1. Commission for Local Democracy (1995) *Taking Charge: The Rebirth of Local Democracy*, CLD/Municipal Journal Books, p.1.
2. Ibid.
3. Bulpitt, J. (1993) Review in *Public Administration*, vol. 71, no. 4, pp. 621–3.
4. Commission for Local Democracy (1995) *Taking Charge*, p. 2.
5. Robson, W. A. (1966) *Local Government in Crisis*, London: Allen & Unwin.
6. Cochrane, A. (1993) *Whatever Happened to Local Government?*, Buckingham: Open University Press, p. 124.
7. For a useful analysis of New Right theory, see King, D., 'From the Urban Left to the New Right: Normative Theory and Local Government', in Stewart, J. and Stoker, G. (eds) (1995) *Local Government in the 1990s*, Basingstoke: Macmillan, ch. 13.
8. HM Treasury (1991) *Competing for Quality*, Cm 1730 London: HMSO, p. 22.
9. Ridley, N. (1988) *The New Right: Enabling Not Providing*, London: Centre for Policy Studies, p. 17.
10. Stewart, J. and Stoker, G. (1988) *From Local Administration to Community Government*, London: Fabian Society.
11. See Leach, S. *et al.* (1994) *The Changing Organisation and Management of Local Government*, London: Macmillan, for a very good overview of the various models. Chapter 10 is particularly useful.
12. Stoker, G. (1995) 'The Struggle to Reform Local Government, 1970–1995', PAC Annual Conference, September, pp. 4, 5.
13. Waldegrave, W. (1993) 'The Reality of Reform and Accountability in Today's Public Sector', CIPFA/PFF Lecture, July 1993, pp. 10, 11.
14. Leach, *et al.* (1994) *The Changing Organisation and Management of Local Government*, p. 75.

15. Rao, N. and Young, K. (1995) *Competition, Contracts and Change: The Local Authority Experience of CCT*, York: Joseph Rowntree Foundation.
16. Loughlin, M. (1994) *The Constitutional Status of Local Government*, CLD Research Report No. 3, London: CLD Ltd, p. 19. See also Loughlin's chapter in this book..
17. Layfield Committee (1976) *Report of the Committee of Enquiry into Local Government Finance*, Cmnd 6543, London: HMSO.
18. 'Labour's Landslide Buries Local Issues', *Local Government Chronicle*, 12 May 1995, p. 9.
19. Jones, G. and Stewart, J., 'No Voters, No Democracy', *Local Government Chronicle*, 26 May 1995, p. 8.
20. Ibid, p. 8.
21. Wilson, D. and Game, C. (1994) *Local Government in the United Kingdom*, London: Macmillan, ch. 11.
22. Hirst, P. (1995) 'Quangos and Democratic Government', *Parliamentary Affairs*, vol. 48, no. 2, p. 341.
23. Young, K. (1994) 'Rethinking Accountability: An Issues Paper', QMC Public Policy Seminar (28 April 1994).
24. Widdicombe, D. (1986) *Report of the Committee of Inquiry into the Conduct of Local Authority Business*, London: HMSO.
25. Lynn, P. (1992) *Public Perceptions of Local Government: Its Finances and Services*, London: HMSO, p. 4.
26. National Consumer Council (1995) *Consumer Concerns 1995*, London: National Consumer Council.
27. Commission for Local Democracy (1995) *Taking Charge*, p. 30.
28. Ibid, p. 31.
29. Young, K. and Rao, N. (1994) *Coming to Terms with Change? The Local Government Councillor in 1993*, York: Joseph Rowntree Foundation.
30. Wilson and Game (1994) p. 212.
31. Ibid, p. 213.
32. Bloch, A. (1992) *The Turnover of Local Councillors*, York: Joseph Rowntree Foundation.
33. Rao, N. (1993) *Managing Change: Councillors and the New Local Government*, York: Joseph Rowntree Foundation.
34. Boyne, G., Jordan, G. and McVicar, M. (1995) *Local Government Reform: A Review of the Process in Scotland and Wales*, London: LGC/Joseph Rowntree Foundation, p. 68.
35. Wilson, D. (1994) 'Facing up to the Democratic Deficit', *Local Government Studies*, vol. 20, no. 2, pp. 193–201.
36. Leach *et al.* (1994) *The Changing Organisation*, p. 183.
37. Wilson, D. (1995) 'Chasing Shadows: Structural "Solutions", for Local Government', ECPR Joint Workshop on The Changing Local Governance of Europe, Bordeaux Joint Sessions.
38. Jones, G. and Stewart, J. (1993) 'When the Numbers Don't Add Up to Democracy', *Local Government Chronicle*, 8 January, p. 15.
39. Stoker, G. (1995) 'Local Governance: A Conceptual Challenge', ECPR Joint Workshop (see note 36 above), pp. 17, 18.
40. Ibid.
41. Ibid.

2 Why does Local Democracy Matter?

Anne Phillips

Introduction

The important issues of democracy no longer revolve around whether citizens should have an equal right to vote in deciding the composition of their governments. There are no interesting arguments against this principle, and none that could win significant popular support. All the questions start from that point onwards. How much more is necessary to deliver on the promise of democracy? Even in its most minimal formulations, democracy seems to imply that each citizen should carry equal weight; in practice it never achieves this. What else can or should be done to fulfil this promise? How much more democracy is possible without setting into motion forces that will prove anti-democratic? And what, if anything, do the different arguments imply about democracy at local level?

The case for democracy has always involved a mixture of the prudential and the ideal. Part of the argument is that the alternatives are just too dangerous, for if decisions are left in the hands of a non-accountable elite, there is too much scope for either tyranny or corruption. If the best policies could be determined with the precision that is sometimes claimed for the natural sciences, we might well choose to entrust ourselves to those most able to identify such policies and most efficient in carrying them through. But, contrary to what Plato argued nearly two and a half millennia ago, the art of good government is *not* comparable to the art of captaining a ship; and while most of us would prefer to see experts in charge of navigating the oceans or designing aircraft that fly, we do not normally consider politics as a matter of technical expertise. Handing decisions over to the experts only makes sense when the issues to be tackled can be regarded as questions of 'objective' truth; when society has established convincing mechanisms for identifying the appropriate experts; and when those selected to make the decisions can be trusted to set their own special interests aside.[1] If we are at all sceptical about any of these conditions, democracy is the safer alternative.

This prudential case for democracy has become particularly important in societies that contain a plurality of moral and religious and political beliefs, with no agreed basis for deciding between them. Part of the background to the development of democracy is a greater tolerance of disagreement and difference, a distaste for final truths about what is best for society, and a reluctance to impose our own convictions on others. This is not to say that people lack firm convictions, for each of us may have very strong views on what ought to be done or changed. But we have become accustomed to what can be quite fundamental disagreement about priorities and principles and goals, and this makes us more resistant to the claims of self-appointed 'guardians' who believe they know what is in our best interest. In the absence of clear and agreed principles for identifying the 'right' judges or the 'right' decisions, we have to fall back on what a freely organised people will choose. This may well result in ill-considered or inconsistent policies; it will certainly produce some policies that some of the citizens detest. It is still much safer than any non-democratic alternative.

This first part of the case for democracy is grounded in the difficulties of knowing which policies are right. It is reinforced by the second justification, which stresses the inevitable variation and conflict of interests. In the heterogeneous societies of the modern world, there is no transparently obvious common interest, or at least nothing that really stands up to scrutiny. At the most general level, we might say that everyone wants a good life, or that all citizens share a common interest in the prosperity and comfort of their nation. Beyond that, there is a complex of different, often opposing, interests, and when some of these gain more weight than the others, the resulting decisions will hardly be fair. The most high-minded amongst us still tend to view the world through our own experiences and interests; the only secure protection against this is the equal representation of all. Where experts are suspect and interests collide, decisions have to be kept accountable through some process of democratic control.

Both these arguments for democracy fit within a pattern of broadly instrumental justifications. They present democracy as a safety net, and they make no strong claims about democracy as a political ideal. The decisions arrived at through democratic pro-

cesses may well prove short-sighted; or they may block the aspira-
tions of one interest group without really satisfying the needs of any
other. The crucial point is that we have no basis for trusting to
anything else. The only legitimate ground for ruling issues outside
the scope of democratic decision-making would be the discovery of
some self-evident truths that no sane person could seriously deny.
When there is, on the contrary, extensive and legitimate disagreement, we are better served by drawing on the full range of citizen
opinion.

These largely prudential considerations are enough, in themselves,
to justify democracy, but may not tell us much about the kind of
democracy we need. The third justification (often described as a
'developmental' view of democracy) moves on to more ambitious
ground, and looks to active and extensive participation to raise the
whole quality of political life. In this more dynamic understanding
of democracy, political participation is often presented as part of an
upwards or downwards cycle.[2] Those who have had no experience of
participating in decisions – perhaps because the kind of job they do
denies them any power over workplace decisions, perhaps because
the kind of democracy available to them has been limited to the
occasional vote – are likely to regard themselves as lacking the
relevant knowledge for political affairs. Those whose life already
offers them some opportunity for influencing decisions are more
likely, in contrast, to consider themselves politically competent. The
inequities in this are obvious, for those who already have certain
decision-making powers will develop in their confidence and claims,
while those who have been more marginal may decline into passive
acceptance. Raising overall levels of political participation is then
seen as part of a strategy for greater political equality. Almost more
important, however, is that higher levels of participation have been
said to enhance the capacity for political judgement and the quality
of the decisions that are made.

This final part of the argument is often directly linked to a case for
more local democracy. Benjamin Barber, for example, argues that
involvement in a flourishing array of local and regional assemblies
would transform the very way people think and behave.[3] In the
isolation of the ballot box, we have little to guide us other than our
inherited party attachments and our immediate material interests.
We do not have to engage directly with others, or consider the
legitimacy of their preoccupations, considerations or concerns. But
once drawn into more active discussion – and provided with genuine

decision-making powers – we are far more likely to develop our mutual understanding and formulate our shared concerns. This is a powerful argument for increased participation in public affairs.

Implications for local democracy

Though it is the last of these arguments that is most commonly linked to more democracy at local level, all have played a role in the defence of local democracy. One standard argument for local government, for example, is that it disperses over-centralised power. This fits broadly within the prudential case for democracy. It presents additional layers of local government as a necessary safety net, protecting the citizens from a potentially authoritarian centre. The American constitution has set up a deliberate system of checks and balances between the legislative, executive, and judiciary; for much the same reasons, it is suggested, the British system of government should balance responsibilities between locality and centre. No matter how well regulated the democratic process, any concentration of power can lend itself to arbitrary and undemocratic behaviour. The more avenues there are for popular government and control, the more hope of combating these dangers.

This is a useful and legitimate argument, but does not, as it stands, make any strong claim about the superiority of local democracy, or what is best dealt with at local level. It operates as a more abstract argument in favour of pluralising the number of places where decisions are made. Left like that, of course, the argument remains vulnerable to the charge that one part of the plurality is less democratic than the other – and this has, indeed, proved one of the weak spots in the defence of local government. Voter turnout in local elections is consistently (and considerably) lower than voter turnout in national elections, and central government is always able to claim a more widely based mandate for its policies and actions. So just as the argument for two Houses of Parliament is undermined when one of these is composed of hereditary peers, so too is the argument for local government undermined if the local proves less democratic than the centre. The case for local democracy needs some additional ammunition, some further basis for claiming that local decision-making is 'better' or more appropriate than decisions that emanate from the centre.

One important addition (still within a largely prudential frame-work) is that local decision-making is best when the decision is of local concern. The people in the locality are better placed than anyone else to know the issues, problems and conditions; and they are, by definition, the only ones who can know their preferences and priorities and concerns. Conditions vary significantly from one locality to another: from urban to rural, from inner city to suburbs, from areas that are ethnically mixed to those more ethnically homogeneous, from areas experiencing high unemployment to those where most adults have jobs. The argument for local decision-making is partly an argument for employing local knowledge, and taking maximum advantage of local experience and imagination and expertise. It draws on that general scepticism about who knows what is best, and translates this into a more local scepticism about the claims of nationally-based politicians or bureaucrats. When there is no sure basis for identifying the 'right' policies, the pre-ference should surely go to those who know the locality. This strengthens the case for local decision-making in matters of local concern.

This too is a useful and powerful argument, and it shifts the burden of proof to those who want to argue *against* local democ-racy. In its simplest formulations, it seems self-evident and uncon-troversial, for the services provided by local authorities often cry out for careful adjustment to local variations in need. But there is a great deal of historical accident in the kinds of services that came to be organised by local authorities, and it is clear enough from recent developments that none of the pattern is immune to change. If we were to start from scratch and work out which services are most appropriately dealt with at local level, it is not so obvious what we would want to include. Probably not the former polytechnics – though these were once under local authority control. But why schools if not universities? And why should we regard public housing as an essentially local concern?

One consideration here is that few decisions are entirely local in their effects, and however strong the case for devolving decision-making to those most immediately concerned, there is always a counter-case for involving others who are also affected. When this dilemma is resolved in favour of the most local forms of decision-making, it can generate the not-in-my-backyard syndrome that ignores any wider considerations. When it is resolved in favour of maximum representation of anyone who can claim to be in any way affected, it can justify a national monopoly over each and every decision. Given the greater difficulties in maintaining accountability at national level, this would set worrying limits to popular control.

An alternative way of approaching this is to stress the importance of local variation, and view local democracy as something that encourages new ideas and initiatives to emerge. This then parallels the case John Stuart Mill made over a century ago in favour of freedom of expression and choice. Mill believed that some principles were superior to others, but he argued forcefully against attempts to impose these on people in advance. He saw all silencing of discussion as an assumption of infallibility, and since no-one *is* infallible, he believed this might rule out opinions that would later prove closer to the truth. But even if the preferred principles were correct (whatever this might mean and however it could be established), the attempt to close down alternatives encourages people to accept things without really thinking. Opinions that never have to be defended become empty of real content or belief; practices that are just taken for granted eventually lose their reason to exist. As applied to local democracy, this provides a potentially powerful basis for maximising local autonomy. Even if others can legitimately claim some interest in the issue being considered, local autonomy may still be preferable in encouraging alternatives to flourish. Since we do not know for sure what is best – whether it is in the sphere of education or housing or policing or transport – a greater variety between and within localities should be valued as a good in itself.

This is a strong argument in favour of decision-making at subnational level, though it too has to be weighed against other objectives of democratic equality. Those who believe, for example, that access to pre-school nurseries should be a basic right for all parents and children are necessarily treading on the toes of local decision-makers. They are saying that the level of provision should be nationally decided, and not subject to where one lives. This might leave considerable scope for local decision over the nature and character of the provision, but it still implies national action to set the minimum standards.

All this leaves the case for a specifically *local* democracy rather indeterminate, and in the face of these various dilemmas, I see the arguments for local democracy as heavily dependent on the notion that an over-centralised decision-making process undercuts the vitality of *all* democracy. If we base the case for local decision-making on what are matters of local concern, this is always vulnerable to counter-claims that the matter is not exclusively local. If we base the case on the value of a flourishing range of local initiatives, this can come up against equally pressing concerns about equalising social provision. But if local democracy can be shown to be one of the cornerstones on which subsequent participation develops, anything that weakens this is going to affect democracy at every level. Local democracy can then rest its claims on being the most accessible avenue for political participation.

In terms of where people are most likely to participate, the claims of local democracy are striking: the most recent and comprehensive study of 'Political Participation and Democracy in Britain' confirms that the bulk of political participation is conducted at a local level, and that when people do participate (most of us don't!) it is typically in their locality and around a local issue.[4] The most likely avenues for raising citizen participation are indeed those that exist at sub-national level, for this is where people feel most competent and are most immediately engaged. Anyone who attaches a value to increasing political involvement and participation is directed to democracy at the local level.

Indeed, even if we have no particular preference between more and less participation, local democracy can claim to be slightly more even-handed in the way its distributes political influence and power. All levels of politics tend to be dominated by more privileged groups – men rather than women, those in professional rather than those in manual employment, organised producers rather than unorganised consumers – but the relative ease of access to local politics usually moderates this pattern. An earlier defence of local government suggested that local authorities were more likely to speak for 'the retired, the young, married women', thereby providing some avenue or voice to otherwise under-represented groups.[5] Later contributions have often noted that women have a higher profile in local and community politics.[6] The greater ease of access helps modify some of the barriers to participation, and this can reduce some of the starker divisions between social groups.

Local councils have, for example, proved more representative in what theorists of democracy call the 'descriptive' or 'mirror' sense than nationally elected assemblies: they have been marginally more open to women, to people in manual jobs, and to people in an ethnic minority. The number of women elected has been consistently higher on local councils than in Parliament, and this trend continues even with recent improvements in the number of women MPs. The election of people from ethnic minorities remains low and patchy, but the concentration of ethnic minority communities in particular urban localities has allowed some of these to achieve the minimum threshold for political presence. Similar patterns can be discerned in the number of councillors who hold manual jobs, for while both national and local assemblies are very much skewed towards those in professional employment, this is less strong at the local level. The cynic might remark that all this testifies only to the declining significance of local government, and that if more power were returned to the localities, this relative advantage would soon disappear. But for the present and foreseeable future, local politics is considerably more even-handed than politics at national level.

Enhancing local democracy

I have suggested that the case for local democracy depends heavily on its role in extending and enhancing democracy, and that this is the cornerstone on which to erect arguments for local democracy. But the idea that democracy can be further extended is itself deeply contentious. We are no longer in the heady days of the 1960s and 1970s, when so many experimented in new forms of direct democracy; we are, on the contrary, in an age of sober reassessment, when even the conventions of representative democracy are under challenge from the free-market right. In the course of the 1970s and 1980s, political theorists began to talk of the 'overloading' of the welfare state, and the tendency of political parties to promise us the moon in order to get themselves elected. From this perspective, governments were being elected on irresponsible programmes of welfare expansion, and their excessive expenditure was being financed by a disgruntled but still silent majority. The fact that people cast their votes for one or other of the political parties was said to tell us little about what they really wanted, for with all parties drawn into a competitive process of public sector expansion, there was no way for voters to blow the whistle. If we really want to know people's preferences, the argument continued, we should look to what they will pay for and use. Service provision should be taken out of the hands of politicians and removed from direct political control.

This substitution of the consumer for the citizen has had particularly acute consequences for local government, which has been variously characterised as unrepresentative, overly bureaucratic, and unresponsive to people's real needs. The market then seemed to capture the high ground of democracy, and accountability was reformulated as something that should take place outside the political process. Where previous generations had debated different possibilities and problems in extending direct citizen control, the new order suggested that politics itself was the problem. Making people pay for each service they used was then justified, not just as a pragmatic response to worsening economic conditions, but as a positively superior mechanism for measuring popular need. The fact that people needed money before they could even enter this market was conveniently forgotten.

Against this rather sombre background, what does it mean to 'extend and enhance' democracy? Earlier debates on democracy tended to revolve around an opposition between representative and direct democracy. The first point to stress is that there no point in arguing against representative democracy *per se*. In any community that has grown beyond the size that can be accommodated in an open meeting, electing representatives to act on the citizens' behalf has to remain the major component – and not only for pragmatic reasons, but also from egalitarian concerns. The great advantage of representative democracy is that elections put the voters on a potentially equal footing, for they make no excessive demands on the citizens' energy or time. The standard alternative proposed by advocates of direct democracy is decision-making by open meeting; the standard objection to that is that only a minority will attend. Voting remains the one form of political participation that is widely dispersed through the population as a whole: it is no longer skewed between women and men; it is not particularly affected by occupation or income. All of us can, and most of us do, vote. The moment when we elect our political representatives is the moment when we come closest to being political equals.

To say this, however, is not to say that electing representatives exhausts all the possibilities for democracy, for representation is beset by a variety of problems that no political system has yet resolved. One immediate difficulty lies in the vagaries of the electoral system, for the British system of first-past-the-post elections is notoriously inexact in translating the numbers who vote for particular parties into the numbers of seats each party then wins. But even setting to one side the strong case for an alternative electoral system, the election of political representatives falls considerably short of what it sets out to do. Representatives are commonly elected on vaguely defined programmes of action which, all too often, they then simply ignore. When we elect representatives to serve on school boards or union executives or some other non-party body, we may be presented with personal manifestos which only the most politically involved can decode. In many such instances, we do not really know what we are choosing. But even in elections organised through the more recognisable labels of political parties, we are usually faced with the general formulations of party manifestos, which few voters ever bother to read. Even if we did, it would make little difference, for the citizens have limited control over subsequent policy decisions. Their main weapon against representatives who disappoint them is to try to evict them next time.

David Beetham rightly notes that 'the fact of the vote casts a long shadow in front of it',[7] and that representatives will act in careful anticipation of what might be unfavourable reactions. To this extent, we do have some continuous control over those we elect to represent us, and we can expect them to respond to our displeasure long before the next election. But politicians retain considerable powers of manipulation in the timing of their most unpopular policies, and this often undermines their accountability to their electorate. Representation may then become a rather empty word.

One response to this (more commonly associated with the political left than the political right) is to establish binding mandates so that representatives have to deliver on what they promised to do. Not that there is any foolproof way of ensuring this: a party might be elected on what is said to be a binding mandate, and still tear up all its promises the next day; a delegate might be mandated to vote for a motion and still ignore this when it comes to the vote. But it is, in principle, possible to reduce the wayward autonomy of representatives by establishing more detailed policy commitments and a higher level of expectation that these will be followed through. Those who abandon their mandate may then expect deselection, or some other form of 'punishment' for failing to follow the pre-agreed line. The more this expectation enters into the practices and conventions of democracy, the less temptation there is for representatives to decide to go it alone.

That said, there are often legitimate reasons why representatives might have second thoughts. It is entirely possible, for example, that an incoming government will uncover a scale of financial disarray that forces the representatives to reconsider what were once firm commitments. When something comparable happens to the elected executive of a tenants' association or some other smaller scale grouping, the representatives have the option of convening a meeting to discuss unanticipated problems. In any context much larger than this, they are forced back on their own political judgements. What is more, there might be reasons why we positively favour this exercise of judgement, and particularly if we consider some of the earlier arguments in favour of enabling people to revise and reformulate their views.

If part of the strength of democratic discussion is that it enables people to recognise the partial nature of their arguments and reconsider their initial positions, then we cannot also expect them to stick firmly to what they started with and never waver from that first point of view. Strict accountability can look very appealing, and it is hard to see what representation is about if not the representatives delivering on what they had promised to do. But if democracy is also about reconciling previously opposed opinion or mobilising new agendas, it cannot rely exclusively on binding mandates. There has to be some room for transformation, otherwise the representatives must endlessly repeat whatever opinions they presented from the start. Some balance has to be struck between allowing the representatives to exercise their judgement, and giving them so much autonomy of action that they can no longer pretend to represent us.

A further complication arises in the context of the widespread concern over the under-representation of women, and people who are in an ethnic minority. This under-representation is increasingly regarded as a problem, and there is a growing conviction that people's interests are not adequately addressed when their 'representatives' are so different from themselves. However well intentioned our representatives may be, they cannot be relied upon to understand experiences very different to their own, or promote interests they do not really share. At the most general level of decision-making, this gap in experience or interests might not seem to matter. If a political party is committed, for example, to introducing equality legislation or expanding nursery provision, then it might not much matter whether the people charged with carrying out these policies turn out to be women or men. Except, of course, that policy decisions are not simply settled in advance by pre-agreed programmes and policies. New issues arise alongside unanticipated problems and constraints, and in the final weighing and interpretation of priorities, it can matter immensely who the decision-makers are. The growing importance now attached to the composition of our elected assemblies reflects this recognition. If democratic representation is conceived in terms of an adequate representation of the different needs and concerns of the electorate, this demands closer attention to the characteristics of the people elected.

This leads, however, in a rather different direction from binding mandates. If representatives were bound in advance to a highly specified set of policy commitments, then politicians could legitimately argue that it was irrelevant whether they were black or white, women or men. Their role would have been reduced to the status of political messengers; it would be the content of the messages that mattered rather than the characteristics of the messengers themselves. It might still seem rather suspect that most of these messengers were white and middle-class and male, but if their hands were tightly tied by pre-agreed policies and promises, it would not be such an obvious problem for democracy. So those who concern themselves with the social composition of decision-making assemblies (how many women, how many workers, how many of the society's different ethnic groups) are taking issue with the naive reliance on binding mandates. The first strategy stresses the content of representation, in the sense of the cluster of ideas and policies and goals, and focuses on keeping representatives accountable to what they said they were going to do. The second looks more closely at who does the work of representation, and regards any pattern of representation that is overly skewed to one sex, one ethnic group, or one class as inherently *un*representative. Both aspects matter in achieving adequate representation, but they do not always work neatly in tandem.

The preceding discussion suggests one avenue for improving democratic control, which is to introduce mechanisms to ensure that representatives are more clearly 'representative' of the society's constituent groups. I have noted that local government already has a better record on this than national government, but even so, there is a great deal more that could be done in this area.[8] The other most obvious avenues for improving the quality of democracy move beyond the sphere of representation to add in elements of direct democracy: the most self-evident being to increase the number of issues on which citizens are enabled to vote directly; and to make more use of the open meeting. There are numerous and well-rehearsed problems with both of these – which is why they should not be set up as *alternatives* to representative democracy – but either could still play some legitimate role in enhancing local democracy.

The first implies more regular recourse to the ballot box, so that instead of abdicating all decisions to those elected as MPs or councillors, citizens would retain direct decision-making powers over some range of political concerns. The referendum *per se* is rarely employed in British politics, but trade unions now ballot their members before taking any strike action, while parents of local school-children may be balloted on whether to opt-out of local authority control. In only slightly more futuristic vein, writers on democracy have suggested that developments in communications could allow us to resuscitate the kind of continuous citizen involvement that disappeared with the ancient Greek democracies.[9]

Both right and left have viewed the referendum as their natural ally, seeing it on the one hand as defending the hard-working citizen against an irresponsible and over-spending state, and, on the other hand, as empowering the poor and underprivileged against the weight of vested interest. When it comes to social issues, the referendum has tended to be rather conservative, and it is not a great device for protecting minority interests. But we can hardly choose our procedures by whether we like their results, and in principle, at least, the referendum looks a highly democratic way of making decisions. It allows citizens to decide directly on the issues, which sidesteps that accumulation of problems about keeping representatives accountable. It also relies on the vote rather than attendance at meetings, which means it is less likely to favour those who are more politically active. There may be practical limits to how many issues can be treated in this way, and good reasons of time or convenience for continuing to rely extensively on elected representatives. But as one possible way of making democratic decisions, direct voting on the issues looks a very good candidate.

The main objection to decision-making by referendum is that it encourages ill-informed or inconsistent decisions. Interestingly enough, this complaint is voiced by half-hearted and strong democrats alike. Giovanni Sartori, for example, has little time for more substantial citizen involvement, and he recoils in horror from proposals for high-tech democracy:

> daily direct democracy in which the citizenry sits before a video and allegedly self-governs itself by responding to the issue in the air by pressing a button. How nice – and how deadly. . . . The

idea that the government of our fantastically complex, interconnected and fragile societies could be entrusted to millions of *discrete wills* that are bound to decide *at random*, with a *zero-sum instrument* – this idea is indeed a monumental proof of the abyss of under-comprehension that is menacing us.[10]

But from his very different political perspective, Benjamin Barber also cautions against unthinking use of the referendum, and stresses the importance of discussion in enabling people to consider the wider ramifications of any decision.[11]

Barber makes a more specific point that could be helpful in exploring the possibilities of putting more decisions to the vote. He notes that the typical referendum offers an over-simple yes/no choice, and that most issues yield a range of more nuanced opinions. Yet this could quite easily be incorporated into a multi-choice referendum, which would then be able to capture the intensity of support and opposition, and the kind of urgency or priority that people give to each issue. (The example he gives is one which has proved highly controversial in America: a vote on state funding of abortion clinics.) A multi-choice set of alternatives would have the advantage of encouraging us to work out more carefully what we think. It might also, however, leave the political elite with more room for manoeuvre in interpreting the outcome of the vote. Since the main reason for putting decisions to a vote is that we cannot trust the representatives to do what we wanted them to do, this might well defeat the purpose.

Though decision-making by ballot is still very under-used in Britain, it has become more prominent with decisions over the 'opting-out' of schools, or whether tenants on a housing estate should opt for alternative management. There are also numerous examples of consultation (over admissions policies to local schools, for example), and these often make use of a multi-choice format. The problem in extending this is only partly that elected representatives are reluctant to lose more power. What always surfaces as the additional worry is the tension between achieving the maximum involvement of all concerned (which points in the direction of the vote) and ensuring full and informed discussion in the light of all possible ramifications. The meeting remains the paradigm for tackling this second concern.

The strengths of decision-making in open meeting should be obvious from what has already been said. The meeting is open to all those who fit into the relevant constituency (which may be defined by area, or by the membership of some party or group), and this potentially works against hierarchical tendencies by empowering people outside the traditional elite. Compared with the isolation and anonymity of the ballot box, decision-making by open meeting also enables people to perceive possibilities they had not previously considered, or recognise the legitimacy of what others have to say. If we just take the preferences people currently express (whether through opinion polls or the market or their casting of an occasional vote), we may be condemning large sections of the population to persistently unjust conditions, for people form their preferences in relation to what they perceive as being possible, and many will adjust their expectations downwards in order to survive and remain sane.[12] One of the virtues of the open meeting is that it exposes us to a wider range of possibilities and alternatives, and this can significantly expand our sense of what we want or need. For those whose expectations are already excessive, the open meeting can have an equally salutary effect, for it may force them to reduce their own ambitions in order to meet with other concerns. The great strength of decision-making by open meeting is that it can reshape the very agenda, mobilising possibilities previously ignored.

The weaknesses, however, are equally obvious – the most potent being that so few people are likely to attend. Decision-making by open meeting inevitably weights decisions in favour of those who bother to participate, and if these prove to be an unrepresentative sample of the constituency as a whole, this cuts across principles of political equality. Decision-making by open meeting may, indeed, actively discourage wider participation, for the very intimacy of the gatherings can act as a barrier to those less involved. Newcomers may feel the other participants all know one another and that they are the odd ones out; their lack of ease will almost certainly prevent them from attending again. Power may then flow to an 'unrepresentative' active minority, pushing the silent majority aside.

Conclusion

The point to take from the above discussion is not that we should abandon any fantasies of a better democracy, but that no one procedure can stand on its own. Each of the mechanisms for democracy has its own strengths and weaknesses, and the deepening of local democracy depends on a clear understanding of these. Exaggerated claims on behalf of any one procedure should be carefully avoided, but as long as the potential problems are recognised, a wide range of possibilities opens up. Context is crucial here, for what might prove a severe disadvantage in one context may develop more promisingly elsewhere.

Where an issue touches on different and conflicting interests, for example, it is particularly important to ensure fair representation of all the conflicting concerns. In such circumstances, the priority must go to those mechanisms that can claim to be more even-handed and inclusive. This might be because they have built into them some proportionate representation of all the relevant groups: producers *and* consumers, for example; women and men; representatives from different ethnic communities; or representatives from different user-groups. More typically, it will be because it relies on the mechanism of the vote, and catches more people in its net. The concern with fair representation is particularly important when a decision involves the allocation of resources between different groups or needs, and where these differences are politically contentious. In such contexts, the emphasis has to be on equalising people's political weight.

Where issues are less intrinsically divisive – either because they deal in limited resources or because there is no obvious conflict of interests between different groups – it is possible to take more risks. The neighbourhood forum, for example, relies on decision-making through open meeting, and is potentially 'unrepresentative' in terms of the kinds of people likely to turn up. If the neighbourhood forum were taking major resource decisions over matters which were deeply divisive, this failure in representation would be a serious concern. But when the decisions under its control can more genuinely claim to be matters of common concern to all local residents, the neighbourhood forum is a good way of mobilising local knowledge and initiative. It makes it possible for people to introduce proposals that would never figure in the party political campaigns for local elections. In principle, at least, it also harnesses a strong sense of the local community and makes this community more real.

These two principles are the central ones for deciding the appropriate balance of democratic procedures, and they can be widened out to consider the relationship between consultation and final decision. One recent innovation in local government has been the development of consultative mechanisms which co-opt representatives from ethnic minority communities and women's groups onto race relations or women's committees. In opening out to these different interests and voices, councillors were acknowledging the partial failure of party political forms of representation. Council elections offer citizens a relatively clear choice between political parties, but they do this in terms that are too broadly defined to capture the full range of local concerns. Additional forms of co-option and consultation have been developed to fill this gap, and this has created some space for policy initiatives coming directly from citizens themselves.

In any strict rendering of democratic accountability, the 'representatives' from women's groups or ethnic groups or voluntary association are not representative: they have not been elected by full and free vote of all the people they might claim to represent. They can claim some level of legitimacy from their networks or their organisational base, but their status more closely resembles that of the individuals who turn up to a neighbourhood forum. In both instances, people may see themselves as representing certain groups or interests, but they cannot claim the same kind of legitimacy that comes from a popular vote. And yet it would be an abuse of democratic principle to dismiss these consultative groups as inherently unrepresentative, or say their members are self-selecting and unaccountable and that their opinions should not really count. The lack of strict accountability certainly limits their 'right' to take the decisions, but it does not undermine their importance in consultation. Additional forms of representation and consultation are a crucial complement to the very general representation that occurs through local and national elections, and we can ill afford to lose these additions.

The substitution of consumer for citizen has presented the market expression of consumer 'preferences' as the better way of finding out what people really want; the retreat from a more active political involvement threatens to reduce the remaining arena of politics to the casting of the occasional vote. Combating these tendencies is no easy matter, for each extension of democracy leads to new problems as well as solutions. But if the case for local democracy rests, as I have suggested, on its role in enhancing and developing democracy, the risks should be confronted and the greater possibilities of democracy released. Even if we consider democracy as little more than a safety net, it calls out for more substantial protections at local level. And if we combine this with the more dynamic understanding of democracy as eliciting a fuller range of political alternatives, the locality can play a crucial role in extending discussion and deliberation and debate.

Notes and references

1. Robert Dahl identifies these as the standard assumptions in the arguments against democracy. See Dahl, R. (1989) *Democracy and Its Critics*, New York: Yale University Press.
2. See, for example, Pateman, C. (1970) *Participation and Democratic Theory*, Cambridge University Press.
3. Barber, B. (1984) *Strong Democracy*, University of California Press.
4. Parry, G., Moyser, G. and Day, N. (1992) *Political Participation and Democracy in Britain*, Cambridge University Press.
5. Sharpe, L. J. (1970) 'Theories and Values of Local Government', *Political Studies*, vol. 18, no. 2, p. 170.
6. For example, Randall, V. (1987) *Women in Politics*, Basingstoke: Macmillan.
7. Beetham, D. (1993) 'Liberal Democracy and the Limits of Democratization', in Held, D. (ed.) *Prospects for Democracy*, Cambridge: Polity Press, p. 63.
8. For a fuller discussion of this, see Phillips, A. (1995) *The Politics of Presence*, Oxford: Clarendon Press.
9. McLean, I. (1989) *Democracy and New Technology*, Cambridge: Polity Press; or Budge, I. (1990) 'Direct Democracy: Setting Appropriate Terms of Debate', in Held, D. (ed.) *Prospects for Democracy*, Cambridge: Polity Press.
10. Sartori, G. (1987) *The Theory of Democracy Revisited: Part One*, Chatham, NJ: Chatham House, pp. 246–7.
11. See Barber *Strong Democracy*, p. 290.
12. This argument is developed by Cass, R. Sunstein. See Sunstein, C. S. (1991) 'Preferences and Politics', *Philosophy and Public Affairs*, vol. 20, no. 1.

3 The Constitutional Status of Local Government

Martin Loughlin

Introduction

On 1 April 1974 a new structure of local government came into existence, bringing to a resolution an intense period of inquiry and review which had taken place over much of the previous decade. This new system was designed to restore the status of local government which had been thought to be in danger of being severely eroded owing to the fact that local government structures no longer 'fit[ted] the pattern of life and work in modern England'.[1] In the following twenty years, the system of local government has been subject to a vast array of changes, many of which challenge the assumptions underpinning the local government reforms of the 1970s and which cumulatively have had a profound impact on the status of local government. The pace of change has been particularly pronounced since 1979 as successive Conservative governments have acted with great vigour to redefine the appropriate relationship between state and society and, as part of this endeavour, have sought to set in place a more limited role for local government. This new role, which is slowly emerging, has proved highly controversial.

These developments raise issues of constitutional significance. Given the peculiar characteristics of the British constitution – in particular, the fact that it is an evolutionary, unwritten constitution which does not incorporate any formally entrenched safeguards – any attempt to engage in such an assessment will inevitably be contested. Nevertheless, since the changes have important implications for the distribution of political authority within the state and the processes through which governmental decision-making is exercised, this type of inquiry cannot be avoided. In this chapter

38

specific changes of the last twenty years will be surveyed and their impact on the constitutional status of local government will be assessed.

The historical development of the institution of local government sets the context for any discussion of its current constitutional status. This history has given rise to the fundamental importance of four defining characteristics of the modern institution of local government.

1. *Multi-functionality* – Local councils as governmental institutions assume responsibility for a broad range of functions.
2. *Discretion* – Local councils have been given a broad discretion which enables them to tailor activities or services to local needs. They have generally been free to decide on the precise pattern of the services which they deliver and even to redefine the nature of the service they provide.
3. *Taxation* – Local councils have possessed an independent power of taxation which long predates the formation of the modern institution. The retention of an independent taxation power has given local government an important source of financial autonomy.
4. *Representation* – Local councils, being the only governmental institutions outside of Parliament which are subject to direct periodic election,[2] are accorded a degree of political legitimacy which other agencies of government do not possess.

Recent strains on the institution are best examined by reference to these four basic characteristics. The modern institution of local government was founded on a set of assumptions – concerning economic growth, the role of government in society, a basic consensus about the role of local government within the wider structure of government, and faith in a public service ethic – which in recent times have all come to be questioned. In order to examine the impact of these changes on the constitutional status of local government it is necessary to simplify a complex set of changes to the institution which can be discussed by reference to the themes of structure, functions, finance and accountability. As other chapters in this book discuss the former two issues, this chapter concentrates upon the institutional changes that have occurred firstly in relation to finance, and secondly in relation to accountability arrangements.

Finance

From the outset, the Conservative government was committed not only to a general reduction in public expenditure but in particular to cutting back expenditure on such services as education, housing and social services over which it had no direct control.[3] It thus proposed a basic reform of the system for distributing central grants to local government which was designed to provide incentives to local authorities to reduce their expenditure.

The enactment of the block grant mechanism in the Local Government, Planning and Land Act 1980 opened a new era in the central–local financial relationship. It was an era which, as the 1976 Layfield committee of enquiry into local government finance had predicted, can be characterised as one of centralisation of power. But it was also characterised both by 'hyperactivism'[4] and 'destabilizing incrementalism'[5] as central government lurched from one mechanism to the next in its quest to control local expenditure. Arising from the financial conflicts of the 1980s came the gradual realisation that increasingly there appeared to be no conspicuous mutuality of objective between central and local government and, ultimately, that the centre apparently no longer viewed the institution of local government as having an important role in the structure of governance. In order to consider this view, the changes introduced to the system of local government finance will be charted and their implications assessed.

Block grant and expenditure targets

Local authorities raise the finance they need to run their services from four main sources: rates, fees and charges, grants and by borrowing. Since local authorities are generally required to finance their affairs on an annual basis, they are not empowered to borrow for revenue purposes. In respect of current expenditure, then, it is the first three sources, and the balance between them, which is of particular importance. Much of the growth in local government during the twentieth century has, for example, been financed largely by central government grants, with the result that the burden on domestic ratepayers (expressed as a proportion of personal disposable income) has remained fairly constant throughout the post-war period. Consequently, the means of allocating grants came to assume a particular importance.

Since the 1950s, grant distribution has been governed by the principle that the bulk of grant aid should take the form of a general grant which is unhypothecated to specific services and, since 1966, that general grant has taken the form of a Rate Support Grant (RSG). This type of general grant – where grant allocation is governed by general principles – protects local government against detailed central control by ensuring that grant is allocated in accordance with a common formula rather than being dependent on central approval of specific local authority services. The basic aims of the RSG have been to compensate authorities for differences in local taxable wealth (the resources element) and for disparities in spending needs (the needs element). Since the mid-1970s the process of technical refinement has been coupled with a concern to incorporate incentives for local authorities to reduce expenditure.

The block grant mechanism enacted in 1980 was explicitly constructed around the concept of equalisation so that up to a notional level of expenditure, called Grant-Related Expenditure (GRE), local authorities were to be fully compensated for differences in rateable values and spending needs. GRE, however, being a central assessment of a local authority's spending needs, also served to trigger an adjustment in grant. By incorporating a tapering provision so that marginal expenditure above GRE attracted a lower rate of grant the block grant mechanism placed the burden of additional expenditure on local ratepayers. The block grant mechanism thus sought to deal with an apparent weakness in post-war grant systems of providing incentives to local authorities to increase expenditure in order to attract more grant. By requiring the setting of individual assessments for each authority, however, an unprecedented degree of central involvement in local government finance was assumed.

The government found that for 1981/82, the first year in which the block grant mechanism was fully operational, local authorities did not react as anticipated to the grant tapering provisions. Many local authorities opted to maintain service levels and to raise additional revenues from the rates. These projections caused the Secretary of State immediately to announce a new set of targets, based on the historic expenditure levels of each local authority. This system of expenditure targets with its associated grant penalty arrangements was engrafted on to the block grant mechanism with retrospective effect in 1982.[6] The target system, which operated until 1986/87, had the effect not only of creating a much more powerful mechanism of expenditure control. It also served both to increase the complexity of the grant regime and to obscure the principles on which the block grant mechanism was based. Furthermore, it was a unilateral act by the centre which transformed the centre's capacity to control local government expenditure.

The government's conduct in the early 1980s has been subject to widespread criticism. Such censure has not simply been because of the shift in the central–local balance, but also because of the rather inept manner in which the instruments of financial control were handled. The government's action seemed to indicate uncertainty or confusion about its goals and, in part, these difficulties appeared to stem from a failure to appreciate the complexity of the system which it was seeking to influence. The most basic criticism was that the government failed to recognise that intrinsic difficulties existed in using the block grant mechanism as a tool of expenditure restraint. Since the primary purpose of block grant was that of rate poundage equalisation, the mechanism entailed a break in the link between the level of local expenditure and the size of the rate bill. The block grant mechanism thus incorporated certain features which prevented it being used as a stringent mechanism for exerting general downward financial pressure on local government[7] and it is perhaps the government's failure fully to recognise this facet of the mechanism which caused much of its subsequent frustration.

The reform of the grant system also exposed certain structural weaknesses in the entire system of local government finance. The shift towards the equalisation of rate poundages had the effect of establishing a close relationship between rate bills and rateable values; but, as a consequence, it highlighted basic inconsistencies in the valuation process and thus exposed weaknesses in the rating system.[8] Again, the government did not appear to have been conscious of this effect of block grant. The most effective method of bringing about a reduction in local government expenditure was to reduce the proportion of local expenditure which central government would support. This was a method which had been shown to work, but only after a period in which rate demands had significantly increased.[9] This, however, was probably a consequence the government was not prepared to countenance.

It is precisely because of these complexities of the system and the tensions in Conservative policy that the government tried to use the grant system to achieve too many conflicting objectives. As a result, it entirely lost control over local government expenditure. By 1984 local government revenue expenditure was 9 per cent higher in real terms than when the Conservatives took office and the consensus of official and academic opinion suggested that responsibility lay firmly at the government's door.

Rate-capping and beyond

Because of the difficulties it got itself into during the early 1980s, the government felt obliged to take drastic action. This took the form of the Rates Act 1984, under which it acquired powers to control the amount of finance which local authorities could raise through the rates. This measure, a direct attack on 'the foundation stone upon which is built the whole structure of local taxation in England',[10] constituted an unprecedented centralisation of political power. However, it is important to recognise that it was 'more out of exasperation than with a conscious sense of direction'[11] that the Rates Act was enacted. Furthermore, far from restoring control, rate-capping threatened 'to undermine what remain[ed] of financial accountability in local government'.[12]

As directive rather than facilitative legislation, the 1984 Act marked a turning point in the drafting of local government finance legislation. It was drafted on the assumption that those to whom it was directed would act as utility-maximisers and explore all available avoidance routes; the Act thus sought to identify these in advance and ensure that these routes could not successfully be taken. As directive legislation, the Rates Act itself was competently constructed. But the unprecedented powers acquired by the government to control the amount which authorities could raise through the rates did not enable the government to control the system. This was because, in the context of the overall system of local government finance, rate-capping was of marginal importance as a control mechanism.

The basic statutory framework laid down in the 1980 Act and on to which the 1984 Act was engrafted had been drafted in the traditional facilitative manner. Rate-capping, in conjunction with expenditure targets, simply caused local authorities to exploit the discretionary aspects of the basic framework either to avoid these control techniques or to ensure that they had a minimal impact. During the 1980s, a major 'creative accounting' industry emerged, in which local authority treasurers and lawyers working hand in hand with financial institutions sought, with some success, to exploit the flexibility within the basic framework.

The problem here concerned the attempt to use law as a determinant of the balance between central and local power. The legal framework relating to local government finance had never been intended to establish the precise rules of the game; its function had been to provide a general framework through which (non-legal) regulatory norms could evolve. With the breakdown in the sense of partnership, both central and local government turned – in different ways – to the law to act as an umpire. It was a role for which the law was patently ill-equipped. The legislation had not conventionally been drafted with the possibility of adjudication in mind and therefore contained many obscurities. Also, since it did not establish a comprehensive regulatory framework, the government was obliged – generally in response to gaps and deficiencies which local authorities had already identified and exploited – to rush to promote new legislation to resolve ambiguities and uncertainties. Eventually, frustrated by a number of legal challenges which had had the effect of threatening the entire system of local government finance established since 1980 the government was obliged to obtain retrospective validation of all its expenditure decisions.[13]

Charging the community?

During the mid-1980s, the government responded to this situation by introducing the most radical reform to the system of local government finance ever proposed in modern times. Though touted as a set of reforms which were 'designed to ensure that local democracy and local accountability are substantially strengthened'[14] in actuality the reforms had the effect of greatly weakening the financial autonomy of local authorities and thus undermined one of the basic pillars of the modern institution of local government.

The government sought to justify its proposals by utilising a model drawn from public choice theory and which focused on the relationship between three local groups which have a direct interest in local government: those who pay for (ratepayers), those who vote for (electors) and those (consumers) who benefit from local services. The financial reforms, which focused explicitly on the relationship between paying and voting, proceeded from the following analysis. In England there are 35 million electors, of whom only 18 million are liable to pay rates, and of these only 12 million, or one-third of the electorate, pay full rates.[15] Further, on average, for every £1 raised locally from domestic ratepayers £1.50 is paid by the non-domestic sector. So although 'the marginal cost of services to domestic taxpayers is reduced by a 60% contribution from non-domestic ratepayers', there is 'no voting right attached to the payment of non-domestic rates'.[16] And, of course, around 50 per cent of local government revenue expenditure is met by central government grants.

In essence the government's reforms, which were implemented in the Local Government Finance Act 1988, aimed to simplify the grant system, to reform the arrangements for the taxation of the non-domestic sector and to establish a closer nexus between voting and paying by making the marginal cost of local services payable by all voters equally. At the core of these reforms lay revolutionary reforms to the rating system, involving the nationalisation of the non-domestic rate and the abolition of domestic rates and its replacement with a 'community charge' (effectively a poll tax). The reform of the non-domestic rate was designed to convert it from a variable, locally-determined tax into a uniform nationally-determined one, the revenues from which would be pooled and recycled to local authorities through the grant system as an equal amount per adult resident. The community charge in principle constituted a flat rate charge on each adult resident of the area.

The consequences of these reforms were profound. The nationalisation of the non-domestic rate had the effect of increasing the proportion of central funding of local government to around 80–85 per cent. In addition to increasing central control, this resulted in the local tax having an extremely high gearing effect, which meant that small variations in a local authority's budget could produce great changes in the level of the charge. Furthermore, such variations might not come from changes in local expenditure at all but from technical adjustments to the grant allocation formula from one year to the next. The Green Paper itself pointed out that, 'if local accountability is to be effective, electors must be able to see how the price they pay relates to their local authority's expenditure decisions and the standard of services it provides'.[17] The combined effect of the high gearing effect and grant volatility indicated that this objective was unlikely to be achieved.

Though the impact of nationalisation of the non-domestic rate was of fundamental importance, the community charge raised even more serious issues. It represented not only a distinct shift from a (household) tax on property to a (individual) tax on persons but also a shift away from the principle of ability to pay and towards the benefit principle of taxation; that is, that payment for the provision of public services should be proportional to the consumption of such services. Even on the benefit principle, however, it was difficult to justify the introduction of a flat rate charge. Local authorities provide a mixture of property and personal services, and there is in fact a significant correlation between property value and benefit obtained from local authority services.[18] The community charge was a highly regressive tax which was not justified even in terms of the benefit principle.

Controls over capital expenditure

In Part VIII of the Local Government, Planning and Land Act 1980 new arrangements for central control of local authority capital expenditure were enacted. However, this system, which was designed to control the capital programme for a particular year, was constructed on the assumptions of the 1970s and, when government began to use the grant system as an expenditure restraint mechanism, the ambiguities in the capital control system were exploited as part of the creative accounting movement which flourished in the 1980s.

Creative accounting tended to involve the rearrangement of the existing resources and commitments of the local authority across different time spans or between different accounting classifications, generally with the objective of maximising the authority's revenue budget for the relevant year. This might, for example, involve the shifting revenue items into capital expenditure, such as capitalising maintenance and repair costs in the housing revenue account in an improvement programme. Most controversially, however, it involved unlocking some of the equity in the local authority's capital assets in return for cash which was used to bolster revenue expenditure (e.g. through a sale-and-leaseback scheme) or actually to embark on capital projects whilst deferring the cost to future years, through deferred purchase schemes.[19]

While the schemes adopted in most local authorities could be viewed simply as an application of the techniques of active financial management to the local authorities capital assets with a view to maximising value for money, the practices of some authorities in using the techniques to spend now while paying later caused much concern.[20] This led to central government action first in 1987 to outlaw deferred purchase deals[21] and then subsequently in 1988 to eliminate virtually all 'off balance sheet' transactions available to local government.[22] The sheer breadth of the restrictions imposed caught local authorities by surprise, particularly since the majority of the transactions affected made financial sense and did not jeopardise local authorities' financial stability. They signalled the fact that the government had lost control of the system; by freezing the market, it was in effect able to acquire the breathing space it needed to devise and enact a new system of capital controls.

This new system was enacted in Part IV of the Local Government and Housing Act 1989. This new regime, which took effect on 1 April 1990, repealed both the controls over borrowing in the 1972 Act and the system of capital expenditure controls in the 1980 Act and replaced them with a new system of credit controls which operated within a much more precise definition of capital expenditure. The 1989 Act also provided, in Part V, for much more extensive central regulation of local authority controlled companies.

The final issue to consider under capital expenditure concerns the issue of capital receipts. Under the 1980 Act, local authorities were free to supplement their capital allocations with such proportions of their capital receipts from asset sales as the government prescribed. With the government's privatisation initiative, and especially the vast sums generated from council house sales, reinvestment of receipts could result in aggregate local authority expenditure significantly exceeding the government's cash limit without any local authority exceeding its allocation. The government thus took steps to curb a local authority's ability to spend its capital receipts. Under the 1989 Act, for example, local authorities are obliged to set aside 75 per cent of capital receipts from council house sales and 50 per cent of any other capital receipt for the purposes of debt redemption. This restriction, together with other curbs on functions such as housing, have caused many authorities to express frustration at their inability to use receipts from asset sales to meet the evident needs of their communities.

Local government finance in the 1990s

The key issues relating to local government finance in the 1990s may briefly be stated. Far from restoring local accountability, the community charge scheme should be understood as an extension in centralisation. The impact of the nationalisation of the non-domestic rate, the volatility of central grant assessments and the high-gearing effect of the community charge seemed likely from the outset to combine to destroy the scheme's capacity to restore local accountability; and its highly regressive impact (together with the retention of capping powers) made it almost impossible for local authorities to diverge significantly from central government spending assessments. Its dismantling, within a year or two of the scheme's implementation, in fact had all the elements of grand tragedy: every informed person could see from the outset that the scheme was both unstable and unworkable. What in the end destroyed it was its widespread unpopularity amongst the public: the estimates that by the end of 1991 7.5 million liability orders had been issued, that non-collection of poll tax amounted to £1.5bn and that 2815 prison sentences had been imposed (the vast majority being suspended) for non-payment[23] simply represent the tip of the iceberg in terms of the costs of the reforms.

The Local Government Finance Act 1992 repealed the community charge and replaced it with the council tax which, as a banded property tax (albeit with personal discounts), marked a return to the basic principles of domestic rates. Criticism can certainly be levied both at the banding structure[24] and at the rather rudimentary valuation methods which have had to be adopted in order to enable lists to be drawn up expeditiously. However, the key issues of the 1990s will continue for some time to be the legacies of the 1988 Act reforms. The community charge scheme all but destroyed the integrity of the local tax system and has made any attempt to restore the taxing capacity of local government an uphill struggle. Furthermore, given the high-gearing effect as a result of 80 per cent of local authority expenditure being centrally provided, local authority budgets are increasingly being effectively determined by central government Standard Spending Assessments (SSAs).[25] Since the introduction of universal capping in 1992, even that limited freedom has disappeared and local councils' budgets seem now to be clustering around their SSAs.[26] This seems thus to be leading to a system in which local authorities assume a degree of formal responsibility out of all proportion to their ability actually to control services.

Accountability arrangements

The tradition of local government which has emerged this century is based on the idea of local councils as multi-functional authorities which are vested with broad discretionary powers to enable them to provide a range of services which meet the needs of their communities. Within this tradition, a distinctive pattern of accountability has emerged which tends to accentuate political mechanisms and to marginalise other forms of accountability. Many of the recent changes affecting local government, however, have been influenced by a desire to strengthen the mechanisms of accountability.

However, accountability is not simply a powerful concept; it is also a complex and multi-faceted one. In order to assess the impact which recent reforms have had on the status of local government, it is important to appreciate the way in which the methods of holding local government to account have, in recent times, been adapted. The tradition of local government which has emerged has thus generated a distinctive pattern of accountability. This pattern is based on the idea of the corporate authority. This idea suggests not only that decisions are taken by, or on behalf of, the entire council and that officers serve the council as a whole but also that local councils are free to regulate their own proceedings and that there are limits on the extent to which the corporate veil should be pierced. Much of the conduct of council business is thus regulated by convention rather than law and the standards of performance of officers is felt to be best enhanced by the promotion of professional standards. The principal control mechanisms are those which are applied as a result of central government supervision. And local accountability is primarily secured through the subjection of elected members to periodic elections.

The recent reforms to local government can be understood to reflect a sense of dissatisfaction over the performance of local government and the government seem to have accepted that the traditional structure of accountability within local government should be viewed as forming part of the problem. The changing forms of accountability thus constitute an important dimension to the recent developments affecting the status of local government.

The challenge

From the perspective of accountability, the essence of the challenge to the institution of local government posed by recent developments is to the ethic of discretion. This is manifested most clearly in the attempt to change the character of local services by altering the mechanisms of accountability for such services. Such reforms possess a number of common features. The most obvious is that they all serve to confine, structure and check the traditional discretionary powers of the local authority and thus they pose a direct challenge to the idea of the corporate authority. Reforms along such lines challenge the traditional role of members and officer-professionals to shape the organisation of the service and even to determine appropriate standards of performance. And it is precisely because they restrict discretion and require precise specification of service standards that they render local government decisions more susceptible to external accountability by consumers, local taxpayers, competitors, central departments, or review agencies. What is of particular importance, however, is that in this process of subjecting local government to these forms of accountability, the peculiarly *public* character of these services and the peculiarly *governmental* character of the institution becomes in danger of being undermined.

We must now consider the institutional reforms which have been promoted to reinforce these new forms of accountability.

The structure of political accountability

Although during the early 1980s the government contemplated a number of initiatives to alter the system of political accountability, the most important reforms followed from the 1986 Widdicombe Inquiry into the conduct of local authority business.[27] The Committee had been asked to pay particular attention to the roles of elected members and their relationships with officers and to make recommendations for strengthening the democratic process.[28] It identified as the key issue the fact that the formal framework did not recognise the existence of party politics in local government nor the needs of modern management, and proposed a range of reforms based on the need to formalise the conventional practices and to bolster the professional position of officers.

Many of the Widdicombe recommendations were enacted in Part I of the Local Government and Housing Act 1989 which provided for the disqualification of members from being senior officers of a local authority, required all appointments to be made on merit, restricted the principle of co-option to council committees, and imposed a duty on the authority to allocate membership of council committees amongst the relevant political groups in proportion to their representation on the council.[29] In addition to the direct regulation of council members, the 1989 Act provided for indirect regulation through the differentiation of political and managerial tasks and through the imposition of new duties on officers.[30] Furthermore, since the new duties on designated officers include the right of officers to determine the resources required to discharge their duties,[31] they marked a clear breach of the tradition of the corporate authority.

Many felt that these reforms to the structure of political account-ability, being skewed to the issue of politicisation, failed to get to the heart of the leadership challenge facing local government.[32] Further-more, it is important to recognise that the reforms marked a change in traditional assumptions underpinning the representative principle in local government as reflected through the idea of the corporate authority. In his classic work on central and local government, Norman Chester identified as two of three vital elements in our local government system the 'right of local electors to elect whom they please to their local Councils' and the 'necessity for a local Council to be able to rely completely on the loyalty of its officials'.[33] The 1989 Act reforms impose significant restrictions on each of these principles.

Financial accountability

One of the primary methods of achieving accountability for the expenditure of public money by local government is through the procedures of external audit. In 1983 audit arrangements were fundamentally reformed as a result of the establishment of the Audit Commission.[34] Under these new institutional arrangements the exercise of regularity audit remained basically unchanged.

The primary impact of this change, however, comes not from the alteration of institutional arrangements for audit but because of amendments to auditors' powers. Under the 1982 Act auditors were placed under a duty to satisfy themselves that the local authority 'has made proper arrangements for securing economy, efficiency and effectiveness in its use of resources'.[35] Since the early 1980s the scale of VFM audit has substantially increased. The Audit Commis-sion has developed methodologies for wide-ranging organisational analysis covering most major areas of local government activity and has moved 'into the ambiguous and treacherous territory of advising local authorities on how to manage their policy-making and policy-implementation processes'.[36] The manner in which the Audit Commission has embarked on this task has been controversial, but there is little doubt that the Commission has been very influential.[37] Further, as a result of Part I of the Local Government Act 1992, which was inspired by the government's Citizen's Charter initiative,[38] it is likely to enter a new phase since that Act empowers the Audit Commission to direct local authorities to publish comparative information on performance, thereby facilitating the publication of league tables of performance.

One concern which arose as a result of central–local conflicts during the mid-1980s over issues of finance was that the auditor possessed powers only to deal retrospectively with misconduct in local government. Under the Local Government Act 1988, then, the auditor was vested with two new powers. First, the auditor is empowered to issue a prohibition order against a local authority, the effect of which would be to require the authority to desist from making or implementing any decision or taking or continuing to take a particular course of action.[39] The second power permits the auditor to apply for judicial review of any decision, or any failure to act, which might have an effect on the authority's accounts.[40] The potential impact of these powers was reinforced by the duty imposed on the local authority's chief finance officer in section 114 of the Local Government Finance Act 1988 to make a report in any case of financial misconduct which arises within the authority. Once the report is issued, the authority is prohibited from pursuing the course of conduct referred to in the report until the report has been considered by the council. Since a copy of the report must be sent to the auditor, the exercise of this power will also alert the auditor to the possibility of financial misconduct.

The new institutional arrangements for audit, the new powers vested in auditors and the new duties imposed on local government officers all serve both to structure the local authority's traditional discretionary power of action and to impose a powerful check on local government decision-making.

Administrative accountability

The main institutional form for examining the propriety of local administration is the Commission for Local Administration, generally known as the Local Ombudsmen, which was established under the Local Government Act 1974. The main function of the

Local Ombudsman is to investigate complaints of maladministration in the conduct of local government business. During the 1980s, reforms have been introduced to address concerns over the accessibility, jurisdiction and remedial powers of the Ombudsman. These issues will be considered in turn.

Under the 1974 Act the Ombudsman could not generally consider a complaint unless it had been referred by a councillor[41] and, for some time, this had been felt to restrict their effectiveness in addressing maladministration.[42] The principle of direct access to the Ombudsman received strong support from the Widdicombe Committee[43] and in 1988 was given statutory effect.[44] During the first year of direct access the number of complaints received by the Commission increased by 44 per cent,[45] a figure which, though not necessarily indicative of increased maladministration, does suggest growing public awareness of the Ombudsman's role and a greater willingness to use the procedure.

There are significant restrictions on the Ombudsman's jurisdiction. They may not question the merits of any decision. As Lord Donaldson put it: 'Administration and maladministration have nothing to do with the nature, quality or reasonableness of a decision.'[46] Nor may the Ombudsman challenge policy, a restriction reflected in the fact that they may not consider complaints concerning action which affects most or all of the inhabitants of an area.[47] And, since a complaint cannot be accepted if an alternative remedy exists,[48] the Ombudsman has no jurisdiction to consider complaints concerning unlawful action. Even within their designated sphere of general competence, there are a number of categories of exclusion, including personnel matters, contractual or commercial matters, internal school proceedings, legal proceedings and the investigation of crime.[49] In recent years there has been some modification of these exclusions but they have been of marginal importance.[50]

More generally, the government has recognised that there is scope for extending the Commissioners' role in improving the quality of administration by developing their capacity to prevent future maladministration. This has been achieved by two legislative changes introduced in 1989: first by requiring local authorities to notify the Ombudsman of the steps they have taken to rectify any administrative shortcomings identified in an adverse report;[51] secondly, by giving the Ombudsman specific powers to publish general guidance to local government on the principles underlying good administrative practice and on common administrative errors.[52] These changes signal an opportunity for the Commissioners to use their investigatory powers not simply to remedy injustice but also to assume the more general role of undertaking an administrative audit.

From the outset, a degree of concern has been expressed about the limited powers of the Ombudsman to enforce remedies. If the Ombudsman finds that there has been maladministration causing injustice, the local authority is obliged to consider the report and notify the Ombudsman of any action they propose to take. However, if the Ombudsman is dissatisfied with the proposed action the only action which can be taken is the issuance of a second report. In 95 per cent of cases in which injustice was found, satisfactory settlements have been reached;[53] but this still leaves 5 per cent of cases in which local authorities have refused to provide a satisfactory remedy. In the 1989 Act the government has tried to strengthen the system by introducing new procedures to require councils to give full consideration to adverse reports and to provide a public explanation if they decide not to comply with the Ombudsman's recommendations.[54] Furthermore, the government has recently stated that, if the new procedures failed to remedy the situation, legislation making the Ombudsman's recommendations legally enforceable would be introduced.[55]

In addition to the reforms bolstering the work of the Local Ombudsman, the government also recently introduced reforms to strengthen complaints mechanisms within local government. In the 1989 Act the duty was imposed on local authorities to establish a monitoring officer whose function would be to report on any action or proposed action by the authority which would give rise to a contravention of law or code of practice or to maladministration.[56] The government has also recently acquired powers to require local authorities to establish a complaints procedure relating to the discharge of their social services functions.[57]

The role of the courts

One consequence of the many changes which have been introduced in reorganising local authority functions and strengthening accountability mechanisms has been, potentially, to render local government more susceptible to judicial supervision. The breaking open of the enclosed, corporate local authority through such reforms as the differentiation of political and managerial responsibilities, the formalisation of the distinction between purchaser and provider functions, the requirement that service units operate on commercial lines and the imposition of new duties on local authorities to avoid anticompetitive practices all serve to subject local government to tighter forms of legal control than has generally been the practice this century. The vesting of new legal rights in the consumers of local authority services provides further opportunities to challenge the decisions of local councils. And the recent reforms to external accountability mechanisms – seen most clearly with audit reforms – tend to provide review agencies with new powers to subject local authorities to more active legal supervision.

The result can be seen in the extent to which disputes concerning certain areas of local government decision-making – such as the allocation of pupils to schools – which have not hitherto generally ended up in the courts are now regularly the subject of judicial review.[58] One consequence of the general trend of recent reforms, then, is to enhance the legal consciousness of decision-makers in local government and potentially to strengthen judicial oversight. Whether our legal system possesses the necessary cognitive, organisational or power resources to be able to handle effectively the control tasks which may be assigned to it remains open to question.

Changing forms of accountability

Many of the reforms designed to strengthen the accountability of local government may be welcomed, in terms both of enhancing the idea of citizenship and of rendering the authority more responsive to the needs of those it exists to serve. But there is little doubt that in general the reforms challenge the idea of the corporate authority and, potentially at least, could weaken the institution of local government. This argument is most likely to be articulated by those who regard public services as being *sui generis* since many of the reforms stem from the desire to simplify local services and thus render them fungible. The critical issue, then, is whether the customer service orientation which seems to underpin many of the reforms can generate a language which is able adequately to encompass and express the interests which citizens hold in the processes of governance.[59]

The constitutional status of local government

Throughout the twentieth century the institution of local government has formed a vital component of the British system of government. Although the functions of local government have been adjusted in the light of changing circumstances, the idea of the elected local council vested with discretion and resources and charged with responsibility for providing those public services which required a local mode of delivery has been generally accepted. Over the last twenty years, however, the stress points have become exposed and, as the Conservative administrations since 1979 have acted to recast the relationship between state and society, those conditions which have sustained the institution of local government within the interdependent network of modern government have subsided. Many of the specific reforms which have been introduced may, considered separately, be justified as part of a need for re-thinking government in a radically changing world. When viewed cumulatively, however, the reforms constitute a sustained attack on the modern institution of local government.

The recent reforms have altered the basic character of local government. The tradition of the self-sufficient, corporate authority which was vested with broad discretion to raise revenue and provide services has been directly challenged. Discretionary powers have been confined, structured and checked and the regime of local government finance is now such that it is virtually impossible for local authorities to diverge significantly from specific, centrally determined spending assessments. Local government has, in effect, been transformed from that of being the basic institution with responsibility for providing those public services which require local delivery systems into a rather discredited agency which, though in fact retaining responsibility for many important services, no longer holds a necessarily pre-eminent status. Local councils have been stripped of governmental responsibility for certain services which continue to be public services but which are now provided by agencies which are funded directly from the centre. New governmental initiatives which are based on localities have invariably been promoted through special agencies which are subject to central control. And, in relation to those functions retained by local government, the centre has generally required councils to adopt a set of internal markets based on a purchaser–provider distinction, the establishment of local council provider units on a commercial basis and the use of competitive tendering for determining delivery of local services.

This may be viewed as being a rather negative assessment. It might be argued that, in reality, the experience of the last twenty years is best seen as a watershed marking a period of transition between an old-style bureaucratic model of local government and a new, streamlined, responsive model of local government which is now emerging. On this analysis, this new model of the enabling authority provides a more effective system: one which replaces a system dominated by producer interests for one in which the consumer interest takes precedence; which builds competition into the structure of local government and thus maintains incentives to enhance the efficiency of public services; which, in differentiating service specification from service provision, requires the council to focus directly on its critical governmental responsibilities; and which, consequently, maintains flexibility so as to be in a position to respond effectively to new challenges.

The difficulty with this analysis may be illuminated by focusing on two closely related issues: the idea of public services, and the ratchet effect of central control. The idea of public services has, as has already been indicated, a vital political dimension. Once public services are subjected to strict market disciplines, however, they are likely to lose their peculiarly political and hence public character; and if those basic attributes are relinquished, such services also lose their local character. Once local services are required to be provided in accordance with market criteria of economy and efficiency they lose the sense of variety which lies at the heart of the justification of local government. Further, if local services are to be provided according to market criteria then the tradition of tolerance in the central–local government relationship will rapidly disappear. The Redcliffe-Maud view that local councils 'can decide for themselves . . . what kind of services they want'[60] will quickly be replaced by the belief that central government 'has a duty to intervene to ensure that local government provides services for the people who live in the area in the most efficient and economical way'.[61]

It is essentially because of these two trends that the positive attributes of the enabling model of local government do not significantly feature in the contemporary framework of local government. Recent reforms in pursuit of efficiency have sought to expunge the basic characteristics of public – and thus local – services and have thereby been associated with the centralisation of power. If there exists an economic benchmark against which all services can be tested, then not only is variety replaced with uniformity but also the centre is no longer able to tolerate difference and is obliged to intervene in order to secure economy and efficiency. Once this position is reached, it rapidly leads to the centre using special agencies, which can more easily be controlled, to carry out local tasks. And if evidence is needed that the government has not in fact discovered the formula which provides the solution to the science of politics, we need look no further than its attempts to reorganise local government or reform local government finance.

The recent reforms thus reflect on the constitutional status of local government precisely because they affect the distribution of political authority, the character of our democracy and, ultimately, our conceptions of politics. The reforms pose a serious challenge to the traditional view that it 'is only by the combination of local representative institutions with the central institutions of Parliament, Ministers and Departments, that a genuine national democracy can be sustained'.[62] That view is in danger of being eroded and with it the idea of democracy as 'an acknowledgement of shared fallibility and shared vulnerability' is at risk of being supplanted with the idea that it is essentially 'a boast of political capacity'.[63] It is in this sense that these recent developments affect not only the status of local government but also the character of our basic constitutional arrangements.

Notes and references

1. *Report of the Royal Commission on Local Government in England* (Chairman: Lord Redcliffe-Maud) Cmnd 4040 (1969), vol. 1, para. 6(i).
2. This position has been modified since 1979 as a result of the adoption of the principle of direct election to the European Parliament.
3. See HMSO (1980) *The Government's Expenditure Plans*, Cmnd 7841, London: HMSO.
4. Minogue, K. (1978) 'On Hyperactivism in Modern British Politics', in Cowling, M. (ed.) *Conservative Essays*, London: Cassell, p. 177.
5. Bramley, G. (1985) 'Incrementalism Run Amok? Local Government Finance in Britain', *Public Administration*, vol. 63, p. 100.
6. Local Government Finance Act 1982, Pt.II.
7. Foster, C. D. and Jackman, R. A. (1982) 'Accountability and Control of Local Spending', *Public Money*, Sept.

8. Jackman, R. (1985) 'Local Government Finance', in Loughlin, M., Gelfand, D. and Young, K. (eds), *Half A Century of Municipal Decline 1935–1985*, London: Allen & Unwin ch. 7, esp. pp. 158–61, 163.
9. Barnett, J. (1982) *Inside The Treasury*, London: Deutsch, pp. 75–6; Pliatsky, L. (1982) *Getting and Spending*, Oxford: Blackwell, p. 112; Gibson, J. (1983) 'Local "Overspending": Why the Government Have Only Themselves to Blame', *Public Money*, December.
10. Redlich, J. and Hirst, F. W. (1958) *The History of Local Government in England* (rev. edn) London: Macmillan, p. 26.
11. Jackman, 'Local Government Finance, p. 170.
12. Ibid.
13. Local Government Finance Act 1987, s.4.
14. Department of the Environment (1985) *Paying for Local Government*, Cmnd 9714, London: HMSO.
15. Ibid, para.1.37.
16. Ibid, paras 2.14–2.18.
17. Ibid, para.7.1.
18. See Bramley, G., Le Grand, J. and Low, W. (1989) 'How Far Is the Poll Tax a "Community Charge"? The Implications of Service Usage Evidence', *Policy & Politics*, vol. 17, p. 187.
19. For a more detailed examination of these various schemes, see Loughlin, M. (1990) 'Innovative Financing in Local Government: The Limits of Legal Instrumentalism', *Public Law*, 372, esp. pp. 377–82.
20. See, for example: Audit Commission (1987) *The Management of London's Authorities: Preventing the Breakdown of Services* (Occasional Paper No.2) which highlighted the case of eight London boroughs which, up to 1987, had cumulatively entered into deferred purchase arrangements amounting to over £550m.
21. Local Government Act 1987, inserting new sections 80A and 80B into LGPLA 1980.
22. Local Government Finance Act 1988, ss.130–132; inserting new s.79A into LGPLA 1980.
23. See Thomas, P. A. (1992) 'From McKenzie Friend to Leicester Assistant: The Impact of the Poll Tax', *Public Law*, 208, 209.
24. Each dwelling is placed in a valuation band, from a list ranging from band A (properties valued at less than £40 000) to band H (properties valued at over £320 000). In less wealthy areas, in which a high proportion of properties are valued in band A, the system operates extremely crudely, with no significant distinction being made between properties which may be worth double those of others in the same valuation band.
25. See Audit Commission (1993) *Passing the Bucks. The Impact of Standard Spending Assessments on Economy, Efficiency and Effectiveness*, London: HMSO.
26. See First Report of the House of Commons Environment Committee, Session 1993–94, *Standard Spending Assessments* (HC 90).
27. *Report of the Committee of Inquiry into the Conduct of Local Authority Business* (Chairman: Mr David Widdicombe QC) Cmnd 9797 (1986) London: HMSO.

28. Ibid, para.1.1.
29. Local Government and Housing Act 1989, ss.1–3, 4, 6, 7–8, 13 and 15.
30. On these developments see Himsworth, C.M.G. (1991) 'Officers, Members and Local Autonomy', in Finnie, W., Himsworth, C. and Walker, N. (eds), *Edinburgh Essays in Public Law*, Edinburgh: Edinburgh University Press, p. 121.
31. See, for example, Local Government Finance Act 1988 s.26(4) (community charges registration officer); 1988 Act s.114(7) (chief finance officer); Local Government and Housing Act 1989 s.4(1)(b) (head of paid service); 1989 Act, s.5(1)(b) (monitoring officer).
32. For implicit government recognition of this point, see Department of the Environment (1991) *Local Government Review: The Internal Management of Local Authorities in England*, London: HMSO.
33. Chester, D.N. (1951) *Central and Local Government*, London: Macmillan, p. 351.
34. Local Government Finance Act 1982, Pt.III.
35. Local Government Finance Act 1982, s.15(1)(c).
36. Day, P. and Klein, R. (1990) *Inspecting the Inspectorates*, York: Joseph Rountree Memorial Trust, p. 16. See also Loughlin, M. (1992) *Administrative Accountability in Local Government*, York: Joseph Rountree Memorial Trust, ch. 3.
37. See: Day, P. and Klein, R. *Inspecting the Inspecorates*; Loughlin, M. *Administrative Accountability*; McSweeney, B. (1988) 'Accounting for the Audit Commission', *Political Quarterly*, vol. 28; Radford, M. (1991) 'Auditing for Change: Local Government and the Audit Commission', 54 MLR 912.
38. *The Citizen's Charter*, Cm 1599 (1991). See further, Loughlin, M. (1992) *Administrative Accountability in Local Government*, York, ch. 6.
39. Local Government Act 1988 s.30, Sched.4 (inserting new ss.25A–25C into the Local Government Finance Act 1982).
40. Local Government Act 1988 s.30, Sched.4 (inserting new s.25D into Local Government Finance Act 1982). This power was successfully used by the auditor in *R* v. *Wirral MBC, ex parte Milstead* [1989] RVR 66.
41. Local Government Act 1974, s.26.
42. See, for example, Commission for Local Administration in England, *Annual Report 1984/85*, ch.3, London: HMSO.
43. Widdicombe Report, Cmnd 9797 (1986) para.9.64.
44. Local Government Act 1988, Sched. 3, para.5(2); amending Local Government Act 1974 s.26(2).
45. Commission for Local Administration in England, *Annual Report 1988/89*, p. 9, London: HMSO.
46. *R.* v. *Local Commissioner, ex parte Eastleigh BC* [1988] 3 WLR 113, 119.
47. 1974 Act, s.26(7).
48. 1974 Act, s.26(6).
49. 1974 Act, Sched.5.
50. In 1988 the exclusion list was amended to enable investigations to be conducted into local authority action in connection with the investiga-

tion or prevention of crime (SI 1988 No.242), and by s.269 of the Education Act 1993 jurisdiction was extended to education appeal committees of grant-maintained schools.
51. 1974 Act, s.31(2B); inserted by Local Government and Housing Act 1989, s.26.
52. 1989 Act, s.23.
53. Commission for Local Administration in England, *Annual Report 1988/89*, pp. 11–13.
54. 1989 Act, ss.26–29.
55. *The Citizen's Charter*, Cm 1599 (1991), p. 43.
56. 1989 Act, s.5.
57. National Health Service and Community Care Act 1990, s.46.
58. See Meredith, P. (1992) *Government, Schools and the Law*, London: Routledge.
59. See Ranson, S. and Stewart, J. (1989) 'Citizenship and Government: The Challenge for Management in the Public Domain', *Political Studies*, vol. 37, no 5; Stewart, J. and Walsh, K. (1992) 'Change in the Management of Public Services', *Public Administration*, vol. 70, pp. 499, 510–16.
60. Redcliffe-Maud Report, Cmnd 4040, p. iii.
61. Howard, M. (1987) (Minister for Local Government), Official Report HC Standing Committee A, col.48 (21 October 1987); quoted in M. Radford, [1988] 51 MLR 747, 767.
62. Redcliffe Maud Report, Cmnd 4040, p. iii.
63. Dunn, J. (1990) *Interpreting Political Responsibility*, Cambridge: Cambridge University Press, p. 214.

4   Participation in Local Elections

Colin Rallings, Michael Temple and Michael Thrasher

Introduction

Victorian reformers charged with creating a system of local government which was both effective and democratic were adamant that
community identity should lie at the heart of the policy. Without
voters who could identify and recognise the community of interest in
the new administrative boundaries the idea of local democracy
would be a sham. A representative local government would fail if
people felt insufficiently motivated to vote, to contribute to the
activities necessary for a sense of civic purpose and identity and to
acknowledge the legitimacy of that local authority.

Despite the radical changes to which local government has been
subject in recent years, most survey evidence suggests that local
government is still valued as an essential element of democracy.
Those members of the public who have contacted their council or
engaged in local participation are generally positive about the
experience. Moreover, there is a remarkable degree of satisfaction
with the standard of service provided by local authorities. Indeed
recent surveys show far more supportive attitudes to local government than those conducted in earlier decades and suggest that local
politicians may have responded to public concerns about accountability and consultation rather better than their critics at central
government level or in the media have ever acknowledged. These
supportive attitudes are bolstered by public feelings of attachment
not only to an immediate locality but also to local authorities
themselves. There is little majority support either for significant
structural or boundary changes or for substantial alteration to the
local democratic system.

A problem of turnout?

However, such feelings of local identity and community spirit as do exist cannot be said to have led to greater participation in local elections. Perceptions of poor levels of turnout continue to dog local government's claim to democratic legitimacy among critics and supporters alike. Compared with other countries within the European Union Britain lags some distance behind in a league table of local turnouts – see Table 4.1. Although some of those countries towards the top of the league have either a legal or quasi-legal requirement for compulsory voting, others do not.

If we extend our coverage of countries, however, marked variations in terms of electoral system and political culture begin to emerge. Table 4.1 again shows how electoral participation is higher for those countries which utilise some form of proportional representation (PR) (largely party list system or single transferable vote) than for those who employ first past the post (FPTP). Various advocates of proportional representation have claimed its introduction would enhance electoral participation[1] while recent research has indicated that, other things being equal, turnout for PR systems is some 7 per cent higher than for FPTP.[2] In a recent analysis of distortions in the seats/vote ratio in British local government resulting from the use of simple plurality elections, we advocated the introduction of the single transferable vote as the best method for restoring accountability without sacrificing the important principle in local elections of voting for the individual and not party.[3]

There are, however, some countries that despite their use of PR for sub-national elections still display relatively low rates of participation. Here, the likely explanation has to do with political culture and attitudes towards the political and governmental system in particular. In the newly democratising countries of Eastern Europe, for example Poland, the initial euphoria surrounding the overthrow of Communism has been gradually replaced by frustration and cynicism on the part of electors. This resentment that the promise of yesterday has not been replaced by the reforms of today has begun to show through in terms of low levels of electoral participation.

Evidence from Table 4.1 suggests that explanations for turnout in local elections may reside in factors which are sometimes structural, sometimes attitudinal and sometimes a combination of both. Academic studies have traditionally approached the matter of electoral

TABLE 4.1 Average turnout in recent sub-national elections

	Mean (%)
Luxembourg^	93
Sweden^	90
Australia* (compulsory)	85
Italy^	85
Belgium^	80
Denmark^	80
Germany^	72
France^	70
Spain^	64
Ireland^	62
Portugal^	60
Israel	57
Netherlands^	54
New Zealand*	53
Poland	43
Great Britain^*	40
Australia *(optional)	35
Canada*	33
U.S.A.*	25

Notes and sources:
These data were obtained variously from official sources; Widdicombe, table 5.8 from 'Aspects of Local Democracy', *Research Volume 4*; and *Keesing's Contemporary Archive*, various years. A * indicates a member country of the European Union. A ^ indicates use of a non PR electoral system. Some Australian states have compulsory voting while others operate a voluntary system.

participation in one of two ways. First, there have been studies considering turnout as part of a wider inquiry into patterns of political behaviour. In such instances the data has often been restricted in time as well as in scope since the research focus has been on the politics of a specific place or organisation. A second method for considering turnout has been to use survey data to investigate relationships between reported turnout and the personal and socio-economic attributes and attitudes of respondents. Findings from such studies have sometimes been contradictory. Researchers have argued variously that patterns of local election turnout are a function of national level electoral movement or, conversely, that the character of the local authority/ward has a bearing on levels of political interest and electoral participation. Some survey research has concluded that those individuals more likely to vote skew election results in favour or against particular political parties; other studies argue that those who vote, and those who do not, are a social and political microcosm of the electorate as a whole.

We will report on these findings in order to summarise the main conclusions and points of dissent to date about the nature of local electoral participation. This will form the basis of a set of questions which can then be examined using data previously unavailable. The Local Government Chronicle Elections Centre now has data on over 100 000 local election results in England and Wales since reorganisation. These data contain information about district wards and divisions, electorates, candidate names, parties and votes relating to every local election since 1973 (in the case of London since 1964). They will prove invaluable as we seek a wider understanding of electoral participation in local government.

Electoral participation: findings from case studies

Party organisation and turnout effects

A number of individual case studies have been conducted consisting of either historical analyses or snapshot inquiries into particular communities. From these we can glean certain evidence about the factors believed to influence electoral participation. Those taking a long-term view of an area have noted the particular impact of the development of a competitive party system on local elections. Studies of Birmingham and Wolverhampton in the late nineteenth century, for example, comment on a rapidly expanding franchise and the need for parties to organise, develop and, on occasion, co-operate to woo sections of the local government electorate.[4] By the end of the last century party politics was a fact of life in the vast majority of the largest towns and cities. In rural authorities the spread of party was not as great and elections in these authorities contrasted with the their urban counterparts in two important respects. First, the absence of competition meant that many councillors were returned unopposed. In Devon, for example, for much of the twentieth century it was normal for most county councillors to be 'elected' in this manner. An analysis of four counties conducted in the 1930s showed that the majority of councillors were returned unopposed.[5] Second, many councillors held no overt party allegiance and fought elections as 'Independents'. In the absence of a party machine such candidates were often left to their own devices in terms of campaigning and canvassing. Over time, however, the spread of parties has embraced more and more rural authorities. In recent local elections both the number of unopposed seats and Independent councillors has declined.[6]

Many studies have examined the link between local party activity and the level of participation in elections.[7] Parties have played a major role in stimulating public interest through election campaigning and facilitating electoral choice by distilling issues for public presentation. Thus, parties present policies for debate, attract media attention and generally instil some vitality into the election atmosphere. Various case studies have confirmed the important link between party competition and higher levels of electoral participation. In the 1964 local elections, for example, Fletcher noted that 'average turnout in non-marginal wards contested by Liberals was more than one third higher than in non-marginal contests where no Liberal stood'.[8] As party organisations developed, however, they became much more than mere campaigning vehicles. Often they became the primary route for the recruitment and selection of new candidates and in this way further facilitated participation in local government.

Parties, therefore, form an important ingredient in the electoral process, encouraging the general public to vote as well as attracting a smaller number of individuals towards a more intense level of political participation. Sometimes the individuals that local parties choose to fight the elections can unintentionally provoke higher levels of public interest and turnout. A study of local elections in Bradford in the early 1960s noted how the presence of Pakistani candidates in some wards appeared to have caused a higher than average amount of interest in the contests, a fact reflected in higher rates of electoral participation.[9]

In reviewing the arguments against parties in local government, however, Byrne observes that the existence of party may have had an adverse effect upon electoral participation. His point is that should one party exert a stranglehold on an authority then voters in such one-party states might see any election as a foregone conclusion and abstain accordingly.[10] We shall test this observation in more detail later.

What evidence exists that electors actually respond to the activities of local parties? A study by Jordan and Dyer of the marked electoral register following elections in Aberdeen was able to determine which electors had actually voted. The authors concluded that two factors appeared particularly influential in persuading people to vote. First, there was the strength of party identification, a sense of psychological involvement which earlier studies had uncovered. The second factor, however, was the level of party activity in the ward. This suggests that other things being equal political parties have a critical role to play in promoting the competitiveness of local elections and in stimulating turnout.[11] A much earlier study by Hill of voting in Leeds had made a clear link between the level of turnout in two Conservative wards and what appeared to be superior organisation in those same wards.[12]

Further evidence of the importance of party upon levels of electoral participation was evident in a study of a Conservative agent in Harrow. The agent diverted party workers away from safe wards into marginal wards producing a significant impact on turnout in those areas. At the following elections when the tactic was abandoned voting returned to its normal levels.[13] Similar effects were noted by Bochel and Denver when they conducted Labour ward campaigns in Lancaster and Dundee. They concentrated especially on frequent canvassing of party supporters in targeted areas. Their activities resulted in increased turnouts in those wards relative to wards in the remainder of the authorities.[14] Another study by the same team replicating a research method pioneered in the United States produced further evidence of the tangible effects of party activity on overall levels of turnout. In the 1970 Dundee elections the failure of the two main parties to fight campaigns in a safe Labour ward delivered the opportunity to conduct an interesting experiment. Two blocks of flats in the ward were selected, each a similar distance from the polling station. One of these blocks was completely ignored while the other was heavily canvassed with each voter visited three times. Electors in the respective blocks were then interviewed the day following the poll to discover whether they had voted. In the block which had been ignored, turnout was 54 per cent, while in the canvassed block it was 64 per cent.[15] Such evidence, therefore, points unequivocally to the link between party organisation, the level of party activity and the state of party competition and the electorate's awareness of local elections and ultimately their willingness to participate.

Ward size and turnout effects

A study in the United States shows a relationship between constituency size and electoral turnout. Cutright and Rossi found that
candidates did better in their home precincts than elsewhere in the
district, indicating that voters were more inclined to support someone they knew when they recognised names on ballot papers.[16]
Further studies have pointed to the importance of what can be
termed the 'friends and neighbours effect' on voting patterns.[17] An
example from Britain suggests that physical space also can have an
effect on turnout. Taylor's study of voting in Swansea demonstrated
the distance an elector had to travel to the polling station appeared
to have an effect on the likelihood of voting. Of those electors
estimated to be within a minute's walk of the polling station no less
than 65 per cent voted, but of those who lived over five minutes
away only 35 per cent did so.[18]

However, a small electorate and/or physical compactness may
have its down side too. In a study of Scottish local elections it was
found that individuals did not wish to stand against an incumbent
who was well known in the district for fear of giving offence.[19] Too
small and wards risk taking the friends and neighbours effect too
far, indeed to the point where electoral competition is avoided
because of its threat to community bonds. Too big and wards cease
to reflect a sense of community identity and electors fail to see the
salience of local elections. Once again, we shall test these observations later using aggregate electoral data.

Ward marginality and turnout effects

The research findings relating to party campaigning suggest party
activists can have an influence on overall rates of turnout. This begs
the logical question: other things being equal, in which wards should
parties campaign the most and, by implication, influence turnout the
most? A study by Price and Lupfer of precinct level canvassing in
Tennessee concluded that party resources are best targeted in the
marginal wards.[20] On this matter, however, case studies in Britain
appear to offer differing sets of evidence. The orthodoxy, it might be
argued, suggests the closeness of party competition within a ward
has an effect on levels of turnout. Fletcher, for example, writing
about the 1960s, concludes the major effect on turnout appeared to
be the closeness of the result – the more marginal the seat the more

parties campaigned and canvassed, the more interest it evoked and the more electors were inclined to vote. In her case study of Leeds, Hill remarked matter-of-factly, 'The general level of political activity (as measured by the turn-out in local elections) upholds the generalisation that it is the marginal wards which have the highest turn-out . . .'[21] Similar findings were reported on party campaigns in London Borough elections.[22]

Another approach, however, has been taken by Newton who argues local voting and turnout were more likely to be affected by national politics and the prevailing mood of the day rather than the marginality of particular wards.[23] Our own turnout data provides some support for both sides to this argument. The sudden rise in turnout at the 'poll tax' elections in 1990 points to the significance of a national controversy on overall levels of electoral participation. However, other things being equal, turnout is higher in marginal wards when compared with safe wards. Competition, it would seem, plays a vital role in stimulating party and electoral interest alike, which in turn can have a beneficial effect on levels of local turnout.

Various case studies have provided *prima facie* evidence that certain factors may play a role in stimulating levels of turnout in local elections. The growth of party organisation and competition have served to bring issues and choices before the local electorate. The drawing of electoral boundaries has been shown to have a potentially critical role in terms of whether voters recognise a community of local interest and display a sense of caring about the outcome of the electoral process. In the next section we examine the evidence on electoral turnout from survey data.

Electoral participation: the evidence from survey data

An explanation of non-voting

Given that the majority of electors do not vote in local elections it is, perhaps, sensible to begin by asking not who votes but rather what sorts of people abstain. Using British Election Study data for the period 1966–74, Ivor Crewe and others investigated some possible explanations for abstention in parliamentary elections. They dismissed the idea that voting was to be regarded as a difficult form of political participation: even respondents who rarely talked about politics or took note of media presentations of politics seemed to vote.[24] The method employed in this study was to observe patterns of voting/non-voting across a sequence of four elections, thereby reducing the effects of random abstention, and increasing the opportunities to identify systematic abstention. The most significant finding, perhaps, was the absence of what we might call the 'serial abstainer'. The research found a mere 1 per cent of respondents had abstained in all four elections. As the authors note, 'Non-voters in a particular election are not part of a substantial body within the electorate who persistently opt out of elections.'

Opinion surveys concerned specifically with exploring the circumstances and motivation for voting in *local* elections have been very few. Even the research commissioned by the Maud and Redcliffe-Maud inquiries in the 1960s touched on this subject only briefly, if at all. Maud, for example, reported its survey had found three-quarters of respondents claiming to have voted in recent district elections – a figure somewhat in excess of the 42 per cent who did actually vote. The survey also found a greater propensity to vote among the elderly compared with the young, and that those with strong feelings about the need to vote were more likely to exercise their vote. Later research carried out for the Redcliffe-Maud commission concentrated on attitudes towards community and local government and did not cover voting.[25]

The best recent information comes from two surveys carried out by NOP (National Opinion Polls). The first a study of over 1000 respondents conducted in November 1985 for the Widdicombe inquiry; the second the re-interview of a panel of 745 of the original sample in May 1986 for an ESRC (Economic and Social Research Council) funded project under the direction of William Miller.[26] In what follows we will concentrate on the evidence produced from the panel survey.

To an extent the panel method employed in the NOP survey replicates the method used by Crewe and others in their analysis of non-voting. Although it is a two-wave study Miller is able to use factor analysis to uncover those variables which appear to be relevant to an individual's decision to vote in local elections. His findings show that, 'local turn-out behaviour *does* vary over time, and the electorate is *not* divided into regular local election voters and regular local election abstainers'.[27] This is precisely the evidence unearthed in the analysis of general election voting but it is surely of greater significance given the differences in abstention rates between local and general elections. In short, the majority who abstain in one set of elections are not necessarily the same majority who abstain in another.

In terms of the personal characteristics of voters and non-voters Miller's surveys confirmed earlier research. The propensity to vote correlated with age and length of residence. Older voters were more likely to vote than other age groups while longer-term residents also had better voting records than other groups. The other variable which the analysis of Crewe *et al.* had identified as significant was housing tenure, noting that council house tenants were more likely to vote than those in the privately rented sector. The size of Miller's sample precluded this distinction within the rented sector but it is worth noting his observation that council tenants were more likely to vote than owner-occupiers. At first glance this finding might appear counter-intuitive, and, of course, it is contrary to findings on voting behaviour in parliamentary elections, but further considera-tion should find it an eminently reasonable observation. Other things being equal, council tenants have more at stake in their local authority and it should not be too surprising that this greater level of investment should manifest itself in their willingness to vote.

The sense of psychological involvement in politics was an im-portant factor in determining the likelihood of someone voting. Miller found that local turnout was closely related to an elector's knowledge of, and interest in, politics. Of those who discussed local politics regularly no less than 74 per cent actually voted in the elections compared with a 46 per cent turnout amongst those who never discussed local politics.[28] Crucially he found a strong correla-tion between turnout and those who could correctly identify their local councillors.

Another category of variables investigated by Miller were labelled 'national mobilisation/constraint factors'. He found that respon-dents' attitudes towards or against particular social groupings, for example trade unionists, did not appear to make any difference to their tendency to turn out and vote in local elections. Would specifically local factors act in either a mobilising or constraining manner? The research found no correlation between a respondent's satisfaction with the council and electoral participation. What did appear to make a difference was whether an actual complaint had been made to the council. In these circumstances the individual was more likely to vote than not. Rate-paying, however, appeared to make no difference to the level of electoral participation. This will disappoint those who believe that a central pillar of local democracy is a clear link between having a financial stake in the activities of the council (through the payment of local taxes) and the holding of elected members to account.

Miller's analysis constitutes the most comprehensive test of opinion about local turnout to date. To a significant extent the findings confirm previous research. A person's age, their sense of psychological involvement in local politics and the strength of party identification all appear critical factors in determining the propensity to vote. But Miller goes on to suggest that while the variables correlated well with turnout they are not necessarily good for predicting turnout itself. The reason for their weak predictive ability appears to focus on the instability of the party identification variable. The process of partisan dealignment has effectively injected a degree of instability into the whole question of a person's sense of party identification. We can no longer be certain that people who identify strongly with a party at one interview will necessarily respond in the same way at a subsequent interview. In short, predicting local turnout on the basis of survey data has become more of a problem than it once might have been. In the next section we shall see whether an analysis of aggregate level data can offer us more scope for understanding electoral participation.

Electoral particpation: the evidence from aggregate data

Analysing local electoral data

Local elections can be thought of as having a set of structural, political and socio-economic contexts. In terms of the structural context we could pose the following questions. What effect, if any, does the size of a council have on turnout? Is there a relationship between people's propensity to vote and the ratio of councillors to electors? Does it make any difference to turnout if elections are held once a year as opposed to once every four years? The political context of local elections generates a different order of questioning. Does the rate at which people participate vary according to the nature of party political control in the ward or authority? Are the electorate sensitive to political marginality and does the closeness of the contest alter the cost/benefit analysis of voting? Finally, what impact do such socio-economic variables as home ownership and unemployment have upon rates of turnout? While survey data have given some clues in this direction it has been but a partial and restricted view. Below, we will offer answers to these questions using aggregate local electoral data.[29]

Local government reorganisation in London took place a decade before that in the rest of Great Britain. It is possible, therefore, to take a longer view of trends in electoral participation in the capital. As Table 4.2 shows, turnout in London borough elections has risen steadily from the 1960s onwards, reaching a maximum of 48.1 per cent overall in 1990, the year of the 'poll-tax' elections, before falling back slightly in 1994. London voters have a generally good record on turnout in local elections compared with the Metropolitan boroughs. Interestingly, the reverse is the case when we compare the two in terms of electoral participation at general elections. Then, the turnout is lower in London than for cities based in the metropolitan areas.

If we examine comparable statistics for the metropolitan boroughs there is a shorter time period to examine but the advantage is that the data are virtually annual because of the nature of the electoral cycle in these authorities.

The metropolitan data in Table 4.3 provide more evidence about the direction and influence of external factors on local turnout patterns. Once again the impact of the poll tax on electoral turnout is apparent. In the 1990 elections turnout reached its peak if we exclude the unusual circumstances of 1979 when voting was simultaneous with the general election. The proximity of a general

TABLE 4.2   Contestation and Turnout in London Elections 1964–1990

GLC			Boroughs		
Year	*%contested*	*%turnout*	*Year*	*%contested*	*%turnout*
1964	100.0	44.4	1964	99.1	35.7
1967	100.0	39.6	1968	98.3	35.8
1970	100.0	34.3	1971	99.2	38.7
1973	100.0	36.6	1974	98.6	36.4
1977	100.0	43.4	1978	99.7	43.1
1981	100.0	44.4	1982	99.7	43.9
			1986	99.9	45.4
			1990	99.5	48.1
			1994	100.0	46.0

TABLE 4.3   Contestation and turnout in Metropolitan elections

Metropolitan counties			Metropolitan boroughs		
Year	*%contested*	*%turnout*	*Year*	*%contested*	*%turnout*
1973	96.3	36.5	1973	97.4	33.4
			1975	94.8	32.7
			1976	98.4	38.1
1977	98.9	38.6	1978	99.1	37.2
			1979	99.1	74.7
			1980	98.4	36.3
1981	99.6	37.9	1982	99.6	38.8
			1983	99.3	42.0
			1984	98.4	39.8
			1986	97.1	39.9
			1987	98.3	44.7
			1988	97.9	40.1
			1990	93.6	46.2
			1991	95.5	40.8
			1992	98.5	32.5
			1994	96.5	38.9
			1995	96.3	32.6

election, perceived or otherwise, also has an effect on local turnout. Hill's study of Leeds county borough provides time series data dating from the Second World War. We can see turnout was above average in years with general elections, falling back quite sharply the following year.[30] In 1983 and 1987 Mrs Thatcher used the local elections as a test of electoral opinion with more than one eye on a summer general election. The voters got the message and turnout rose above the average. In 1991 many thought John Major would repeat this practice and turnout rose once again. It is, perhaps, too early to judge the dramatic slump of 1992 where the local elections followed just a month after a general election. Initial thinking might suggest that general voter fatigue plus dispirited Labour voters combined to reduce turnout in the metropolitan authorities to their lowest ever level. However, turnout in 1995 struggled to beat even this low and may presage a return to the lower turnout levels of the 1970s.

The turnout data contained in Table 4.4 for the shire counties and districts in England is difficult to interpret. The problem stems from the fact that in the shire districts local authorities have the option of

TABLE 4.4   Contestation and turnout in English shire elections

	Counties			Districts	
Year	*%contested*	*%turnout*	*Year*	*%contested*	*%turnout*
1973	86.2	42.6	1973	81.2	38.6
			1976	74.0	44.2
1977	87.2	42.3	1978	93.0	42.4
			1979	72.4	76.6
			1980	93.1	38.9
1981	95.9	43.7	1982	96.9	41.8
			1983	82.5	45.6
			1984	95.1	40.2
1985	97.9	41.6	1986	97.1	41.9
			1987	88.7	47.8
			1988	95.7	41.5
1989	97.9	39.2	1990	96.3	48.6
			1991	87.6	48.1
			1992	96.6	37.8
1993	98.3	37.2	1994	96.3	42.6
			1995	91.7	40.3

conducting annual or quadrennial elections although most district councils have all-out elections every four years. Just under 40 per cent of the shire districts hold annual elections where a fraction, normally one-third, of seats are contested. In this sense, therefore, we are not comparing like with like when we compare turnouts on an annual basis. The safest approach is to take the quadrennial cycle from 1983 onwards and examine those years for any pattern. Certainly, the results confirm the findings of the London and metropolitan authorities, that local turnout is generally rising over a 20-year period, is above average when general elections are perceived as imminent, and falls away significantly in the aftermath of a general election. Once again, however, data from 1995 present a slightly contrary view. Although the proportion of wards contested was over 90 per cent for the first time in this cycle, turnout was about 6 per cent below average. Much of this may be explained by the lack of speculation about a general election, but as in the metropolitan authorities there is just the hint that turnout may be declining again as local government personalities, policy and finance no longer occupy the centre stage they were accorded through much of the 1980s.

Is there a pattern to local turnout?

When we have examined turnout by tier of local authority the data suggest a slight increase in turnout over time. The standard deviation in turnout levels *between* authorities within each tier has remained fairly constant or slightly decreased. This suggests that most authorities within each tier have conformed with a general trend. If we ignore the figures for 1979, the highest mean turnout figure in each tier is accompanied by relatively high minimum and maximum scores among individual councils. Likewise, the lowest mean turnout for a tier of local government similarly produces low minimum and maximum individual turnouts. In short, when turnout rises across a tier of local government it does so across the board, and similarly when it falls it does so across all authorities.

There should be a word of caution at this point. Turnout *may* have increased partly as a result of declining numbers on the electoral register, with those citizens inclined to vote in any event less likely to take themselves off the register than those whose participation was always low. This would produce an increase in recorded turnout even if no more, or indeed, fewer people were going to the polls. A recent study by McLean and Smith has explored the effects of the poll tax on the composition of electoral registers. They estimate the total shortfall from the electoral register because of the poll tax to be some 600 000 people.[31] An alternative view of the declining register, however, could be that electoral registration officers are proving more efficient at compiling their registers. Thus whereas, in the past, electors who had died or moved out of the area might have been left on the register, the ease of computerising registers means that alterations can be made more rapidly. This also implies that registers of electors may have been too large prior to computerisation, especially when registration officers were less assiduous at weeding out redundant names. This may have contributed to artificially low turnout figures.

Just as there seems to be evidence that the pattern of turnout in local authorities as a whole responds to similar impetuses, so it is the case that individual councils tend to occupy a largely unchanging position in any league-table of turnout. Two pieces of evidence can be used to support this claim. In the first place, there is a very high correlation in turnout across local authorities between pairs of elections – or put another way a local authority which enjoys high turnout in one election is likely to have high turnout at subsequent elections. Although the relationship is strongest between adjacent elections, it is impressive that it is still present for elections more than ten years apart. The correlation between contests in 1990 (poll tax elections) and 1992 (aftermath of general election) is especially interesting. Those two sets of elections produced first the highest and then the lowest local turnouts for more than a decade, but the still high inter-election correlation suggests that the absolute change in turnout levels had little impact on individual local authorities' records as relatively good or relatively poor performers. Voters in some authorities appear good at participating while in other authorities they show a marked reluctance to use their vote.

This pattern of enthusiasm or indifference can be confirmed by looking at where local authorities appear in an election by election rank order of turnout in their tier. The same authorities appear time and again at the top or the bottom of the respective lists. Thus, for example, the London borough of Richmond upon Thames consistently finishes in the top three of a league table of London authority turnouts while Hackney repeatedly picks up the metaphorical wooden spoon. The pattern extends itself to the metropolitan boroughs. Here, it is Sunderland which finishes at or near the bottom of the 36 boroughs while Stockport is rarely far from first place. Of course local authorities can find that their position in the league table of turnout rises or falls. Where changes do take place there is usually a *prima facie* explanation readily available. For example, the movement of Liverpool and Westminster from near the bottom to near the top of their respective 'leagues' and the unusually high turnout in Bradford in 1990 would appear to be related to specifically local political events in those authorities.

Compactness and rates of electoral participation

If one of the aims of local government is to bring decision-making closer to the people, it might be expected that participation in local elections would vary according to the size and compactness of the local authority unit. In London there is a consistent, though declining, inverse relationship between population density and turnout: in short, the higher the population density the lower the turnout. Although the connection is not as stark as in the 1960s (when some inner city boroughs recorded turnouts below 20 per cent), population density still appears to define different attitudes to elections in the capital. By contrast, the relationship between population density and turnout in the metropolitan boroughs is both weak and inconsistent. The boundaries of these authorities are drawn in such a way that, unlike London, high population density does not in itself act as a surrogate for likely Labour party strength. Barnsley, for example, with a low population density has low turnouts, many uncontested seats and unchallenged Labour rule. Liverpool, by contrast, has a high density with relatively high turnouts and a more fiercely contested party system. In the shires, population density rarely features as an explanation of much force or significance for variations in turnout. The compactness of a local authority, therefore, does not appear to be significantly related to the electorate's propensity to vote.

Aside from the local authority itself, it might also be hypothesised that the size of each individual ward might have an impact on turnout. We can measure this in one of two ways. First, we can use the number of electors in each ward as the indicator, or second, the number of electors per councillor. In single member wards these ratios are, of course, the same. In London the relationships between representative ratios and turnout are, in fact, extremely modest. Similarly, in the metropolitan boroughs, ward and councillor/elector ratios seem to have negligible impact on turnout. In the counties, over time, size of electoral division is inversely correlated with turnout – the more electors in a division the lower the turnout. In the districts, although the correlation between representative ratios and turnout is small, the comparison of means does indicate a drop-off in participation at over 3000 electors per councillor and at over 7000 electors per ward regardless of the electoral cycle which districts adopt.

Political influences on turnout

Previous literature has suggested substantial support for the idea that levels of turnout are influenced by the political marginality or safety of a local authority/ward. Local authority marginality – here defined as the seats held by the largest party as a proportion of the whole – is likely to reflect at one and the same time socio-economic conditions less conducive to turnout as well as electors' reactions to living in an authority where party politics is perceived to be non-competitive. It is rational that electors in politically 'safe' local authorities should feel less need to record their vote simply because that vote is likely to make very little difference. In London, and to a lesser extent the metropolitan councils, we find that the safer the political control the lower the turnout in that authority. This inverse relationship is particularly strong for Labour-run councils. In the counties, the inverse relationship between turnout and marginality generally applies, while among the districts the same pattern is, once again, particularly noticeable for Labour-controlled councils.

Ward marginality – now defined as the percentage lead of the first over the second placed party at the previous election – appears to be a major influence on turnout in most types of authority. There is a consistent relationship between turnout and marginality, suggesting that when electors believe the outcome in their ward is in doubt they are more willing to incur the costs associated with voting. As far as the parties are concerned it is noticeable that there is a positive correlation in recent elections between Liberal Democrat share of the vote and turnout. Many of the party's local government successes seem to have been based on persuading an absolutely larger number of people to vote. On a more general level we can also observe that the growth of party competition has had a positive effect on levels of electoral participation. Other things being equal, the more parties contest and campaign for the seat the higher the turnout. Put another way, electors whose preferred party does not offer them a candidate at a given election will be less likely to turn out.

Social factors and turnout

Previous studies have suggested an individual's social circumstance can influence their willingness to participate in local elections. The conclusions of an analysis we carried out were unequivocal. In London boroughs, for example, there was a negative relationship between turnout and local authority affluence. Boroughs with high unemployment, high levels of council housing and an overcrowded housing stock were particularly prone to record low turnouts. Some boroughs, however, consistently appear to either out- or under-perform their predicted turnout. Richmond upon Thames is more than one standard deviation above its 'natural' turnout on every occasion; Barking and Dagenham and Newham are always at least that far below theirs.

A similar pattern is apparent in the metropolitan authorities in terms of both the relationship between measures of socio-economic status and turnout and the tendency for certain authorities to have consistently and statistically unexpectedly high or low levels of participation. In the shires, however, social and economic variables do not appear to be as powerful an influence on turnout as they are in London and big conurbations.

Conclusion

We have approached the issue of electoral participation from three different directions. First, we reviewed a series of case studies of either individual local authorities or aspects of party political behaviour. This literature pointed in general to the importance of party competition, particularly in respect of the closeness of that competition, electoral campaigns and the size of wards as factors in persuading electors to exercise their vote.

Next, we looked at the evidence from survey data, beginning with the valuable research on voting/non-voting in general elections conducted by Crewe, Fox and Alt. They discovered that age, residential mobility and housing tenure were significant factors in determining the propensity to vote. In addition an individual's psychological investment in the political process also appeared critical. Miller's two-wave panel survey confirmed many of the earlier findings with the additional observation that council tenants were more likely to vote than owner-occupiers. Arguably the most important finding of the survey data is that there do not appear to be electors who habitually abstain from voting in either national or local elections.

Our third and final approach has been to examine the data from local elections over a twenty-year period, or almost thirty in the case of London. In addition to confirming the link between marginality, party competition and turnout together with the influence of socio-economic variables on participation we were able to shed new light on levels of electoral participation. Over time, turnout in local elections has been rising, although we issued a cautionary note about the possible effects of the electoral register on these data. In general the creation of one-party states in local government has a negative effect on turnout. A healthy local democracy (judged in terms of local turnout) appears to be one where party competition is high and where no seat can be adjudged safe. There appeared also to be a number of external political factors having a significant effect upon turnout.

The proximity of general elections seemed to galvanise the local electorate and persuade more to vote than otherwise might be the case. Equally, there was a sense of general election hiatus when, in the year following, local turnouts would fall. Political controversy also appears to have a beneficial effect on turnout. As a general case the 1990 elections proved beyond doubt that the electorate will vote if stimulated – or perhaps 'provoked' would be a better description. Localised examples of the same kind of stimulus can also be found in authorities such as Liverpool, Westminster, Bradford and Basildon.

This still leaves those electors in certain authorities who defy the trends. Regardless of socio-economic status, regardless of the scale of party competition, regardless of the state of council and ward marginality, voters in authorities such as Rossendale, Richmond upon Thames and Stockport appear to turn out in greater numbers than we might expect. At the other extreme the reluctance of voters in Newham, Barking and Dagenham, Wigan, Sandwell, Stoke on Trent and Hull to go to the polls cannot be explained by the variables we currently have at our disposal.[32]

Notes and references

1. Lakeman, E. (1974) *How Democracies Vote: A Study of Electoral Systems*, London: Faber; Powell, G. B. (1980) 'Voting Turnout in Thirty Democracies: Partisan, Legal and Socio-economic Influences', in Rose R. (ed.), *Electoral Participation: A Comparative Analysis*, Beverly Hills: Sage.
2. Blais, A. and Carty, R. (1990) 'Does Proportional Representation Foster Voter Turnout?', *European Journal of Political Research*, vol. 18, pp. 167–81.
3. Rallings, C. and Thrasher, M. (1991) *Electoral Reform for Local Government*, London: Electoral Reform Society.
4. See Hennock, E. P. (1973) *Fit and Proper Persons*, London: Arnold; Jones, G. W. (1969) *Borough Politics*, London: Macmillan.
5. Self, P. (1947) 'Local Government and the Community', *Fabian Quarterly*, vol. 53, March, pp. 15–22.
6. See Rallings, C. and Thrasher, M. (various years) *Local Elections Handbook*. For an authority-by-authority breakdown see Rallings, C. and Thrasher, M. (eds) (1993) *Local Elections in Britain*, Plymouth: Local Government Chronicle Elections Centre.
7. See Gregory, R. (1969) 'Local Elections and the "Rule of Anticipated Reactions"', *Political Studies*, vol. 17, pp. 31–47; Pimlott, B. (1972)

'Does Local Party Organisation Matter?', *British Journal of Political Science*, vol. 2, pp. 381–3; Pimlott, B. (1973) 'Local Party Organisation, Turnout and Marginality', *British Journal of Political Science*, vol. 3, pp. 252–5; Bruce, A. and Lee, G. (1982) 'Local Election Campaigns', *Political Studies*, vol. 30, pp. 247–61.

8. Fletcher, P. (1967) 'The Results Analysed', in Sharpe, J. (ed.) *Voting in Cities*, London: Macmillan, p. 301.

9. Spiers, M. and Lelohe, M. (1964) 'Pakistanis in the Bradford Municipal Election of 1963', *Political Studies*, vol. 12.

10. Byrne, T. (1985) *Local Government in Britain*, Harmondsworth: Penguin, 3rd edn, p. 121.

11. Dyer, M. and Jordan, G. (1985) 'Who Votes in Aberdeen? Marked electoral Registers as a Data Source', *Strathclyde Papers in Government*, no. 42, Glasgow: University of Strathclyde.

12. Hill, D. (1967) 'Leeds', in Sharpe (ed.), *Voting in Cities*, p. 140.

13. Brown, J.(1958) 'Local Party Efficiency as a Factor in the Outcome of British Elections', *Political Studies*, vol. 6, pp. 174–8.

14. Bochel, J. and Denver, D. (1972) "The Impact of the Campaign on the Results of the Local Elections', *British Journal of Political Science*, vol. 2, pp. 239–42.

15. Bochel, J. and Denver, D. (1971) 'Canvassing, Turnout and Party Support: An Experiment', *British Journal of Political Science*, vol. 1, pp. 257–69.

16. Cutright, P. and Rossi, P. (1958) 'Party Organisation in Primary Elections', *American Journal of Sociology*, vol. 64, pp. 262–9.

17. O'Loghlin, J. (1981) 'The Neighbourhood Effect in Urban Voting Surfaces: A Cross National Analysis', in Burnett, A. and Taylor, P. (eds) *Political Studies from Spatial Perspectives*, New York: Wiley, pp. 357–88. See also, Eagles, M. and Erfle, S. (1989) 'Community Cohesion and Voter Turnout in English Parliamentary Constituencies', *British Journal of Political Science*, vol. 19, pp. 115–25.

18. Taylor, A. (undated) 'Journey Time, Perceived Distance, and Electoral Turnout – Victoria Ward, Swansea', *Area*, vol. 5, pp. 59–63.

19. Masterson, R. and Masterson, E. (1980) 'The Scottish Community Elections: The Second Round', *Local Government Studies*, vol. 6, pp. 63–82.

20. Price, D. and Lupfer, M. (1973) 'Volunteers for Gore: The Impact of a Precinct-Level Canvass in Three Tennessee Cities', *Journal of Politics*, vol. 35, pp. 410–38.

21. Fletcher, 'The Results Analysed', and Hill, 'Leeds', in Sharpe (ed.) (1976). For a discussion of the same phenomenon at national level, see Denver, D. and Hands, G. (1985) 'Marginality and Turnout in General Elections in the 1970s', *British Journal of Political Science*, vol. 15, pp. 381–98.

22. Rowley, G. (1971) 'The Greater London Council Elections of 1964 and 1967: A Study in Electoral Geography', *Transactions, Institute of British Geographers*, vol. 53, pp. 117–32.

23. Newton, K. (1972) 'Turnout and Marginality in Local Elections', *British Journal of Political Science*, vol. 2, pp. 251–5.

24. Crewe, I., Alt, J. and Fox, A. (1977) 'Non-Voting in British General Elections 1966 – October 1974', in Crouch, C. (ed.) *British Political Sociology Yearbook*, volume 3, 'Participation in Politics', London: Croom Helm, pp. 38–109.

25. *Report of the Committee on the Management of Local Government* (Maud) vol.iii, 'The Local Government Elector', London: HMSO, 1967; *Royal Commission on Local Government in England*, 'Research Study 9: Community Attitudes Survey', London: HMSO, Cmnd 4040, 1969.

26. See Miller, W. (1986) 'Local Electoral Behaviour', in *The Local Government Elector, Research volume 3, Report of the Committee of Inquiry into the Conduct of Local Authority Business*, London: HMSO, 1986; Miller, W. *Irrelevant Elections?*, Oxford: Clarendon Press.

27. Miller, *Irrelevant Elections?*, p. 91.

28. Though such findings once more highlight the propensity to over-report turnout in all survey-based studies of electoral participation.

29. We have chosen to make our report on the aggregate data analysis as non-technical as possible. For this reason we will comment only generally about the findings, excluding the usual statistical information accompanying such analysis. The interested reader should examine Rallings, C. and Thrasher, M. (1990) 'Turnout in Local Elections – An Aggregate Analysis with Electoral and Contextual Data', *Electoral Studies*, vol. 9, pp. 79–90 for a more technical approach to this topic. Similar data are discussed and analysed in more detail in Rallings, C. and Thrasher, M. (1994) *Explaining Election Turnout: A Secondary Analysis of Local Election Statistics*, London: HMSO.

30. Hill, 'Leeds', p. 138.

31. McLean, I. and Smith, J. (1993) 'The Poll Tax, the Electoral Register, and the 1991 Census: An Update', paper given to Elections, Parties and Opinion Polls group, University of Lancaster, 1993. For a US view of similar issues and turnout see Rosenstone, S. and Wolfinger, R. (1987) 'The Effects of Registration Laws on Voter Turnout', *American Political Science Review*, vol. 72, pp. 22–45.

32. A qualitative study of authorities with consistently high and low turnouts is currently being conducted by the authors with funding from the Joseph Rowntree Trust.

5 Central Government Perceptions of Local Government

George Jones and Tony Travers

Introduction

Local government in Britain has been reformed relentlessly during the past 20 or so years. The structure, functions and finance of local authorities have been changed, though rarely in a co-ordinated way. Between the mid-1970s and 1994, local government moved from being a traditional, powerful, provider of public services to a more strategic and less autonomous institution.

For a number of reasons the relationship between local and central government degenerated during the 1980s. Factors contributing to the failed relationship included the fact that local government moved steadily away from Conservative control and into the hands of the opposition parties. This inevitable mid-term effect was compounded by wide political differences between a radical Conservative government and a number of equally radical Labour councils. In addition, efforts to hold down public expenditure led to continuous clashes between the government and local authorities of all parties.

Local government featured extensively in the government's legislative programme throughout the 1980s. By some counts there have been 150 Acts of Parliament affecting local authorities since 1979. Several of the most important of these pieces of legislation, for example the Local Government Finance Act 1986 (poll tax) and the Education Reform Act 1988 (grant-maintained schools, national curriculum, polytechnic transfer), were the size of telephone directories and required huge numbers of complex regulations to make them work.

In the United Kingdom's unwritten constitution Parliament is free to change local government on any occasion it can secure a majority for reform. This fact is important, as local government is itself an element within the country's constitutional arrangements. Throughout the years from 1979 onwards (and even before, during the period of financial retrenchment from 1975 to 1977) ministers and civil servants have, in effect, played God with British local government. Each time there has been a real or imagined problem with local government, ministers reached for the statute book. The idea that periodic local elections would solve such problems does not appear to have been a sufficient comfort for ministers bent on changing important elements of the country's political and economic system.

Functions have been transferred from elected local government to central departments, to government-appointed bodies, to trusts and to the private sector, while limited new powers have been given *to* local government, notably for community care. Local spending has been subjected to grant penalties, capping and two massive tax reforms. Structural reform took place in the metropolitan areas in 1986 and London in 1986 and 1990, and is currently being visited upon the rest of Britain.

Within a political system where local government is subject to continuous and massive reform, it is inevitable that ministers and civil servants play a key role in shaping policy and the legislation which implements it. Where the reforms themselves lead to increased central control over aspects of local provision, ministers and officials also become more closely involved with the detail of local services. The transfer of grant-maintained schools from local government control into the oversight of the Department for Education and its newly-created Funding Agency for Schools is a good example of this phenomenon. As ministers and civil servants have taken ever-greater interest in local government and local public provision, the attitudes of the individuals charged with the duty of making and implementing reforms are of considerable importance to the future of both public services and local democracy. This chapter is concerned with these attitudes. It is the first piece of research explicitly to examine what ministers and civil servants think about local democracy in general and local government in particular. The purpose of the study was to find out what ministers and civil servants believed about the constitutional position of local government, the appropriate role and functions of local authorities, funding arrangements, the competence and professionalism of local government and possible improvements to the form and operation of local government. In addition, the more subjective question of how senior politicians and civil servants view their own (home) local authority was also addressed. Views on this final subject were used to inform more objective responses to the other topics outlined above.

Any study which seeks to unravel the attitudes of government ministers and their officials risks controversy. Constitutional theory states that Cabinet members share collective responsibility. Indeed the whole of a government is deemed to have but a single view on any particular subject. Serving civil servants are, again in theory, merely the servants of their political masters, and cannot have personal views that differ from those of the government of the day. Thus, in as far as this project approached serving ministers and civil servants, it risked running up against the doctrine that 'the government' (embracing both ministers and civil servants) had a single view on all matters, including local government.

Elements of this doctrine were the subject of a report by the Treasury and Civil Service Committee of the House of Commons,[1] which wished to commission an attitude survey of civil servants. The government refused to allow such a survey, largely on the grounds that the results of a survey could threaten the political impartiality of the civil service, though also because civil servants cannot have views that differ from those of their ministers. In a letter to the Committee the Chancellor of the Duchy of Lancaster (William Waldegrave) explained it was a condition of employment in the civil service that civil servants shall 'not take part in their official capacities in surveys or research projects, even unattributably, if they deal with attitudes or opinions on political matters or matters of policy'.[2] In another letter to the Committee, Mr Waldegrave noted that civil service attitude studies had generally been turned down because 'the civil service has no constitutional existence other than as an arm of the Government of the day'.[3]

This study of attitudes in Westminster and Whitehall intrudes deeply into territory which the Chancellor of the Duchy of Lancaster believes must not be penetrated. Notwithstanding such potential limitations, this study has interviewed ministers and ex-ministers from the three major political parties, as well as civil servants with recent and contemporary understanding of civil service attitudes at all levels. The views of a distinguished academic commentator and an ex-political advisor were also sought.

George Jones and Tony Travers

The constitutional position of local government

Textbooks generally attribute to local government an important position within Britain's unwritten constitution.[4] Official inquiries have also accepted that local government has a constitutional role.[5] Governments have generally been less forthcoming in their views about the constitutional position of local government. The attitudes of those in government to the constitutional aspects of local government have, thus far, been unrecorded. In the array of white and green papers published by successive governments during the 1960s, 1970s and 1980s the constitutional position of local democracy was barely mentioned or implied. Government consultative papers appeared to start from the basis of an unstated understanding of the constitutional position of local government. Perhaps it was felt unnecessary to make an explicit statement about the constitution.

Continuous expansion of local authority expenditure in the period from the 1950s to 1975 had ensured that (by the standards of the mid-1980s) the relationship between local and central government was relatively smooth. In the wake of the IMF visit in 1975 (and consequent public expenditure reductions) local authority spending was cut, leading to a growth of tension between Whitehall and town halls. A battery of initiatives to reduce spending in the years after 1979 led to accusations that the government was acting 'unconstitutionally'.[6] Yet consultative documents rarely referred to the constitution, still less discussed it. For example, in the 1981 Green Paper *Alternatives to Domestic Rates*, a section blandly entitled 'Wider Considerations' considered the degree of influence that central government should exercise over local authorities. The section concluded: 'The case for the Government taking such powers [to impose direct limits on individual councils' spending] has to be judged against the very considerable constitutional and practical difficulties that would be involved'.[7] However, there was no discussion of the constitutional position.

The 1983 White Paper entitled *Rates* also touched on constitutional matters: 'We live in a unitary and not a federal state. Although local authorities are responsible to their electorates, they derive their powers from Parliament. Their structure, duties and functions have been subject to frequent modification as the needs of the country have changed.[8] Then in 1986 the Green Paper that initiated poll tax briefly stated: 'In the United Kingdom, all the powers of local authorities derive from Parliamentary legislation. The structure of local government, the services it provides, and the way in which it finances those services are all subject to statutes passed by Parliament.'[9]

These limited forays into the subject of local government and the constitution suggest that even during the 1980s when, by common consent, changes were taking place which affected the unwritten constitutional position of local government,[10] the government was little troubled by such wide questions. Each initiative taken by the government was a short-term reaction to some actual or supposed problem in local government. There was little time to consider the way in which local authorities fitted into the wider constitutional picture.

Interviews with ministers and civil servants who were (and, in some cases, are) responsible for local government (and in departments which are responsible for local authority services) have made it possible to build up a picture of the constitutional views held by those who are responsible for the legislation and administration affecting local government. Virtually all our interviewees – ministers and ex-ministers of all parties, and civil servants – appeared to accept the *ad hoc*, unwritten, British constitutional arrangements as being virtually inevitable. There was no strong pressure to change the constitution, and thus to alter local government's position within it. Policy-makers and their officials appear to accept that the British constitution is a fact of life. Indeed, most interviewees talked little about the conventional academic debate which sees local government as one of the 'checks and balances' within the constitution. As one official put it, 'I just take it [local government's position in the constitution] for granted . . . I suppose there will always be things that have to be done at a level below central government.'

A minority of ministers and officials believed that there is, as one recent senior Cabinet minister put it, 'an awkward gap' in the constitutional arrangements which means that the position of local government cannot be guaranteed. If there *were* to be a written constitution, a number of officials believed that the position of local government should be codified within it. However, there was no expectation that there would be such a constitution. Nevertheless it was widely accepted that local government maintained political diversity, particularly during a period when one party is continuously in power in Parliament. (One dissenting voice, a former political advisor, said that the Conservative Party in government during the 1980s had believed that 'local democracy had collapsed'.)

At its most elegant the 'pro diversity' view was seen as having developed from a constitutional settlement at the end of the nineteenth century. Lord Salisbury's government operated in two spheres: the Imperial Parliament and local government. By leaving local government to run domestic services, Parliament could remain uncluttered by drains and schoolbooks. This settlement was broken by the creation of the National Health Service which made central government responsible for direct service provision. From 1948 onwards the centre became increasingly involved with domestic provision.

Several interviewees believed that the constitutional position of local government had changed in recent years. As one civil servant put it, 'local government is at the mercy of governments with strong views'. Another observed (quoting Anthony Crosland): 'Opposition parties defend local government. But once in power, the government does not want to hear about local autonomy.' Rate capping was the high-water-mark of the constitutional debate. Both capping and the purposes that underlay the community charge (poll tax) were, in constitutional terms, 'uncharted territory'.

The Thatcher government, in the view of a senior ex-civil servant, saw local government as part of the (left-leaning) Establishment. This sclerotic edifice was, in her view, in need of radical overhaul. As Mrs Thatcher stated in her autobiography: 'socialism was still built into the institutions and mentality of Britain'.[11] Thus, the changes made by Mrs Thatcher's administrations were not deliberately designed to change the constitution, merely attempts to reform the political economy of Britain. Constitutional reform was an accidental by-product of other changes.

Those who were in Westminster and Whitehall during the 1980s agree that, in the words of an ex-Cabinet minister: 'Local government had upset the accepted constitutional balance by challenging the power of the government, conferred on it by Parliament, to pronounce on public expenditure policy. . . . The challenge over spending was not just from labour councils: some Conservative authorities argued they were a special case and should spend more.'

Ministers and civil servants who had been in power before the Thatcher government were unanimous that local government's position within the constitution had been different before 1979. The relative strength of local authority leaders in those days did not derive from an understanding of constitutional principles, but rather because senior politicians from big cities such as London, Manchester, Leeds and Birmingham were seen as power-brokers. A minister in the Wilson and Callaghan governments made the point that 'council leaders were more important than a junior minister . . . ministers would always find time to see them'. On the other hand, the same minister observed, 'though important, they were not as important as trades union leaders'.

Whitehall was more reverential towards local government during the 1960s and 1970s than it is today. 'The Director of Education for Liverpool, and in other cities, was a great figure'. Local authorities and their leaders were seen as part of the Establishment. The authority of political power was shared between central and local government. Local government was seen as a good service delivery mechanism. Yet the relative strength and importance of local government in these earlier times was not the result of a conscious constitutional settlement. Indeed, a senior member of 1960s and 1970s Labour governments stressed that 'there is no sovereignty of local government. Parliament is sovereign, and has always been so. . . . From time to time Parliament will change things. . . . No body other than Parliament can (or should) determine local government structure and finance.' The period from 1975 to 1979 showed that 'no government that believes in macroeconomic policy can avoid influencing the total of local expenditure'.

What appears to have been common to the 1960s, 1970s, 1980s and 1990s is the perception that local government is primarily a service provider – either in its own right or as an agent of the centre. The importance of local authorities as providers of education, social services, rubbish collecting and other services seems to be a far greater preoccupation for Whitehall and Westminster than constitutional niceties. More recent ministers and civil servants stressed that local authorities should be 'service commissioners' rather than direct providers. Some favoured the fragmentation of local services and the client/contractor split. Regardless of such modernisms, there is a strong thread of belief (over many years) that service provision/ enabling is the pre-eminent role of local government.

Of all the senior ministers who have published memoirs in recent years, Nigel Lawson (Chancellor of the Exchequer from 1985 to 1990) provides the most detailed consideration of the constitutional position of local government. As several of our interviewees laid great stress (though rarely in a flattering way) on the importance of the Treasury, it is worth quoting Lawson's view. He was, after all, one of the more powerful members of any recent government, and a considerable intellectual force. Lawson wrote: 'We suffer from an unfortunate constitutional set-up in this country as a result of our consistent pursuit in every way of the middle way.' He compared Britain with West Germany and the United States, where there is a 'genuine federal constitution and where local authorities . . . are genuinely held to account. They are independent authorities and the electorate understands the responsibilities that these authorities have for managing their own affairs. That does not work too badly.' France has the opposite arrangement, where they have 'a unitary constitution . . . where nearly every decision is dictated from the centre – Paris – and the head of the *Département*, the *préfet*, is appointed from the centre. That works out not too badly. We have a curious mixture because our constitution is mid-way between the two: we have a unitary constitution but nevertheless the local authorities have considerable autonomy'.[12]

The ex-Chancellor's constitutional doctrine boils down to the notion that there are two acceptable constitutional arrangements within which a local government system might fit: either one where local authorities are free to manage their own affairs and are locally responsible, or one where all decisions are centrally determined. The British system, a 'curious mixture' compared with the straightforward systems in other countries, is, by implication, less successful. Either the Treasury should take complete control over local authority expenditure or else it should require councils to fund all their spending from local taxes.

Nigel Lawson was unusual among his ex-colleagues in including a section on local government in his memoirs. A number of other senior Conservatives who have written about the Thatcher years (for example, Lords Carrington, Pym, Hailsham, Young, Parkinson, Whitelaw and Sir Norman Fowler) do not reflect on local government at all. Two former members of Thatcher Cabinets have written about local government and its constitutional position. In 1987 Michael Heseltine wrote: 'Parliament cannot be equated with local government. Democratic accountability lies in Parliament, from which all the authority exercised at local level is derived. . . . Parliament is the centre of our democracy, but that does not argue for tightly centralised control. Conservatives distrust the concentration of power.'[13] Sir Ian Gilmour went further than Heseltine, arguing that 'the most damaging of the Thatcherite offensives against what de Tocqueville called "secondary powers" was the relentless campaign against local government. . . . Thatcherism was at direct variance with the Conservative tradition' of 'diffusion of power'.[14]

There was a tendency among some (but not all) interviewees to elide government and Parliament: few attempted to distinguish between the two. The House of Commons was often equated with Parliament, with little distinction between the Commons and Lords. There appears to be a wide acceptance that the government, because it has the confidence of the House of Commons (a Parliamentary majority) should always get its way. This is the old view of Crown (Executive) dominance. It has a responsibility to promote policies in the national interest. It is a Jacobin attitude. Those who hold such views do not think in terms of checks and balances on a potential, or actual, all-powerful government. They lack any sense of the need for constrained government, which is the essence of constitutionalism. According to such a view, Parliamentary sovereignty smoothly becomes governmental sovereignty. The 'unitary state' means that everything is not just under Parliament but under government too: local government should not seek to frustrate what the government wants.

One further point was raised by a number of ministers and civil servants with experience of government in the late 1980s and early 1990s. The courts and the judiciary have increasingly played an important role in providing a constitutional balance to central government. Governments now write legislation in such a way as to be 'judge-proof' and in so doing are conceding that the courts have assumed considerable importance as a limitation on the government of the day. Michael Heseltine concurs with this view in his book *Where There's a Will*: 'more and more the courts tend to side in judicial review with the Davids who challenge the central government Goliath. While wealth and power continue to move towards London and Brussels, we should take care before we weaken any institution which resists this movement'.[15] In constitutional terms, local government is now seen as a less important check on the power of the centre than the courts.

The role and functions of local government

Both the role and functions of local government in Britain have been radically altered in the past twenty or so years. Provision has passed from local to central government control, while Parliament has required local authorities to provide a number of new or expanded services. The way in which provision has been secured has changed. Local authorities have become less directly involved with the day-to-day delivery of services and more concerned with ensuring that other organisations are contracted to deliver effective public provision.

One politician who had been much involved with the reforms of recent years conceded that 'enough has been enough'. There was now a need for consolidation and a period of reflection. There was a remarkable degree of agreement among interviewees from both ministerial and civil service backgrounds that firstly things were different – generally better – in the past and that secondly further service reforms were likely in the future. Interviewees generally accepted that the role and functions of local government in 1994 are little more than an historical accident. As one experienced ex-civil servant put it, discussion of what were the most appropriate roles and functions for local authorities was 'for the birds'.

Nevertheless, in contrast to the above section, where the constitutional function of local government was revealed to be of relatively minor interest to most ministers and officials, service provision was seen by virtually all of our interviewees as the most important reason for having local authorities. An official with experience of both spending departments and the Treasury observed, 'it is absurd to think that central government can deliver many services . . . local government is better at delivering services than many government agencies . . . local government doesn't run out of money half way through the year in the way the NHS does . . . even Mrs Thatcher was convinced that community care should be passed to local authority control given its capacity to budget effectively'.

However, there is a wide variation in the views of ministers and civil servants about the precise role and functions to be adopted by local government. Those now in government stressed the need for local government to be, as one minister put it, 'a regulator, a commissioner of services and a regenerator'. Councils should regulate in services such as environmental health; should commission the provision of services like education; and should be the 'assembler of local resources, the organiser and catalyst' to assist with economic restructuring in the light of late-twentieth-century industrial and social change. In essence they would be 'administrative holding companies'.

This post-modern vision of local government appears to have been accepted by civil servants, though some had to be prompted to discuss the 'enabling' concept. Some officials still appear to think more in terms of direct provision. The notion that councils should secure the provision of services, rather than directly provide them with their own labour, appears to have taken root, though it is unclear whether the majority of officials really feel it is a good thing. The fragmentation of what had previously been single-structure local departments or services into smaller operating units (locally managed schools, contracted-out homes for the elderly, direct service organisations for manual services) was seen by several ministers, ex-ministers and officials as offering the possibility of producing genuinely *local* provision within the oversight and control of elected local government. On the other hand, ministers and ex-ministers expressed considerable concern at the growth of appointed bodies. As an explanation of how local, elected, bodies had been gradually supplanted by quangos, one of our interviewees, still in government, stated 'Mrs T. didn't trust the conventional mechanisms of government and set up a parallel structure to get things done.' This parallel structure now causes concern in Whitehall and Westminster.

A senior ex-Cabinet minister believed that local authorities could adopt a 'consumer voice' or 'select committee' role in future, particularly in dealing with appointed bodies. However, this notion of local government as consumer advocate or champion was not mentioned by other ministers or civil servants. Several politicians said the regulation of planning and environmental matters had grown in importance and would continue to do so in the years ahead. There is a future for local government, but it will have to adapt and change to meet the needs of its electorate.

The services to be run by local government are subject to wide disagreement: there appear to be many and different views about what is appropriate for local authorities to do in future. Recent and current ministers see little future for local government in housing, certainly not as a direct provider and landlord. Education, police and fire services appear to fall in a grey area: some would transfer them out of local government, others see a (reduced) future role. There is unanimous agreement that planning, environmental services and regulation will remain local government duties.

Nigel Lawson consistently supported the removal of the financing of education from local government. Central funding of education 'would have greatly improved local accountability by substantially reducing councils' reliance on central government funding'.[16] Norman Tebbit saw local government in far more minimalist terms, stating that 'education no more needs local political control than does the provision of groceries'. Regulation (for example, planning) and protection (for example, of children and other vulnerable groups) were acceptable services for elected local government. Even refuse collection, street lighting and other local services could be subject to nationally imposed standards, with some local discretion to spend above national benchmarks.[17]

A number of officials and two ex-ministers expressed concern about the continuing difficulty for central government because of the conflicting pressures for, on the one hand, local autonomy and, on the other, uniformity of service provision in different areas of the country. Political demands for more local freedom had to be viewed alongside pressures for similar provision throughout the country. The system of grants to local authorities (the equalising purposes of which were widely accepted) was based upon the assumption that services should be broadly the same everywhere. This idea was inimical to local democracy. Nevertheless, councillors and the public pressed for ever more sophisticated equalisation.

A final observation concerns the structure of local government. There was general criticism among ministers and officials of the confusion brought about by having two tiers of local government. Unitary local government was seen as offering improvements (though few interviewees explicitly said so). A minority of ministers and officials expressed an almost romantic attachment to 'community' based local government. One ex-official cited Switzerland, France and the United States, where there was still a genuine level of 'commune' or 'neighbourhood' government. Britain's system of local government was seen as often being too remote, and thus not very interesting.

The funding of local government

Few political issues have been as widely debated as the taxing, spending and borrowing powers of local government, particularly in the light of the poll-tax fiasco. Several interviewees were quick to raise the spectre of the Treasury once local government finance was mentioned. An ex-advisor at both the Treasury and the Department of the Environment stated baldly: 'the Treasury sees local government as an unnecessary encumbrance the country can ill afford' and as 'a hole in cost control . . . a threat to macro-economic policies'. Moreover, this view would be the Treasury's under a government of any party.

One of the key ministers in local government during the 1980s agreed with the above formulation, adding 'the Treasury dominates much of the debate about local government'. Indeed, the Treasury 'was responsible for the decline of Britain'. More modestly, an official believed that 'even when local authority spending was excluded from the public expenditure planning total, the Treasury still took an interest in it . . . the Treasury needs cracking on public spending matters'.

A leading academic commentator pointed out that the Treasury sees itself as the embattled defender of the public purse. Treasury officials see local government (in common with such institutions as the defence Chiefs of Staff, the intelligence services, the Scottish, Welsh and Northern Ireland Offices, the arts and many other lobbies) as little more than a pressure group for extra cash. The Treasury does not differentiate between local government as part of the constitution and local government as a lobby for higher spending. Moreover, if the Treasury is interested in financial control, other departments appear to have centralist instincts over aspects of policy. Within spending departments the interests of their particular service are generally paramount. 'Why spend months making a case for the public expenditure round, and then allow local authorities to use the money for other services?', as an official with experience of a major spending department put it. An ex-advisor at both the Department of the Environment and the Treasury saw the DoE as real constitutionalists, prepared to defend the rights of local government against the depredations of both the Treasury and spending departments.

The general view was that local authority expenditure was no different from the expenditure of departments of central government: all should be controlled by the government. There was little or no sympathy with the view that local authority expenditure financed from its own taxation should not be of concern to and controlled by the centre. Local discretion should be tolerated only at the margin and (generally) above nationally determined minimum standards.

There was unanimity among interviewees – ministers, ex-ministers and officials – that local government raises too small a percentage of

its income from local taxation. Rather than lamenting the reduc
in local government income sources, Kenneth Baker observed in
autobiography: 'One of our biggest mistakes was to give loc,
authorities more duties which could only be financed properly by
central government grants rather than by locally raised revenue'.[18]
Capping of local expenditure and/or taxes was also seen as highly
undesirable, though not all would abandon it. Proposals for how to
move forward to an improved situation were many and varied.
However, there were no heroic proposals for new local taxes or
radical shifts in the funding of local government. Local income tax is
seen as a total non-starter, with local sales tax as only slightly more
likely. The best bets (in Whitehall and Westminster, at least) appear
to be an increase in the amount raised by council tax, possibly
supplemented by reforms to non-domestic rates. One minister who
served in governments during the 1980s and early 1990s saw a
vicious circle in which 'a lack of interest in local government leads to
low levels of participation, which in turn produces a lack of
accountability and thus failed revenue pressures'. Unless finance
ensured accountability, local government would continue to be
weakened.

A number of current and recent ministers would like to follow the
approach proposed by Nigel Lawson. Education would be funded
(and thus, in effect, controlled) by central government, possibly
along with other services such as police and fire. The remaining
provision within local responsibility could then be largely funded by
local taxation and specific grants (for agency services such as
housing benefit). Those more recently involved with local government appear enthusiastic to reintroduce some degree of freedom
over non-domestic rates (NDR). The yield from the NDR has fallen
steeply since it was nationalised in 1990, and local authorities now
have every incentive to reduce the local yield. There is a concern
within DoE to enhance discretion over the business rate.

There is also an awareness, particularly at the Department of the
Environment, that there is 'an obsession with equalisation' in
Britain. No other country equalises to the same extent. In the words
of one minister, 'I wonder whether we need quite such a beautifully
calibrated system?' There is also a realisation among a number of
ministers and officials that the egalitarian purposes of equalisation
have, ironically, been pursued more zealously during the past five or
ten years then ever before, and certainly more than overseas where
'a greater degree of local freedom to differ appears to have been

accepted'. Only one of those interviewed mentioned capital expenditure and control. Almost all attention in Whitehall and Westminster is concentrated on revenue expenditure and local taxation. There was little discussion of the amount of capital investment, or of its funding.

Professionalism and competence in local government

The question of professionalism and competence, more than any other asked of interviewees, elicited a gut reaction about councillors and officers in local government. Given that this study was to examine attitudes in Westminster and Whitehall, we probably received a clearer view in response to this enquiry than any other. None of the major autobiographies and memoirs examined included any analysis of the quality of local government officers and members. (There was, on the other hand, a great deal about alleged political extremism during the 1980s.)[19]

There were mixed views about politics in local government. A number of senior ex-civil servants believed that local authorities were too political. The possible advantages of elected single-purpose authorities (for example, school boards) were mentioned by officials. Some ministers and ex-ministers felt that local government politicians were likely to 'go native' with the opposition, and were not political enough. Responses to questions about the quality of local authority members and officers varied wildly, from 'good' (always applied to officers in a minister's constituency) through 'mixed' to 'poor' (generally applied by both ministers and officials to councillors in general). It is clear that civil servants in some departments, particularly the Treasury, though also some divisions of service departments, have little or no contact with either officers or members.

The extent to which ministers and officials have dealings with local authority officers and members affects the way Whitehall and Westminster view local government. Thus, ministers (who have much experience of councillors, through delegations, surgeries and their constituency parties) may have a more sympathetic view of local elected members than do civil servants. On the other hand, one ex-minister produced a highly derogatory view (one sometimes imagined to exist, though rarely articulated) of local authority members and officers. 'Local government is a lower-middle-class activity, of course with some exceptions. The top mandarins of the civil service come from different social strata from those in local government. There are more graduates in Parliament than in local councils. These differences point to differences in quality. . . . Local government people have limited vision. There are some good chief officers, but a lot are pretty ordinary. Mayors are chosen on Buggin's Turn: they have no ideas and cannot speak. Parties find it hard to get good candidates to stand for election.'

Confusion in the minds of the public about what constitutes an MP's duties and what is the responsibility of local councillors was seen by some ministers and ex-ministers as being the fault of local government.

Ministers were generally impressed by senior local authority officers (notably chief executives and directors of finance). This relative enthusiasm arose from constituency rather than ministerial contacts. Several interviewees believed 'the quality of elected members has declined because of the lower status of local government in society', as one recent ex-minister put it.

Civil servants were generally more critical than their masters of both local authority members and officers. Several interviewees rarely, if ever, met councillors either in the course of their work or as local residents. Officials from service departments and the Treasury appear to be very unlikely to meet councillors. A leading commentator felt that although senior civil servants may have stereotyped (usually unsympathetic) views about councillors, they were similarly very critical of MPs and ministers. Nevertheless, a number of views were expressed by officials about councillors, who are generally felt to be boring (at best) and possibly mildly corrupt (at worst). The academic commentator put it simply: 'local government comes high up their (civil servants') hierarchy of ennui'. A number of civil servants and ex-civil servants feel that local government should be revived by reforms such as elected mayors and/or the creation of a Westminster-style Cabinet and backbencher system. As one official put it: 'At least the GLC made local government interesting with policies such as Travelcard and Fares Fair . . . I couldn't even tell you the name of my local borough leader.' Other, less sympathetic views, suggested councillors were a bit dim and often self-important. Unlike their political masters, civil servants do not appear to believe that local authority elected members are politically extreme.

In the words of one official who had had extensive dealings with local authority senior officers, 'I have enormous admiration for officers, particularly in busy, inner-city areas.' But another believed that 'local government officers whinge all the time about the way they are treated by the centre . . . whether it is justified or not, it can be boring'. Service-orientation is still believed (by Whitehall) to be deeply entrenched in local government. (Although this study is not about local government attitudes to Whitehall, it is fair to assume this criticism is reciprocated.) An experienced ex-official is convinced that the quality of management grew steadily during the 1980s (as it had in DoE), improving the responsiveness of local services. Reform had sharpened up the act of local authority officers.

There is sympathy in some parts of Whitehall for local government, and evidence of strongly held views in some central departments about the quality of other (central) departments. As a former Treasury civil servant observed: 'central government makes hopeless demands on local government which it could never meet itself'. Indeed an experienced Whitehall official with experience in a number of positions went further: 'civil servants often push out junk . . . to be on the receiving end of the DFE must be very demoralising'. Indeed the DFE are seen by a number of other departments as 'wanting power without responsibility' and thus 'making local government's life virtually impossible'.

Whitehall views about local government may have been affected by relative changes in earnings among middle-ranking and junior civil servants. We were told that while older and more senior officials generally live in well-to-do suburbs, middle-ranking and junior officials often have (for financial reasons) to live in mixed, inner-city, areas. The service failures of some inner London authorities in recent years are likely to have affected the views of many officials who now live in such areas. 'It becomes all to easy to believe the *Daily Mail*'s view of the world.'

A gap of understanding exists between central and local government, much of which appears to be based on simple ignorance (or worse still, mistaken, stereotyped, views). Civil servants appear, in some cases, to have little understanding of what local officers and elected members actually do. It is possible that local authority members and officers are similarly ignorant. Having said that, a number of ministers and civil servants appear to believe that the quality of local government members is not as good as it used to be, and not good enough by any standards. The mundane nature of many local services appears to encourage (at least some) civil servants to believe that they possess: 'Rolls Royce minds, while local government officers have motor cyclists' minds'.

Possible improvements to the form and operation of local government

All interviewees were asked what, if anything, they would do to bring about immediate improvements to the way in which local government in Britain worked. The responses suggested widely varying priorities for local government policy across Whitehall and Westminster. Results were not systematic, either among ministers/ex-ministers or civil servants. The two most popular possible improvements to local government (among interviewees) were firstly changes to internal management to make local authorities more visible within their communities; and secondly, greater financial freedom. Two other propositions were also supported by a number of interviewees: 'link local government more closely to community' and 'reduce the importance of quangos'.

These responses were consistent with the interviews as a whole. The idea that local government needed reviving and that it should be made more interesting to the local electorate was a regular theme in discussion with both ministers and their officials. Elected mayors/ chief executives received support from a number of interviewees, though two others (both politicians) were strongly opposed to elected mayors. Greater financial autonomy for local government was also a regularly mentioned factor during interviews. However, as explained above, the way of reaching this improved state was rarely spelled out. A number of politicians would favour the Lawson route of removing funding responsibilities from local government closer to the point where income (from council tax) would match expenditure. There were no detailed descriptions of how local income sources might be increased so as to come closer to local government's existing spending requirements.

Linking local government more closely to 'community' feeling is a more weakly favoured policy. As with attitudes towards funding, this proposal appears to be an aspiration rather than a thought-through policy. The notion that the number of quangos should be reduced, and their services made more democratic, is a more easily enacted suggestion. Civil servants, it was observed, would probably prefer a return to a steady state of policy. Running a consistent and stable administrative machine was more attractive to them than overseeing a continuous revolution.

There is not, it can be observed, a clear body of opinion in Whitehall and Westminster about the future of local government. Ministers and civil servants (or recently active ones) have been bombarded by reform in much the same way that local government itself has. The sum total of this activity has left central government with a number of partly thought views about what should happen next, but no corporate view (either official or private) about how policy should develop from here onwards. The very fragmentation visited upon local government by Whitehall and Westminster appears to have had an effect on the capacity of the central political and administrative machine to develop a rigorous view of what might happen in future.

Conclusion

This study, based on interviews and the published views of senior politicians and civil servants, comes to a number of conclusions:

The constitutional position of local government

Whitehall and Westminster does not spend much time thinking about local government's constitutional position: this position is taken as given. Furthermore, the lack of a written constitution does not produce pressure in Whitehall and Westminster for constitutional reform. Service provision is seen as local government's prime purpose and local government's role and functions are seen as an *ad hoc* development within British government.

The role and functions of local government

In relation to the role and functions of local government there is little agreement within Whitehall and Westminster about the appropriate functions for which local authorities should have responsibility. Many recent ministers favour reducing local government provision, particularly for housing, education and the police, and the growth of appointed bodies is viewed with suspicion by both ministers and civil servants.

The funding of local government

The recent war between local and central government over finance has left Whitehall and Westminster with a limited view of possible future reforms. The Treasury is seen as a massive constraint on improvement although there is universal support for increasing the proportion of local government income raised from local taxation and the capping of expenditure is seen as undesirable. Some recent politicians favour matching local spending to council tax income by removing education, police and fire services from local control.

Professionalism and competence in local government

Conclusions in relation to professionalism and competence in local government are not complimentary towards local administrators: ministers are (in general) more sympathetic to councillors than civil servants; many civil servants hardly ever meet a councillor; some ministers and civil servants believe that councillors are inferior and dim; and some ministers and civil servants believe that standards of local authority members have fallen and are continuing to decline although some ministers and civil servants are impressed by individual councillors and a few senior council officers (particularly chief executives and directors of finance).

There is little agreement in Whitehall and Westminster about the future of local government in Britain. Ministers and civil servants (and their immediate successors) have views as individualistic and developed as any other group. This diversity is perhaps surprising given the amount of legislation and debate on the subject during the past twenty years.

Two views, one put to us by a senior minister from the last Labour government, and one from a minister in the present government, probably come close to summarising our findings. The minister from the Labour government told us 'if central government treats local government like an outcast, it will behave thus'. There is clearly a current realisation in Whitehall and Westminster that some of the changes and policies of the 1980s have gone too far. Or, at least that 'enough is enough'. The second quotation is taken from Michael Heseltine's 1987 book, and neatly summarises the slightly Fabian, interventionist, approach that appears to represent a reasonable distillation (on the basis of our research) of Whitehall and Westminster's attitude to local government: 'There can be only one

Chancellor of the Exchequer. Above all there is an obligation to intervene where a local authority's performance prejudices social conditions, the local economy or the stability of local industry. Central government must ensure that local authorities deliver adequate local services, and do not indulge in conspicuous waste and extravagance in order to provoke political confrontation with central government'.[20]

Notes and references

1. *Proposed Attitude Survey of the Civil Service*, Fourth Special Report from the Treasury and Civil Service Committee, HC 460, Session 1993–94.
2. Ibid, Appendix 2.
3. Ibid, Appendix 9.
4. See, for example, Jones, G. and Stewart, J. (1983) *The Case for Local Government*, London: George Allen & Unwin, p. 5.
5. See, for example, *Royal Commission on Local Government in England 1966–1969*, Cmnd 4040, London: HMSO, 1969, para. 28 pp. 10–11.
6. See, for example, Geoffrey Rippon MP, House of Commons, *Official Report*, 17 January 1984, col. 193.
7. *Alternatives to Domestic Rates*, Cmnd 8449, London: HMSO, 1981, para. 1.14.
8. *Rates*, Cmnd 9008, London: HMSO 1983 para. 1.2.
9. *Paying for Local Government*, Cmnd 9714, London: HMSO, 1986, para. 1.4.
10. See, for example, Alexander, A. (1985) 'Structure, Centralization and the Position of Local Government', in Loughlin, M., Gelfand, M. and Young, K. (eds) *Half a Century of Municipal Decline 1935–1985*, London: George Allen & Unwin, pp. 72–6.
11. Thatcher, M. (1993) *The Downing Street Years*, London: Harper-Collins, p. 306.
12. Lawson, N. (1992) *The View from No. 11: Memoirs of a Tory Radical*, London: Bantam Press, p. 563.
13. Heseltine, M. (1987) *Where There's A Will*, London: Hutchinson, p. 131.
14. Gilmour, I. (1992) *Dancing with Dogma: Britain under Thatcherism*, London: Simon & Schuster, p. 212.
15. Heseltine, M. (1987) *Where There's A Will*, London: Hutchinson, p. 132.
16. Lawson, N. (1992) *The View from No. 11: Memoirs of a Tory Radical*, London: Bantam Press, p. 575.
17. Tebbit, N. (1991) *Unfinished Business*, London: Weidenfeld & Nicolson, pp. 61–3.
18. Baker, K. (1993) *The Turbulent Years: My Life in Politics*, London: Faber & Faber, p. 112.

19. See, for example, Thatcher, M. (1993) *The Downing Street Years*, London: HarperCollins, pp. 123, 306, 339, 599, 642.
20. Heseltine, M. (1987) *Where There's A Will*, London: Hutchinson, p. 132.

6 The Demise of the Public Service Ethos

Lawrence Pratchett and Melvin Wingfield

Introduction

Public servants are an important, though often overlooked, element of modern democracies. The large bureaucracies which are a feature of all contemporary governments have a major role to play in sustaining democratic structures and practices, especially by providing for a mix of technical expertise and impartial advice within a pluralist framework of representative democracy. Within local government the 2.2 million full and part-time employees[1] must be juxtaposed against the 20 000 elected members who are their political masters.[2] Often better paid, better qualified, better informed (through professional networks and so on) and more experienced than their political counterparts, it is difficult to deny that local government officers make a significant contribution to the overall policy process in local authorities, and to the more general nature of democracy at the local level. It is important, therefore, that the behaviour of these officers is informed and guided by an underlying culture which supports and understands the political context of democratic local government.

This sense of *public service ethos* is a defining characteristic of traditional local government which has been a distinguishing feature of employment in the service.[3] There is a growing concern, however, that the traditional attitudes and values of the public service ethos in local government are under threat from a barrage of changes which have fundamentally altered the structure, organisation and management of local authorities over the last two decades (see Chapter 1). This is not simply a concern that the opportunities for corrupt or inappropriate behaviour in the public sector are increasing, although such anxieties are being expressed.[4] It is also a concern that the deep-rooted traditional values of public life are being eroded. Consequently, there is disquiet that the distinctive spirit, character and attitudes of public servants,[5] which provided the essential cohesive force for traditional public administration, are being lost.[6] In other words, there is a belief that the changes of the last fifteen years are subverting and undermining the public service ethos that has characterised public organisations throughout the twentieth century.

This chapter reports on research that was conducted during the summer of 1994, which investigated the extent to which recent changes are undermining the traditional values of the public service ethos. It offers an empirically based analysis of the changing values of local government officers, and the implications of these changes for both traditional and emerging concepts of local democracy. Thus, this chapter raises questions over whether there is an erosion or evolution of the public service ethos, and the implications of such trends for those who would seek to revitalise democracy at the local level.

Defining the public service ethos

The public service ethos is a spirit that is often referred to but rarely, if ever, identified or defined.[7] It is something that is alluded to in discussions of the special qualities required of those working in the public sector, and suggests that there is some consensus over the values and principles of those employed in publicly accountable organisations which guides their behaviour and directs their actions.[8] Such accounts assume that the public service ethos is something intrinsically virtuous, to which all public servants should (and do) aspire. It remains, however, an ambiguous and elusive concept.

Before exploring the generic features of the public service ethos, it is important to recognise that the current definition is informed and influenced by two factors. Firstly, the term 'public service ethos' would appear to be a relatively new one. This is not to argue that the existence of a culture and ethos that is shared throughout a cross-section of public employees is new. On the contrary, this chapter assumes an evolving set of values and ethics that have their roots in the institutional development of public administration in the UK. It does argue, however, that interest in the subject is relatively new,[9] and that this interest is in large part due to the perceptions of both senior practitioners and academic commentators who are suggesting that these values are now being eroded.

Secondly, the public service ethos remains a largely intangible concept. Most references to it are vague and imprecise, combining professional ethics and customs with elements of democratic and bureaucratic theories, to prescribe the behaviour of public servants. Plowden[10] in his discussion of the civil service, offers one of the few attempts to define this abstruse concept when he argues that the composite ethos of civil servants:

> does and should embody certain attitudes likely to be peculiar to government: a respect for the democratic political process in the sense that its outcomes are accepted as legitimate even when uncongenial or absurd; a respect for the rights of the individual citizen that do not relate, as will often be the case in a business context, to the citizen's purchasing power. 'Managing in a political environment' calls for technical skills, and also for genuine political sensitivity plus some professional humility – that is, the capacity to recognise that the technically correct solution may simply be inappropriate. One might add to the list, more explicitly than expressed here, the willingness – in Aaron Wildavsky's phrase – to 'speak truth to power'.

This definition can be built upon to consider the generic features of the public service ethos in local government.

For the purposes of analysis it is possible to recognise at least five distinct but related features that cut across the various professional and institutional boundaries of public administration, and which are of particular relevance to local government:

1. *Accountability* – Accountability is concerned with the local government officer's acceptance of the legitimacy of the political institutions and processes that govern, and an awareness of the officer's role in upholding these.
2. *Bureaucratic Behaviour* – Bureaucratic behaviour in this context refers to a whole range of qualities that are generally associated with public servants. They are the classical Weberian qualities expected of the bureaucratic public official, and include such attributes as honesty, integrity, impartiality and objectivity.
3. *Sense of Community* – There is an awareness amongst public servants that their collective responsibilities are not confined to the immediate boundaries of their employing organisation, but also extend to the community which the organisation serves, and

indeed, beyond. Hence, there is a belief that local government staff hold the wider concerns of the community at heart.

4. *Motivation* – Related to a sense of community, the motivation of local government officers is perceived as being different from those employed in other sectors of the economy. Their motivation is not based primarily in any concerns for profit (either individual or organisational), but involves some element of altruism.

5. *Loyalty* – Loyalty is closely related to the other characteristics of the public service ethos. It is derived from a combination of features including an understanding of political legitimacy and accountability, and a sense of community. Officers, therefore, subscribe to a concept of loyalty that is more than simply a loyalty to the employing organisation, or a loyalty to individuals within it. Whilst the precise locus of this loyalty may be confused and ambiguous, it includes loyalties to the employer (and possibly departmental loyalties within it), professional loyalties, general institutional loyalties (for example, loyalty to the institutions of government) and community loyalties (that is, loyalty to the community as a whole, or to sections within it).

The changing public service ethos

The absence of a clear and established definition in traditional accounts of values and perceptions amongst local government officers makes it difficult to indicate from where the fundamental values of the ethos have emerged. The most obvious source within local government is the institutional structure itself. That is to say, the organisations of local government are imbued with the value systems of the public service ethos, and that these cultural principles are instilled into individuals as part of a general induction into the world of local government. Unfortunately, there is little evidence to support such a notion. Individuals enter into local government service through a wide variety of routes, and with a very broad cross-section of qualifications and educational backgrounds. Once in local government, the training that they receive varies considerably, not only between different grades and occupations, but also between authorities. Even the formal codes of conduct – the standing orders – of individual councils vary significantly in both their format and content. For example, it was not until 1974 that a

'National Code of Local Government Conduct' was formulated for elected members.[11] Although terms and conditions of employment are consistent across local government, these ensure a uniformity of terms and conditions for staff, rather than imposing or inculcating specific values on those receiving them.

Furthermore, the national associations concerned with local government have demonstrated very little interest in creating education or training facilities to develop a unique local government ethos. There is no local government equivalent to the Civil Service College, created in the wake of the Fulton Report.[12] The activities of the local authority associations remain largely concerned with the lobbying of central government,[13] and the new unified association proposed for representing the reorganised local government system (in the aftermath of the Banham reviews) does not appear to differ significantly from this lobbying basis. In addition, the Local Government Management Board, whilst offering a range of training and development resources for local authorities, does not fulfil the role of instilling a specific value system across local government. At a national level, therefore, there is little evidence of any agencies undertaking the role of generating or sustaining a public service ethos.

The importance of key professions in local government, on the other hand, may well be the source of the features that distinguish the public service ethos. The idea of a distinctive set of values within the public sector and specifically within local government has been clearly identified by a number of authors concerned with the professions in local government.[14] The professional bodies that dominate local government departments are able to impose their own values and culture through a number of related mechanisms. Firstly, the lengthy training process of most professions, culminating in professional examinations, offers ample opportunity for the instilling of the values of the profession, both directly, in the form of prescribed training, and indirectly, through the use of mentors and role models. Indeed, a major part of most professional training is to ensure that the individual understands and subscribes to the general ethical standards set by the profession. Secondly, the internal ethics of the profession ensure a commonality of behaviour amongst members, once qualified. Thirdly, the policy networks that the professions are centred around[15] lead to a consensus on policy that emerges from the general ethos of the profession. This extends well beyond the ethical behaviour expected of the profession to define the overall attitudes and perceptions of the profession which guide the behaviour of individuals in particular circumstances. For example, Dunleavy's study of high-rise housing in Britain in the post World War Two era identifies a complex of professional standards and networks for the widespread development of 'tower-block' housing.[16] The professions, especially those that are concentrated around local service provision, therefore, bring a number of distinctive values and features to the management of local government.

Rather than seeing these features as homogeneous, however, the disparate nature of the public service ensures that values are manifested as those relating to individual professional bodies, and not local government *per se*. The issue here is whether or not they all add up to something more than the sum of their collective parts. That is, do the divided and unco-ordinated value systems of disparate professional bodies unite to form a public service ethos? Alternatively, it may also be the case that the distinctive characteristics or culture of each independent and functionally differentiated professional body militates against any generic public service ethos. Thus Laffin and Young[17] highlight the contrasting languages of different professions, and the ambiguity that flourishes where the activities of professions intersect one another.

This dichotomy is useful in setting a context for the role of the professions in local government. Professions bring a particular set of values and ethics to local government. The same values, however, may not be shared across different professions, creating a tension over the nature of the public service ethos, rather than a consensus throughout local government. In striving to construct unity between differentiated professions, the public service ethos may simply be the lowest common denominator.

Traditionally, local government has reserved its senior positions for professionally qualified staff.[18] If the influential nature of the professions is accepted, this offers a further proposition for the public service ethos in local government. It suggests that local government has attracted an homogenous group of people that bring with them a set of values and attitudes towards public life. Thus, the local government professions attract people from particular social and educational backgrounds who share common values. A corollary to this is that particular functions in local government may attract individuals who share the values that are identified with the public service ethos. In particular, those individuals involved in the caring professions, especially the personal social services, housing and education, may exhibit the values and attitudes of the public service ethos simply by the very nature of the job that they undertake. If this is the case, these values are not so much a shared ethos across the whole of local government, as a service related functional/professional ethos.

The professional basis of the public service ethos has significant implications for the impact of change on the behaviour of individuals. Collectively, organisational, managerial and political changes in local government appear to be inexorably eroding the fundamental nature of the public service ethos. But it is important not to exaggerate the impact of such changes on the values and attitudes of those involved in them. Is it really the case that simply because staff are moved into a more competitive environment, their attitudes and perceptions change? The professional basis of the public service ethos suggests that the erosion of the public service ethos is anything but certain. Professionals moved into the private (or voluntary) sector will not change their values overnight. Professional bodies will continue to promulgate the same culture and ethos regardless of the institutional location of individual members. Functions that attract individuals with particular qualities that are closely aligned to the public service ethos will still exist, although in a transformed way. Consequently, it is important to recognise that many of the characteristics of the public service ethos that appear to be under threat from current changes, may well be preserved, albeit somewhat altered, in the emerging local government structure.

An empirical study of the public service ethos[19]

Although it is difficult to establish the institutional basis of the public service ethos it is nonetheless useful to consider the ways in which its various features are being influenced by recent changes. It is only by empirical analysis of this ethos that the implications of both the underlying culture of local government officers and the impact of the recent changes on this culture can be understood. Consequently, the authors undertook a series of case studies of the public service ethos conducted in four local authorities during the summer of 1994. The research involved a postal questionnaire to 471 randomly selected employees of the four authorities, combined with a series of six 'group discussions' involving a further 48 randomly selected staff. In total, 519 individual employees in the four local authorities were given the opportunity to participate in the research, of which 319 did so. The research concentrated around the five features of the public service ethos identified earlier, and questioned participants on the extent to which they subscribe to these different values, and the extent to which their attitudes and perceptions had changed (and were continuing to change) in relation to them. In particular, the research was interested in analysing whether organisational, structural, political and managerial change was leading to different emphases within or between these features.

Accountability

> You have to have accountability otherwise it's a waste of time having local government. You have to have some kind of [democratic] accountability to know why you are doing what you are doing. (survey respondent)

Whilst 72 per cent of respondents thought that accountability was important, the lines of accountability were notably confused. Alexander and Orr[20] have charted the growth of the fragmented authority and note that 'as service delivery fragments, collective accountability weakens as the distance between political responsibility and service delivery increases'. The questionnaire results support this contention. Over 35 per cent of respondents thought that accountability was most important at a departmental level, while only 3 per cent thought that staff should be accountable at a political level. Moreover, 37.5 per cent of all respondents were departmentally orientated. They thought that the department was the 'most important' actor in relation to their work, while 33 per cent felt that the primary locus of their 'loyalty' was the department.

Nevertheless, there was a general consensus amongst all the discussion groups that the electoral process performed an important and legitimate role in making local government accountable. Although other forms of accountability were also considered important there was general agreement that accountability to the elected members was the overarching level of accountability that provided a broader accountability to the local community:

> I don't think that we are accountable to the councillors, we are
> accountable to the public through the councillors. (survey respon-
> dent)

Many participants were also of the opinion that the policies of the
council were an accurate reflection of the wishes of the community,
and that only by being accountable to the elected members could
they be sure that they were undertaking the wishes of the community.

The conclusions of the group discussions as they relate to
accountability as a feature of the public service ethos, therefore,
are twofold. Firstly, a sense of democratic accountability, as well as
hierarchical accountability, is still an important feature amongst
local government staff. The need for such accountability, in the
perception of staff, does not appear to have diminished with the
onset of a more competitive and fragmented environment in local
government. Secondly, however, the means by which this accountability is translated into the day-to-day activities of officers is
confused. This is not necessarily a product of recent changes in
local government. It may well have been the case that officers have
always been unclear about how electoral accountability relates to
their own day-to-day activities.

Bureaucratic behaviour

> People working in local government are still living as if the good
> old money tree is still firmly planted in the back garden and
> bearing as much fruit as it ever has. (survey respondent)

Participants considered the proposition that they were governed by
bureaucratic rules and procedures as a largely disparaging and
pejorative reference to their attitudes. Nevertheless, in discussing
the concept, they exhibited many of the features that characterise the
traditional bureaucrat. Thus, there was a general belief that local
government officers behaved with greater honesty and integrity than
those in the private sector:

> I'm not saying that those in the business sector are necessarily
> dishonest – it's just that they're not always as honest as they might
> be. They don't tell you the whole truth, they only tell you what
> suits them. We're much more honest than that. We'll tell you the
> whole truth even if it's not what you wanted to hear – or what you
> would like to hear. (survey respondent)

The implication here was that the bureaucratic integrity of local government officers is such that they do not operate with a hidden agenda, but ensure that all information is made available to those who need it, even if such information is not in the best interests of the individual bureaucrat.

The pejorative belief that local authorities are bastions of bureaucratic behaviour, however, was disputed by those answering the questionnaires. Some 63 per cent thought that rules ensured that services were provided fairly by the staff and that they safeguarded staff from allegations of bias or favouritism. The majority of respondents, 84 per cent, were of the opinion that equitable treatment was the main feature of the bureaucratic structure, and that this was the purpose of bureaucratic rules. In answer to a separate question, however, 49 per cent of respondents thought that it was acceptable to 'bend' the rules to assist those in need, and over half of all respondents, 56 per cent, thought that local authority rules and procedures acted as an impediment to staff initiative. This suggests that a large proportion of staff would value the greater discretion and innovative roles that new public management claims to offer.

When asked to identify the five characteristics (from a list of ten) that are most important in a local government officer, there was a high level of correspondence with the features of classical bureaucratic behaviour. Thus, there was a great deal of consensus over such qualities as honesty (82 per cent), integrity (78 per cent), professionalism (91 per cent), impartiality (68 per cent).

Consequently, the rules and procedures that predominate in bureaucracies were generally seen to be a means of ensuring equity between customers, but there were some tensions that arose here with other features of the public service ethos. In particular, there was an argument that rules should be 'bent' where it met a wider social good. Indeed, there was widespread consensus amongst the groups that rules were often bent as one way of achieving the wider social aims of the council. This introduces a more worrying notion into the public service ethos. If staff are prepared to bend the rules in order to fulfil wider social or political objectives, then their impartiality has to be questioned. In bending the rules they assume a paternalistic role, presuming that they know better than the policy-makers who framed the rules. Of course, this concern is blurred by the fact that most rules are subject to a degree of interpretation by the individual officer, with the result that the paternalism of working within 'the spirit of the rules' is an inevitable feature of bureaucracy.

Finally, there was a significant element of dissent over the value of bureaucratic rules and procedures in the modern local government environment. This concern was raised especially, although not exclusively, by those involved in the more competitive aspects of local government. The concern was that the traditional emphasis upon rule-bound bureaucratic behaviour prevents individuals from exercising any initiative or entrepeneurialism. One participant listed the features of bureaucracy that most frustrates such enterprise:

> It stifles initiative; people are demoralised by but resigned to red tape; all of us are undervalued; our expertise is not acknowledged externally – and sometimes internally; there's little stimulus or challenge; there's a lack of progression and opportunity; and there's no sense of pride or ownership.

Another person went further, suggesting that local government was characterised by 'petty bureaucracy and woolly minded liberalism'.

Such sentiments were echoed, although not always so vehemently, by a number of participants who were responsible for managing the competitive functions of local government.

Two features of this bureaucratic behaviour are worth emphasising. Firstly, respondents identified more closely with the concept of professionalism than with any other characteristic (91 per cent). This suggests, in part, an emphasis upon behaving in a professional manner. It also supports, however, the contention that the professions are the source of much influence over the public service ethos, both directly and indirectly. Secondly, a significant minority of respondents also valued many of the features that are not traditionally associated with the public service ethos, but may well feature in its erosion or evolution. Most significantly, enterprise (29 per cent) and business acumen (25 per cent) were highly regarded amongst a number of respondents.

Sense of community

> One cares about outcomes – that links a whole range of public sector areas. The outcome is important to the people delivering the service. (survey respondent)

Related to the general belief in equity, the group discussion participants also exhibited a sense of community. This was not simply associated with a sense of accountability to the wider community, although this was a factor, but also concerned a broader desire to work on behalf of the community. This sense of community, therefore, dominated the value systems of many participants, giving them the intrinsic motivation to undertake their work. For these, a 'concern for the community as a whole' was fundamental to the public service ethos.

A more important aspect of this sense of community, however, was the extent to which individuals felt that they existed within a local government community. There was a general optimism that the public service ethos in local government is strong enough to resist the fragmentatory pressures of competition:

> I view them [client/contractor splits] as artificial splits that are imposed from above, and what happens is that all the way until we legally have to be split, and afterwards, we will be working together for the corporate good. (survey respondent)

The majority of questionnaire respondents (70 per cent), however, quite clearly identified the conflict that can arise between community needs and the needs of the local authority. Policies may be introduced by the local authority that are not coterminous with the wishes of much of the community. The officers working on such contentious issues were particularly conscious of the democratic way in which they had arisen. For most respondents (95 per cent) inter and intra organisational competition was perceived as a negative factor. There was, however, considerable confusion over whose interests were most important to officers.

In terms of commitment to different parts of the organisation, and to the wider concept of the local community, there was also an absence of consensus. A significant proportion of respondents identified their immediate work colleagues or department as being those whose interests were most important to them (37 per cent). A further 22 per cent felt that the council as a whole was the most significant concern. Significantly, 35 per cent of respondents aligned their own interests most closely with those of the local community.

Motivation

> What I do is for the whole of the area. Whilst I make some profit from doing it [i.e. in the form of a salary], I resent the thought that

someone might want to make a profit out of my service to the community. It shouldn't be like that. The whole community should profit from what I do, not just shareholders. (survey respondent)

Questions about what motivated staff in local government elicited some strong responses from the groups. Important in this motivation was a belief that local government employees are distinguished from the private sector because they are 'service orientated not profit motivated'. Indeed, the 'not for profit' motive of local government employees was one of the most frequently cited characteristics of the public service ethos in the group discussions.

Furthermore, financial remuneration was not one of the main factors respondents considered important when deciding to work for a local authority – only 14 per cent considered local authority employees' pay to be good. As some respondents indicated, once they had decided to follow a certain profession, local government was the major employer in that field and they had little choice but to work in that institution. Nevertheless, 87 per cent of all respondents did not wish to work for a private sector company. When asked to select from a list of 11 the three best features of working in local government, serving the community (63 per cent) and interesting work (69 per cent) were by far the most frequently cited features.

Conclusions over motivation as an important feature of public service are, therefore, mixed. There was a strong belief amongst participants that they worked for the benefit of the whole community and that this was closely associated with a 'not for profit' motive. Equally, however, there was also an acknowledgement from some that they were motivated primarily by professional values and the pride that they get from doing a 'professional' job. This suggests that whilst altruistic motives are important in local government, there is scope for many professional jobs to be undertaken outside of the institutions of local government without any significant erosion of the public service ethos.

Loyalty

I've always considered myself to be a loyal sort of person – but loyal to who? It's difficult to know who to be loyal to when they're all trying to kick you at the same time. The council are only loyal while it suits them and Joe public are even more fickle.

. . . I try to be loyal to the local government tradition but I keep asking myself 'what's the point?' (survey respondent)

Surprisingly, there was less consensus over where employee loyalties should lie, than for any other feature of the public service ethos. Some participants felt that the council had failed to show them the loyalty that they deserved during a period of extensive and profound change.

Others, however, returned to the wider sense of community that they felt, and argued that they owed a loyalty to the community through the council:

I owe it to my residents to do the best job I can, regardless of the pressures that are put on me from above – or from outside of the council. (survey respondent)

Overall, opinion was divided over loyalties to different parts of the organisation, to the elected Council, to the community, and to the institutions of local government, with no clear pattern of loyalties emerging amongst particular groups or professions.

The public service ethos

When respondents were directly asked if they believed that there was a public service ethos 77 per cent replied positively. As one respondent commented the public service ethos manifests itself in a belief that staff are:

Motivated by the desire to work for the community at large, and the disadvantaged or unrepresented in particular, for mutual advantage and the improvement of the quality of life across the authority area.

Table 6.1 profiles the respondents by authority, gender and their own belief in a public service ethos.

Some important features of the changing public service ethos emerge from this profile. Firstly, as anticipated, those employed in the authority most closely associated with the contracting out of services (Rutland) questioned the existence of a public service ethos much more readily than their colleagues in other authorities. Whilst the average number of respondents who did not believe in the public

TABLE 6.1   **Profile of respondents with and without a sense of public service ethos**

Authority	Without public service ethos[¥]		With public service ethos[¶]		Total number*
	Female	Male	Female	Male	
London Borough of Greenwich	7	6	26	35	74
Leicestershire County Council	13	6	42	42	103
Rutland District Council	10	7	9	9	35
Tameside Metropolitan District	5	6	11	28	50

Notes:
[¥] Denied a belief in the public service ethos.
[¶] Confirmed a belief in the public service ethos.
* Total is less than 271 due to uncompleted questions.

service ethos was 23 per cent across all authorities, in Rutland it was 49 per cent. This suggests that the political priorities of the council, and particularly its position over recent reforms, do have a profound affect upon the sense of public service ethos amongst its staff. Secondly, the county council, metropolitan district and London borough all exhibit similar levels of staff who believe that there is a public service ethos. Type of authority, therefore, would not appear to be a significant influence on the public service ethos. Thirdly, the profile shows a significant disparity between the responses of males and females in relation to the public service ethos. In total, 28 per cent of females denied the existence of an ethos, in contrast with only 18 per cent of males. This suggests that gender could be a significant feature in determining the characteristics and importance of the public service ethos in contemporary local government. It is beyond the scope of this research, however, to speculate over the reasons for this disparity.

Finally, the age of individual respondents does appear to be significant, as Figure 6.1 demonstrates. This shows a marginal increase in the percentage of respondents believing in the public service ethos for each age band. It implies, therefore, that a belief in

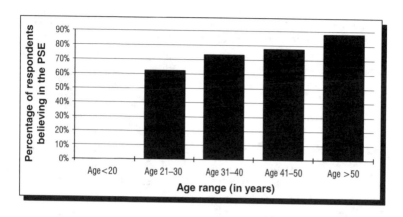

FIGURE 6.1   Age range by belief in the public service ethos (PSE)

the public service ethos is age related: the older the employees, the more likely they are to believe in the public service ethos.

It is useful at this stage to highlight two of the more general themes that emerged from the group discussions. Firstly, whilst many of the outcomes of the group discussions were similar, the overall attitudes and values of the participants varied along two dimensions. The first was that of proximity to a competitive environment – those engaged in more competitive work were notable in proclaiming other values not traditionally associated with the public service ethos. The second dimension was that of political context. During the group discussions it became apparent that those employed in more overtly left of centre authorities demonstrated a closer affinity to the traditional values of the public service ethos than those with less definitive political positions. The most likely explanation for this is that radical political policies have generated a more politicised environment for staff, thus making them more aware of the values and culture that underpin their working ethos, regardless of whether or not they support the political party in power. It follows from this argument that the degree of politicisation in local government may have a significant affect upon the public service ethos.

Secondly, the group discussions show that some of the traditional values of the public service ethos are losing their credibility in the face of new and emerging values. They recognise that some of the traditional features of bureaucratic behaviour are giving way to a new spirit of innovation and enterprise. What is less clear, however, is the extent to which these changing values amount to an erosion of, or an evolution in, the public service ethos.

Erosion or evolution?

There can be little doubt that contemporary organisational, managerial and democratic changes in local government are having a profound and sustained impact upon the attitudes and perceptions of those working either directly or indirectly for local authorities. But do such changes amount to an erosion of the public service ethos, or an evolution of values?

The findings clearly identify an erosion of some of the values of the public service ethos: interpretations of accountability are shifting away from democratic accountability towards contract and market accountability; the acceptance of bureaucratic rules and procedures is diminishing, especially amongst those who have been or are about to be exposed to competition; the fragmentation of local government into discrete business units is having a profound affect upon the collegial sense of community that characterised the traditional environment of local government, encouraging individuals to place the interests of their own part of the organisation above those of the wider organisation or community; and loyalties are being moved away from the traditional council wide focus towards more personally located loyalties. The changing nature of these features demonstrates that the principal foundations of the public service ethos are being eroded and undermined by current changes in the organisation and management of local government.

The dual impact of market competition (especially through compulsory competitive tendering – CCT) and the internal reforms of the 'New Public Management' (NPM) must be held responsible for this erosion. The division of functions between client and contractor that are engendered by market competition have led to antagonistic and adversarial relations between different parts of the same organisation, encouraging more reticent and secretive behaviour within and between local authorities. These problems have been compounded by the NPM-led reforms that have shifted attention away from the traditional focus on procedural integrity, to concentrate much more upon efficiency and performance measurement. This again has encouraged a more self-interested and insular approach which contrasts with that encountered in traditional local government. The consequence of these changes has been an identifiable shift in the attitudes and perceptions of those employed in local government: that is, a significant, and perhaps irreversible erosion of the public service ethos.

At the same time, however, it is also necessary to acknowledge that whilst an erosion in some features of the public service ethos has been witnessed by this research, it is also evident that other features of it are evolving rather than diminishing. Accountability, for example, has not diminished, it has simply changed its focus. Similarly, the 'not for profit' motivation of many of those who work in local government has not been radically altered by competition, and many of those affected by change were able to identify significant public benefits that had come about through competition. In this respect, the public service ethos is evolving, rather than declining. This evolution is being augmented by the emergence of new features: a greater dedication of officers to the provision of qualitatively better and more efficient services; a more innovative and flexible approach to the management of functions that comes from a competitive and entrepreneurial environment; and an acceptance of the need for objective measures of organisational and individual performance. It is these features that make up the new and evolving public service ethos.

The case studies emphasised that the functional/professional location of the individual is fundamental to the meaning that is given to specific values of the public service ethos. The very different and contrasting functions of local government (for example, the contrast between social work and civil engineering), and the role of the professions in dominating these functions, are the key to understanding the differing attitudes of individuals within the same local authority. In exploring these cleavages within the group discussions, the role of the professional bodies in instilling particular ethics into their members was emphasised consistently. Many participants stated that their behaviour and attitudes were conditioned by the professional training that they had received, and by the values that underpinned 'professional practice'. It emerges, therefore, that the professional bodies are the main sources of the value systems that comprise the public service ethos, and that the professions dominate the development and dissemination of this ethos throughout local government.

There are two consequences of this professional underpinning and domination of the public service ethos. Firstly, because the professions are functionally differentiated in local government there is very little overlap between them. This leads to differing emphases on particular features of the public service ethos, and explains why different individuals from the same authority can have contrasting perspectives on the relative importance of specific features. Secondly, and more significantly, because the public service ethos emerges from the professions rather than from the democratic institutions of local government, it is clear that it is not dependent upon local government or local democracy *per se* for its continued existence. Hence, the stability created by professional domination will ensure a continuation of the values associated with the public service ethos, regardless of whether functions are provided in the public or private sectors.

Conclusion

In recognising the weakening of some of the pillars of the traditional public service ethos and the emergence of a new set of dominant values, the real concern is whether the evolving set of values are those which are appropriate for local government. The public service ethos in local government is sufficiently ambiguous and flexible to adapt to meet the pressures that it currently faces. The real issue is whether, in adapting to meet the needs of modern local government, the new-look ethos is one that will complement or compound contemporary changes. It has already been noted that the domination of the professions in the propagation of the public service ethos means that simply by moving functions from the public to the private sector will not necessarily change the underlying values and culture of professional staff. But as new 'professions' come to dominate in functions that have traditionally been the domain of local government (for example, accountants without a public sector background), then the professional basis of the public service ethos may be lost.

The simultaneous erosion and evolution of the public service ethos collectively signals a form of local government that will be fundamentally different in the future. These differences will not be limited to the structure, organisation and management of local government. It is the underlying culture and values of those involved in providing local government services that is now at stake. The key feature about the emerging ethos of local government service is that it emphasises a competitive, contractual, insular and adversarial culture. This new ethos will not provide cohesion in the face of fragmentation, but will gradually compound the divisive elements of the new local government, leading to a disintegrated and disunited range of local services. Most importantly, the emerging culture of public service is ignoring and subverting the democratic principles which traditional bureaucracies have sought to uphold: such attributes as bureaucratic impartiality and objectivity, a collegial sense of community, democratic accountability, and a motivation centred around service to the community rather than profit-centre performance. Of all the changes that have occurred in local government over the last two decades, therefore, the changes in the public service ethos threaten to be the least conspicuous but most profound in their impact.

Notes and references

1. Audit Commission (1995) *Paying the Piper: People and Pay Management in Local Government*, London: HMSO.
2. Wilson, D. and Game, C. (1994) *Local Government in the United Kingdom*, London: Macmillan.
3. Poole, R. (1978) *The Local Government Service in England and Wales*, London: Allen & Unwin.
4. See, for example, Harrison, A. (1994) 'Showing a Willingness to Play by the Rules', *Local Government Chronicle*, 22 July 1994.
5. Throughout this chapter the terms ethos, values, attitudes, culture and belief systems are used interchangeably to indicate the deep-rooted perceptions of public servants. Whilst it is acknowledged that such terms can have very different meanings, these will not be explored in this chapter.
6. For example, in relation to the Civil Service: Plowden, W. (1994) *Ministers and Mandarins*, London: IPPR. In relation to local government: Maldé, B. (1994) 'The Return of the Public Servant', *Local Government Studies*, vol. 20, no. 1, pp. 7–15.
7. For example, the Oughton Report (1992) of the Prime Minister's Efficiency Unit, which reported on an opinion survey of 4250 British civil servants, highlighted a concern that 'the public service ethos is being eroded', but did nothing to further define or explain the nature of either the ethos, or its apparent erosion (cited in Plowden (1994) ibid, pp. 60–74).
8. For example, Maldé, 'Return of the Public Servant'.

9. For example, the late John Smith MP was one of a number of politicians to use the concept of public service ethos as a party political tool – See Smith, J. (1991) 'The Public Service Ethos', *Public Administration*, vol. 69, no. 4, pp. 515–23.
10. Plowden, *Ministers and Mandarins*.
11. Cmnd 5636, *The Redcliffe-Maud Committee on Local Government Rules of Conduct* (1974), London: HMSO.
12. Cmnd 3638 *The Civil Service: Report of the Committee 1966-68*, London: HMSO.
13. Rhodes, R. A. W. (1986) *The National World of Local Government*, London: Allen & Unwin.
14. For example: Poole, *The Local Government Service. . .*; Laffin, M. (1986) *Professionalism and Policy: The Role of the Professions in the Central-Local Government Relationship*, Aldershot: Gower; Young, K. (1988) 'The Changing Nature of Professionalism in Local Government', *Policy Studies*, July 1988.
15. Marsh, D. and Rhodes, R. A. W. (1992) *Policy Networks in British Government*, Oxford: Oxford University Press; Smith, M. (1993) *Pressure, Power and Politics*, London: Harvester-Wheatsheaf.
16. Dunleavy, P. (1981) *The Politics of Mass Housing in Britain 1945– 1975*, Oxford: Clarendon Press.
17. Laffin, M. and Young, K. (1990) *Professionalism in Local Government: Change and Challenge*, London: Longman.
18. Cunningham, I. and Fahey, U. (1976) 'Administrators and Professionals in Local Government', *Local Government Studies*, vol. 2, no. 4, pp. 19–29.
19. The authors are grateful to the Institute of Chartered Secretaries and Administrators for their financial support for this empirical work, and for their continued interest in the issues raised by the research.
20. Alexander, A. and Orr, K. (1993) *Managing The Fragmented Authority*, Luton: Local Government Management Board.

7 Political Parties and Local Democracy

Chris Game and Steve Leach

Introduction

The period immediately following local government reorganisation in 1974 saw, particularly in more rural areas, a marked acceleration of the party politicisation of local government. One major cause of this development was the structural reorganisation itself: the boundary changes and the amalgamation of small and independent-dominated authorities into larger and more overtly partisan ones. An additional cause was the incorporation of formerly 'independent' councillors, associated with, and even members of, the Conservative Party into the Conservative mainstream as a result of explicit pressure being placed upon them to stand in future as officially adopted Conservative candidates, or risk facing the opposition of such candidates. As a result, in the years since reorganisation, the number of 'non-partisan' councils and independent councillors has continued to fall, although the latter are still in a majority in nearly one council in ten, and retain a significant presence on at least the same number again.

The catalytic impact of reorganisation – the boundary changes and the amalgamation of the smallest authorities with or into larger and more partisan ones – can be seen by examining the situation after the first election to the newly created authorities. The proportion of 'partisan' authorities[1] rose immediately to well over three-quarters, while the figure for county councils shot up more dramatically still – to nearly 90 per cent, leaving in England just three counties (Cornwall, Shropshire and the Isle of Wight) where Independents remained the largest political grouping.

In the succeeding decade this trend continued. By 1986, at the time of the Widdicombe Committee, 'non-partisan' councils constituted just 15 per cent of the total in Great Britain and only 12 per cent in England and Wales. The previous year's elections had seen the completion of the party politicisation process among English county councils as, even on the traditionally staunch non-partisan Cornwall County Council, Independents were displaced by the Liberals as the largest single group.

Table 7.1 presents the picture in 1995 in a slightly more differentiated form, distinguishing, for example, the 16 (4 per cent) completely or predominantly non-partisan councils and the 46 (10 per cent) we have defined as 'weak partisan'. These are councils on which Independents still retain a significant presence, but that is by no means to imply that they have been completely supplanted elsewhere.

In many rural authorities the fact that many, or even most, councillors nowadays are elected under party labels does not necessarily mean that council business is conducted or power and influence exercised entirely through party political channels. Other forms of status system survive. Similarly, party group discipline and voting cohesions are much more common urban phenomena, as is the use of manifestos in election campaigns. Young and Davies in their 1989 survey of 'post Widdicombe' political change suggest that differences in practice and inclination will persist.[2] The likely continuing displacement of Independents themselves by party-labelled members does not imply any homogenisation or inexorable urbanisation of practice.

The intensification of political partisanship

The same post-reorganisation period has seen not just a spread of formal party politics, but an *intensification* and, particularly during the 1980s, a polarisation *of partisanship* in local government. One feature of this growing partisanship has been a tightening of group discipline across all parties. Labour and Conservative party groups both operate extensive *whipping systems* which have increased in scope and effectiveness in recent years. Liberal Democrats operate in a more informal way, but they too, as they have come to control or share power in increasing numbers of authorities, place growing emphasis on party cohesion and public displays of party unity. This increasing replication of an almost 'Westminster-style' approach to party discipline is arguably less appropriate in local government, where it is known that considerably higher proportions of electors vote on the basis of their knowledge of the candidates than in parliamentary elections, and where it is frequently claimed that a

TABLE 7.1 Party systems in local government, Great Britain, May 1995

Party system and definition	England					Wales	Scotland	Great Britain	
	New Unitaries	Counties	London Boroughs (1994)	Metropolitan Districts (1995)	Non-Met. Districts (1995)	New Unitaries	New Unitaries	Total	%
Substantially non-partisan (60% or more seats held by Independents)	–	1	–	10	–	3	2	16	4
Weak partisan (20–59% of seats held by Independents)	1	–	–	38	–	4	3	46	10
Multi-party/fragmented (20% or more seats held by 3rd party/parties)	19	7	3	63	3	1	–	96	21
Two-party (80% of seats held by 2 parties, neither over 55%)	9	3	6	29	1	–	1	49	11
One-party dominant (55–60% of seats held by one party)	C 1 Lab 6 LD 2	– 7 –	– 8 –	5 32 31	– 1 –	– 3 –	C – Lab 10 LD – SNP 1	6 67 33 1 ⎫ 107	24
One-party monopolistic (70 % or more seats held by one party)	C – Lab 1 LD –	3 10 2	– 19 –	– 59 7	– 8 1	– 11 –	C – Lab 10 SD – SNP 2	3 118 10 2 ⎫ 133	30
Total	39	33	36	274	14	22	29	447	100

relatively high proportion of committee business is essentially 'non-partisan' in nature.

Notwithstanding all the encouragement in its Memorandum of 'the maximum amount of flexibility', of 'elasticity' and free votes,[3] Labour groups continue, as in the past, to operate the strongest whipping systems, with group decisions being binding on most votes. This is automatic for most groups and most whips spend their time making sure that members are actually present to vote and that they know which way they are supposed to vote. There are, however, a number of situations in which normal whipping expectations are explicitly or implicitly relaxed. Issues of conscience and where a member's ward is adversely affected – for example, through a school closure – are the two most common examples. There is a variety of practice on whether, in such circumstances, members are permitted to vote against the group line, expected to abstain, or expected to absent themselves at the time of the vote.

Whipping systems in Liberal Democrat groups are usually nothing like as formal as Labour's. Group standing orders expect members to stand by group decisions, but even then leaders often have to persuade, rather than automatically expect, their group members to stand by majority decisions. Some Conservative groups, particularly in smaller and more rural authorities, are also relatively 'flexible' about discipline, sometimes preferring to use the collective responsibility of group executives – formal or informal – to give the group the lead on voting, rather than what might be considered the heavy-handedness of formal whipping.

The trend towards an increasingly pervasive group discipline is continuing. There remain differences in the extent to which these changes have affected group cohesion in different types of area. Young and Davies show that, on all measures of party cohesion, partisanship is at its highest in urban areas and at its lowest in rural areas: for example, 32 per cent of controlling party members in urban authorities reported never voting with the opposition at committee meetings, while in rural authorities the figure was just 3 per cent.[4] The diversity of practice which was such a strong feature of the Widdicombe research evidence thus remains. Nevertheless, the overall conclusion from the Young and Davies survey is clear:[5]

Not only have the last four years seen a sharp increase in partisanship, with councillors behaving in a more cohesive way and abjuring support for opposition viewpoints in those committee meetings where, traditionally, party differences have generally been put aside, but that this is likely to be driven in part by changing expectations within the party group itself. What we see here is . . . a tightening of party political organisation.

The formal decision to discipline a member for voting against group is largely in the hands of the group and the leadership itself. Most groups have a sliding scale of discipline with only persistent offending punishable by expulsion. Most leaders are reluctant to expel a group member because it can easily be counterproductive. All members have the right of appeal to the party and that can often result in a publicised and conflictual investigation. Liberal Democrats are the most tolerant of wayward voters.

Changing patterns of party control

Following the recent almost unbroken sequence of poor local election results for the Conservatives, the Labour Party is currently, and unprecedentedly, the overwhelmingly dominant party in the country's local government. The Conservatives are becoming increasingly marginalised, controlling in 1995/6 just six of Britain's 127 major spending councils. The cataclysmic nature of the decline of the Conservative Party's fortunes in local government is illustrated by the figures in Table 7.2. In 1985, the year the Widdicombe research was carried out, the Conservatives still controlled more councils on a majority basis in Britain than Labour, even after six years of Conservative rule nationally. It was only in 1986 that Labour overtook the Conservatives in this respect. In 1993, further decline in the party's fortunes at the local level had left them in control of 99 councils (19 per cent of the total), now way behind Labour (32 per cent) but still comfortably in second place. What followed in 1994 and 1995 were two of their worst years in recent comparable history.

The 1994 elections were bad enough. The Conservatives were defending an already woefully weak position resulting from the 1990 'poll tax elections', which they were hoping significantly to improve upon. Instead, they suffered net losses of a further 429 seats and 20 councils, leaving them in control of just 15 of the 198 borough, district and regional councils being contested. With a projected national share of the vote of 27 per cent – their lowest in any

TABLE 7.2   **Pattern of control of local authorities in Great Britain: May 1986, May 1993 and May 1995**

Type of control	1986		1993		1995	
	No.	%	No.	%	No.	%
Conservative	144	28	99	19	21	4
Labour	156	30	165	32	210	41
Liberal Democrat	9	2	28	5	55	11
Independent	79	15	58	11	47	9
No overall control	127	25	164	32	182	35

post-war set of nationwide elections – the Conservatives were at least 13 points adrift of Labour and, possibly even more embarrassingly, fractionally behind the Liberal Democrats. Statistically, then, there can be very little doubt that the Conservatives' 1994 results were the worst in recent comparable history. In the 36 metropolitan boroughs they won a total of just 77 seats, an average of barely two per borough. In over a third of metropolitan boroughs (13) and over one in eight shire districts (33) they failed to win any seats at all. In London's all-out elections, as in the metropolitan boroughs, the Conservatives' worst ever share of the vote (31.3 per cent) lost them seats almost everywhere, the gains being shared between Labour and the Liberal Democrats.

But 1995 was even worse. The Conservative Party lost control of its sole remaining metropolitan district stronghold (Trafford) and a further 57 shire districts to Labour (15) Liberal Democrats (4) or no overall control (38). In addition none of the new unitary authorities in Scotland, Wales or England (Humberside, Cleveland and Avon) were won by the Conservatives, who were left in control of a mere 19 authorities. Given that in councils where there is no overall control, co-operation between Labour and Liberal Democrats is much more common than co-operation between Conservatives and Liberal Democrats, it is apparent that Conservative influence in local government has been well and truly marginalised. There are precious few 'potential model Conservative authorities' left, anywhere in the country.

Labour have benefited significantly over this ten-year period of local Conservative decline, particularly in the metropolitan and urban areas, but increasingly too in rural and suburban areas not usually associated with Labour local government. Even so, 1995 was a particularly good year with Labour gaining control of 37 councils (and losing none) and experiencing a substantial net increase of councillors. However, over this period the Liberal Democrats have also made impressive progress, both in terms of councils won on a majority basis and their influence in councils with no overall control.

The rising profile of the Liberal Democrats

If 1995 was a very good local election year for the Labour Party, 1994 had been equally so for the Liberal Democrats – and 1995 wasn't that bad either! In 1994, the number of councils controlled by the Liberal Democrats increased by nearly 50 per cent (from 28 to 40). In 1995 there was a further net gain of 13 councils taking the Liberal Democrats overall total to 55, well ahead of the Conservatives (21) and for the first time overtaking Independent-controlled councils (46).

But Liberal Democrat influence on local policy is by no means confined to the councils it controls on a majority basis. After the 1995 elections there were 182 councils (35 per cent) in which no one party enjoyed overall control. After Labour-controlled councils no overall control is by far the most common category in British local authorities. This figure represents a steady increase since 1985, when there were 104 (or 20 per cent) of councils with no overall control. But of equal importance to the numerical increase, has been the increasing politicisation of hung (or balanced) councils, reflecting (*inter alia*) the changing patterns of predisposition to inter-party co-operation amongst the three major parties. In 1985, Liberal Democrat/Conservative co-operation in such circumstances, although not as prevalent as Labour/Liberal Democrat co-operation, was by no means uncommon. By 1995, given the growing *rapprochement* between these two parties and the formal statement from the Liberal Democrats of eschewing the policy of 'equidistance', the number and proportion of Liberal Democrat/Conservative pacts or agreements had declined significantly. Thus the influence of the Liberal Democrats extends well beyond the 55 authorities they now control. In the majority of the councils with no overall control they are influential partners (typically with Labour) and in many other cases hold a pivotal position on councils in which there is little formal inter-party co-operation.

The growth of Labour/Liberal Democrat co-operation

The pressure towards inter-party discussion, accommodation and co-operation has developed significantly since the mid-1980s by virtue of the increase in the number of hung authorities. The preparedness of local Labour and Liberal Democrat party groups to co-operate programmatically as well as procedurally and administratively has increased markedly since 1991. Such a process inevitably decreases the influence of the local party especially for Labour Party groups. Whether this is seen as a healthy or unhealthy development in terms of local democracy depends upon one's view of the merits of internal party democracy – for example, the influence of local party or party group – as opposed to the benefits of inter-party compromise and the openness of governmental procedures within the council itself. Both can be seen as legitimate conceptions of local democracy.

The national party dimension is of particular interest here because of the potential impact of inter-party co-operation locally on voter perception of party distinctiveness, or the lack of it. These perceptions may be subsequently translated into voting preferences at a general election. For this reason, and because of the increasing extent to which newsworthy examples of deals or repelled advances in local government are appearing in the national and local press, all three major parties have an understandable concern about what happens in hung authorities.

Hung councils can choose from essentially four forms of administration. Initially most common was the *minority administration*, still to be found in about a third of all hung authorities. One party, usually the largest numerically, is prepared and permitted to take all chairs and vice-chairs and, in this sense at least, to 'govern' as if it were in overall majority. In 1993, following the county council elections which returned hung councils in 26 of the 39 English counties, minority administrations were formed by Labour in Cumbria, Norfolk and Warwickshire, and by the Liberal Democrats in Devon, West Sussex and, until they gained majority control through an October by-election victory, in Dorset.

Between a fifth and a quarter of hung councils have *no administration* or party spokesperson systems, in which chairs are shared or rotated for procedural purposes amongst two or more parties but are stripped of any policy significance. Ten counties adopted this model, which in some instances was accompanied by regular 'behind the scenes' policy discussions between two of the usually three parties involved – for example, between Labour and Liberal Democrats in Cambridgeshire and Wiltshire – but without approaching any formal shared administration.

The commonest form of administration in 1993/4 was *power-sharing*, in which two or more parties agree to share chairs but normally play down or avoid any formalised joint policy programme, and invariably expressly deny that there is a coalition or any form of 'deal'. Among the 1993 hung counties Labour–Liberal Democrat power-sharing agreements were concluded in Essex, Suffolk, East Sussex, Hereford and Worcester and Shropshire. The two examples of chair-sharing between Conservatives and Liberal Democrats were prompted less by any striking similarity of views on policy than, in Cheshire, by the wish to minimise the influence of a large Labour group and, in Surrey, by a small Labour group's concern to retain its ideological distinctiveness.

Ironically, the rarest form of hung council administration is the one that, albeit perhaps misguidedly, tends to receive the most attention in a parliamentary context: the *formal coalition*, where a sharing of chairs is backed by a publicly agreed shared policy platform. The closest approach to a formal coalition among the shire counties is probably in Berkshire or in Lincolnshire, where, in a Council press release, the Labour Leader and Liberal Democrat Deputy Leader announced 'a major package of new policies to be implemented county-wide'.

In reality, there is a grey area between power-sharing and formal coalitions where the two become difficult to distinguish. There is relatively little positive Labour–Liberal Democrat co-operation in Essex, but a good deal in Suffolk, despite the fact that both technically have power-sharing administrations. The main difference between 'power-sharing' and 'coalition' may lie in the use of labels rather than in the extent of co-operation, or commitment to shared programmes.

Attitudes to party groups

There are significant differences in the major parties' organisation of their local government activities, particularly between the more centralist and hierarchically organised Labour Party and the more decentralist Conservative and Liberal Democrat Parties. In some ways, though, these differences are greater in theory or potential than in day-to-day practice. Even in the Labour Party, examples of deep-rooted conflict between a party group on council and the wider party – locally or nationally – are relatively rare, and, certainly compared with the mid-1980s, there are fewer local Labour parties today attempting to push groups in policy directions to which the latter are resistant.

It is important to appreciate that party groups from the three different parties in local government expect different things from their party machinery, reflecting differences in their political ideologies and culture. For example, the Labour Party has the strongest sense of a hierarchy, with local party groups expected to follow national guidelines. Labour is also the only party to give formal policy-making responsibility at the local level to the local party, as opposed to the party group. Conservative and Liberal Democrat groups have much more policy-making autonomy, but can expect, in the case of the Conservatives, to be subject to periodic exercises of 'internal diplomacy' within a wider local and national party network, and in the case of the Liberal Democrats to conform to the ethos of participation and 'resolution through discussion' which has been such an important factor in the party's success at the local level.

The Labour Party

In the case of the Labour Party, there is still validity in Gyford and James's observations that the party's commitment to the principle of state intervention, 'to the idea of equality through legislation and centrally determined standards of public provision' is not easy to reconcile with 'ideas of local autonomy'.[6] A similar tension can be identified in the party's internal organisation which, certainly for local government purposes, is the most formally hierarchical of the three major parties and has an institutionalised separation of the party organisation and its locally elected representatives.

The rationale behind this separation is to promote discussion and debate before any major decision is reached. The party is seen as consisting of many other actors beyond the group in council and they all have a right to an input into local party policy-making. There is a sense of a wider movement to be accommodated and the formal structures reflect this. Formally, the party decides both policy and rules at its Annual Conference and all members are bound by those decisions. But there is also a traditional emphasis on ongoing consultation between local politicians and the local party where local policy is worked out between the two. There is a sense that the politicians must respect the wishes of the wider movement and this can only be done through debate and at times internal conflict. Thus some Labour leaders find they have to spend far more of their time manoeuvring and negotiating at district and county party level than do their Conservative or Liberal Democrat counterparts.

Most party group leaders, while accepting the supremacy of Conference and the NEC, report that they have never had much dealing with it on a policy level and have little to do with the national party. In fact, over local government reorganisation there have been some complaints that the national party has not enforced its policy of unitary authorities on local parties and groups. Despite its potential power within local Labour politics, the national party tends to be viewed in the main as a rule-enforcement agency. The few instances encountered of direct influence from the NEC or any of its sections have been mainly in relation to its rulings in major membership disputes, often involving 'fringe groups'. More typically, perhaps, the national party is used as an appeal of last resort. It interprets the rules, lays down guidelines for model standing orders and for the conduct of local group and party business.

The Conservative Party

The Conservative Party is one which did and still does place a great deal of weight on internal diplomacy in the conduct of its affairs, not least, as Gyford and James point out, because it has no formal constitution to integrate the workings of its parliamentary, local government, or organisational wings.[7] 'It's not our style to write down rules and regulations', as one senior party official explained to us; 'we hold meetings, dozens of meetings'.

The spirit behind Conservative Party structures is neither to direct nor to decide on policy on an open and democratic basis. It is much more informal than that. The party is there to advise, 'air views', be a sounding board, and to build goodwill and consensus. Much emphasis is placed on loyalty rather than debate and conflict. The 'voluntary' party, as the constituency level is often termed, is there to raise funds and get the vote out during election time, not to decide policy or in any formal sense to set agendas, especially at the local level. Any role the party plays in affecting policy is still through 'internal diplomacy', where the idea is quietly to find out what is and what is not acceptable.

Nationally the Conservative Party structures – both the Local Government Department at Central Office and the Local Government Advisory Committee of the National Union – have limited impact on local groups and local Conservative politics. There is a role for them to play, and it is one that would almost certainly expand if the party were to go into opposition nationally, but it is essentially one of advice and support: mechanics and tactics rather than policy direction and discipline. There is, for example, a rough equivalent of the Labour Party's Local Government Rules, but, instead of Labour's twenty almost annually amended pages, it consists of just five typewritten A4 sheets and was apparently last revised in June 1977. The most committed supporters of the national party organisations tend to be local Conservative politicians from areas in which they are in a 'permanent minority', such as Tyne and Wear. It is an arena for them to make contact with the wider party and get their voices heard.

There remains no real role for the national party in local policy-making. Several Conservative leaders told us that if the national party tried to impose a view on their groups, or on them personally, they would ignore it. No actual mechanism exists to impose party policy upon party groups.

The Liberal Democrat Party

The idea of a strong party is anathema to the Liberal Democrats. There is no central organisation with responsibility for local government. The Association of Liberal Democrat Councillors (ALDC) exists as a separate organisation from the Liberal Democrat Party and is affiliated to the party rather than a sub-section of it. Yet local government and participatory democracy occupy very important positions in Liberal Democrat thinking. This is partly because local politics has sustained Liberalism for such a long period and partly because of the Liberal Democrats' continuation of the Liberal emphasis on 'community politics'.

As Gyford and James argue:

[Recent] attempts to define community present a view of a modified form of the traditional liberal individualism, in which society consists not just of a series of independent individuals and a central state, but of individuals grouped together in communities. These buffers between the individual and the state are potentially self-interested and self-protecting. Community politics seeks to mobilise this potential. It therefore involves a specific pluralistic view of society that may not be shared by other political parties.[8]

As a result, the prevailing ethos of interaction between Liberal Democrat party groups and the wider party emphasises qualities such as consultation and participation, backed by a highly effective source of advice – the Association of Liberal Democrat Councillors – used, however, purely at the discretion of the individual local party group.

The national party has little formal influence in the affairs of local party groups. There are no mechanisms for handling complaints about the behaviour of local groups. In the case of the alleged racism on the part of Liberal Democrat councillors in Tower Hamlets, a special 'panel of enquiry' had to be set up. Yet all the leaders interviewed told us that they would not ignore national party policy and wherever possible try to advance it. The party does try to co-ordinate its policy and campaign at national and local levels, with the local groups, to quote one leader, 'putting local flesh and bones on policy which the national party has drawn up'.

The Yorkshire-based ALDC provides a significant national resource for local groups. It regularly sends out to groups ideas on good practice, how to campaign, or on what has worked elsewhere. The ALDC has no mandate as such; groups can ignore it if they so choose. Its influence comes not from any institutional authority but because of the support and advice it provides. Groups look to the ALDC for these services and many have come to rely on it.

In summary, although the Labour Party operates with the highest degree of potential control by the centre in relation to the policies and operations of party groups on local authorities, in reality Labour groups do not appear to be significantly more constrained or hidebound than other party groups in this respect. Sanctions are rarely used (except for explicit breaches of disciplinary rules) and the desire of party groups of all parties to support (or at least, not jeopardise) what the national party is doing is the strongest informal control in this respect.

National parties and local groups

The Labour Party

The balance of influence in the Labour Party between party group and local party has shifted since the mid-1980s towards the party group, for two major reasons: firstly the removal of the power of the local party to deselect sitting councillors (although this power was reinstated in 1993), and secondly, because of the hard lessons learnt from the disqualification and surcharge of councillors from Lambeth and Liverpool in 1987, and the fact that this outcome was only narrowly avoided in a number of other authorities. This experience proved a salutary reminder of the dangers of responding to outside pressure even when applied through legitimate channels.

Of the three major parties, the Labour Party stands alone in making party groups on council accountable in some senses to local party machinery. As Figure 7.1 shows, Labour's main sub-national unit of organisation, as for the other two parties, is the constituency party, whose main task is to select (or re-select) a parliamentary candidate and to maximise the chances of his or her subsequent election. In the Labour Party, however, there is an additional level of party organisation corresponding to the local authority area – county, Scottish region, district or London borough – with a specific remit in relation to local government. This level of organisation is not found in the other two major parties.

Formally the position of the local party is the same in relation to all party groups and is spelt out in the party's regularly revised Local Government Rules. These rules and memoranda of advice are interesting and important in their own right – both for their detailed content and for the carefully chosen phraseology in which they are expressed. Nowadays, it will be noted, the prevailing tone is much more exhortatory than directive:

> . . . *It is proper that* the group . . . should consider and take account of any views which the local party may desire to express. . .
> . . . the success of consultative arrangements depends not so much on standing orders as on a *spirit of co-operation and goodwill* among those concerned.
> *It is also important* for the Group to foster a good relationship with local Labour MPs, MEPs and the wider party. (our emphases)[9]

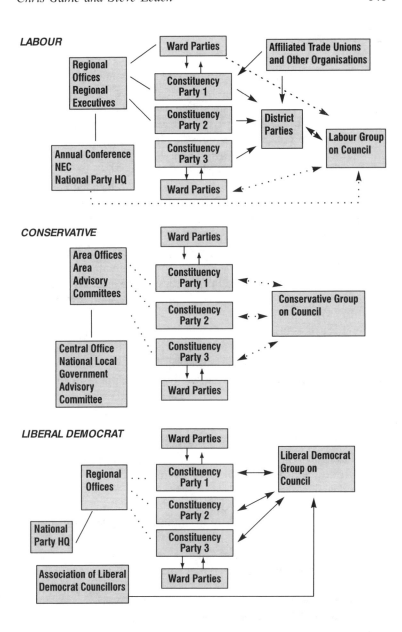

FIGURE 7.1   Local party networks (in a metropolitan district embracing three constituencies)

Inevitably, the nature of the party–group relationship varies considerably in practice. In some areas the local party is powerful. We found no equivalents of the Liverpool situation of the mid-1980s, where the district party dominated the council party group through a network of Militant-influenced councillors and district party members. But we have identified a range of different circumstances in which the local party was almost irrelevant in terms of influence on the party group. The interesting question is: *in what circumstances is the local party likely to be more or less influential?*

One important factor is *frequency of election* in the local authority concerned. Given that the key tasks of the local party are to draw up an election manifesto, select candidates and organise the campaign for local elections, it follows that in authorities where there are elections three years out of four – metropolitan districts and about a third of English shire districts – there is a greater impulse to sustained action than in those authorities where elections are only once every four years – London boroughs, shire counties and about two-thirds of shire districts.

The effect of election timing may obviously be overridden by the existence of a *major controversial issue.* Thus the heyday of activism for many local government committees in London boroughs was the period of the central–local battle against rate-capping in the mid-1980s, when many of the so-called 'new urban left' dominated Co-ordinating Committees in the affected boroughs pushed hard for resistance, and generated some of the strongest pressures on party groups (often themselves divided on the best course of action) that councillors can remember. One of the striking differences between party–group relations in the mid-1990s and in the mid 1980s is the relative dearth today of such manifest dramas.

Local parties can themselves be an important source of ideas and policies. The district parties in Walsall and Rochdale, for example, were not only the originators of the decentralisation policies in those boroughs, but have also played a key role keeping the issue on the agenda over the years. Such policy innovation was again most prevalent in the early and mid-1980s, when the 'new urban left' were seeking an increasingly active role in local parties, yet often finding their vision resisted by a more traditional group of Labour councillors. In such circumstances, if the party group on council was seen as being unimaginative or unrepresentative of the wider party, it could happen that the local party would use its formal responsibility for the local election manifesto as a means of seeking to change the group's policies and priorities. Thus another condition for an active and potentially influential local party is the existence of a *critical mass of activists* who do not feel that their priorities are adequately reflected in the actions of the party group on council.

Again, however, the existence of this condition on its own is no guarantee of success. Much depends on the *balance of forces* within the local party, for its effective sanctions are limited. Local parties can be 'managed' and defused, through the legitimate involvement of sitting councillors. A manifesto produced by the local party can be ignored – albeit with some difficulty – or reinterpreted by a party group which is not committed to it. The power of a local party to deselect a sitting councillor, except for disciplinary reasons, disappeared in 1986, and although it was recently reintroduced, it is still only rarely used – a factor attributable at least in part to a dearth of what the party terms 'candidates of good standard' in many areas.

The most common situation currently lies somewhere between the extreme of an active, hypercritical local party and a docile, almost moribund one, managed by local councillors. The key elements in the most typical form of relationship are as follows:

- A significant overlap of membership between party group and active local party, but a strong sense of the distinctiveness of the two pieces of machinery.
- An acceptance that the local party should take the lead in manifesto preparation, but with input from committee chairs into relevant manifesto 'working groups' to ensure a sense of realism in manifesto proposals.
- A leader who takes the local party seriously, reports back regularly, and who tries to generate local party support for, or at least acceptance of, proposals from the group on council – but who will ultimately resist pressures from the local party if it is out of line with a legitimate interpretation by the party group of its brief.
- Considerable use of informal channels between key actors in the local party and the party leadership, and a recognition that most problems can be resolved in this way rather than by the passing of formal resolutions.

The Conservative Party

Although the traditional autonomy of Conservative party groups from any kind of national party direction has continued into the mid-1990s, what has changed is the traditional collective commitment to an outward show of unity. Although some council groups enthusiastically espouse the national party's programme for local government, increasing numbers of Conservative groups are privately critical of some of the recent measures of their colleagues at Westminster, and are prepared to be publicly critical of the effects of such measures: for example, council tax-capping. This is particularly true of Conservative groups who do not run local administrations.

With the Conservatives having been in power nationally since 1979, there has developed an undeniable tension between the traditional freedom of party groups to pursue local policies and the demands of loyalty to the government, including its policies of cutting back on public spending. It might be argued, then, that when the Conservatives are in power at Westminster, they do not need a mechanism to impose national party policy. Anything the government passes as law is national party policy. Indeed, this is reflected in the briefing notes circulated from Central Office, which are essentially summaries and reminders of government policy in different local government service areas.

Some Conservative party groups have, of course, enthusiastically espoused government policies in relation to ratecapping, the introduction of competitive tendering, and the enabling/purchasing philosophy. Westminster LB, Wandsworth LB, Wansdyke DC in Avon and Rochford DC in Essex all provide examples. But, more recently, increasing numbers of Conservative groups have become critical of what they perceived as the unfairness of the SSA (Standard Spending Assessments)-based revenue support grant distribution and the arbitrariness of community charge and council tax-capping limits. The way in which the move to grant-maintained schools has been encouraged and in some cases the principle itself have been issues of contention for some groups. For others local government reorganisation has proved a divisive and incomprehensible government initiative.

There are occasions when a council leadership will seek the support of its constituency associations in a dispute with a national government of the same political persuasion, and there is thus a 'reverse influence' of group on party rather than party on group.

This is what happened in Warwickshire in 1991 and 1992, when the Conservative-controlled County Council appealed against what it regarded as an unfair RSG (Rate Support Grant) settlement and expenditure limit – although the pressure was most strongly focused on the county's Conservative MPs.

This example illustrates the importance of the informal links between local and national Conservative politicians. Much use is made of networking, telephone chats and lunches. Sometimes it is a case of Conservative leaders talking directly to government ministers: sometimes MPs are used as intermediaries or local spokespersons, although some MPs will resist this role for fear of jeopardising their reputation within the parliamentary group. Conservative national leaders do listen to what is being said and know what the local concerns are, but representation of views mostly takes place outside any formal channels.

The Liberal Democrat Party

There are today *stronger links between national and local Liberal Democrat policies* than there were in the past. This may have much to do with the sense Liberal Democrat councillors have of being part of a coherent and developing network, while 10–15 years ago the picture was more one of isolated local pockets of Liberal power or influence. The continued effectiveness of the Association of Liberal Democrat Councillors (ALDC) has also had a powerful influence on the consistency of local party group policy and the nationalisation of local experience. The influence of local Liberal Democrat policy and politics on the national party is, inevitably, greater than the corresponding influence of locality on centre in the other two parties reflecting the former's lack of experience and realistic expectation of majority power at the national level.

Because much of the Liberal Democrat success nationally has been built up from a strong local base, and because the party cannot in the foreseeable future realistically aspire to being 'the party of government' at national level, the 'locality' emphasis of the party machinery tends to be stronger than in the other parties. Those constituencies in which Liberal Democrat MPs have been returned or have a realistic prospect of success tend – albeit with some notable exceptions – to be in those areas in which the party has achieved control (or a significant level of representation) on the local authority. Success at both levels has been built, amongst other things, on community politics and the Focus Newsletter, both of which require a sizeable and active group of party members. It follows that in authorities where Liberal Democrats hold or share power at the local level there is likely to be active and participative local party membership in which local councillors and candidates play a significant but not necessarily dominant role – comparable to the role of Labour councillors in some district parties. There is often much active discussion of council affairs amongst the wider membership, a situation which is invariably welcomed by councillors.

Membership overlap in local party networks

One reason for the normally broad congruence of view between a council party group and the local party is the considerable membership overlap in local party networks, most of which tend to be dominated by relatively small – and, in the case of Conservatives, declining – numbers of activists. As local party networks constitute the strongest, and often the only, external influence on party group behaviour, it follows that any such influence is confined in many cases to a relatively few key individuals. This in turn raises the question of the extent to which councillors can uphold any claim to be representing or accountable to the wider community beyond their own local party network.

It is at local party level that the greatest potential exists for influence upon the party group on the local council and its decision-making. In all three parties the local party network has a much richer set of channels of communication with the party group on council than does the regional or national machinery, and for that reason alone it is potentially a more powerful and consistent source of influence.

In political science terminology all three parties can be seen not as centralised bodies, but as stratarchies: stratified hierarchies, which acknowledge that a high degree of central control is both difficult and injudicious, that any influence has to be achieved through communication, persuasion, debate and common agreement, and so devolve power or responsibility to local institutional networks.[10] To understand the operation of these political networks, which, despite the different formal status accorded to local Labour parties exhibit many similarities of behaviour, it is useful to explore the concept of 'party network' at the local level in more detail.

Figure 7.1 outlines the *formal* local network of each of the three main parties. As in most voluntary organisations, though, it is the 'position holders' who devote the most time and energy and have the greatest potential for influence. Thus it is the chairs, vice-chairs and secretaries of constituency/district/county parties, together with the leader, office holders and chairs (or spokespersons) of the party group on the council who are likely to form an 'inner network' of influence within the wider political network. Other prominent actors will be the party agent (if one exists), the local MP(s) and/or the local prospective parliamentary candidates.

When one studies the *informal* operation of particularly these inner networks, two significant features become apparent:

1. There is often considerable overlap of membership, particularly in key positions.
2. The informal network of communication, consultation and persuasion is often a more commonly used and effective vehicle of influence than are formal procedures (for example, resolutions from the district party). Even in the Labour Party attempts to use formal procedures or sanctions in furtherance of a policy disagreement tend to be reserved for occasional divisive and controversial issues. In most party networks, for most of the time, they are not invoked in this way.

The phenomenon of multiple channels is more significant for Labour than it is for the two other parties, and particularly in the Conservative Party, where, as we have seen, the role of the constituency is normally very low-key in relation to local authority matters. But in all three parties the overlap of active membership explains whey there is so often a broad congruence of view between a party group and local party: the two groups frequently comprise a similar set of individuals!

More typically, however, membership overlap is a force for consensus, and in particular provides a rich mesh of channels for resolving problems informally. A district party has the right to pass formal resolutions requesting the party group to carry out a particular action. But it is much more likely that the request will be conveyed and responded to informally – if the district party secretary, for example, happens to be a party group member.

If several of the limited number of political careerists have, as it were, overlapping 'careers' on more than one council, on council and in the party, or at more than one level in the party, it will be understood how effectively local political debate and influence can come to be confined to relatively small numbers of individuals. The numbers of party activists and members will vary considerably depending on local circumstances. More typically, however, in a district dominated by a particular party and coterminous with a constituency held by the same party, the number of 'political careerists' on the above definition may well not exceed 40–50, of whom perhaps around 20 might be considered 'key influentials'.

The outcome can be a distinctively limited, exclusive version of 'local democracy', as indeed the Labour Party itself has come explicitly to acknowledge with the introduction of its representative National Policy Forum and joint policy commissions. The party's frank self-analysis set out in its brief policy-making guide is directed primarily at national party institutions but, in our observations, has at least as great a relevance to policy-making at the local level, and not just in the Labour Party:[11]

> There is a general lack of membership involvement in the policy-making process. Members need to know that they can contribute their ideas and views in the process of policy development, that are valued and can make a difference. They need to be a part of the policy-making process, not removed from it.

Conclusion

There is a difficulty in reconciling the two major contrasting trends in local party politics during the past quarter century. Parties used to be in a class of their own as the main agencies of political participation: locally grounded mass membership organisations offering individuals a variety of ways in which to assert their distinctive political identities, interests and commitments. Today's parties reflect the dramatically changed nature of our political system: severely depleted memberships, increasing dependence on limited numbers of ageing activists, and their 'relevance' challenged by ever proliferating numbers of single-issue groups, and also by the growing interest in alternative and innovative forms of democratic participation and debate: consultative referendums, citizen-initiated ballots, citizens' panels and juries, and deliberative opinion polls.

Yet they dominate the operation of our local councils as never before. If there is a 'problem' of the role of political parties in present-day local democracy, that would appear to be it.

Notes and references

1. 'Partisanship' is here defined on a minimalist basis – over 50 per cent of seats held by self-proclaimed members of political parties
2. Young, K. and Davies, M. (1990) *The Politics of Local Government since Widdicombe*, York: Joseph Rowntree Foundation.
3. Labour Party (1995) *Memorandum to Party Groups*, London.
4. Young and Davies (1990) p. 48.
5. Ibid, p. 50.
6. Gyford, J. and James, M. (1982) *National Parties and Local Politics*, London: Allen & Unwin, p. 50.
7. Ibid, p. 37.
8. Ibid, p.72.
9. Labour Party (1995).
10. See Eldersweld, S. (1964) *Political Parties: A Behavioural Analysis*, Chicago: Rand McNally.
11. Labour Party (1993) *Meeting the Challenge of Modern Times*, London.

8 Quangos and Local Governance

Alan Greer and Paul Hoggett

Mapping the terrain

Concern about quangos is not new but has again become a much publicised theme within contemporary debates on the nature of government. Whilst national and regional bodies such as the Housing Corporation and the various funding councils for education have a significant impact on the governance of localities, the focus of this chapter is on those local quangos which have proliferated in recent years and which now deliver a considerable portion of the policies, programmes and services which affect people's everyday lives. Specifically the approach is to survey eleven kinds of non-elected public body (despite the terminological confusion hereafter referred to as quangos) which operate at the local level in the health, education, housing, training and urban development sectors: District Health Authorities (DHAs), Family Health Services Authorities (FHSAs), and NHS hospital trusts; Higher Education Corporations, Further Education Corporations, grant maintained schools, and City Technology Colleges (CTCs); Housing Action Trusts (HATs) and housing associations; Urban Development Corporations (UDCs), and Training and Enterprise Councils (TECs). The central contextual factor is that there are well over 4800 local quangos with a total budget of over £37 billion, that is almost two-thirds of the equivalent allocation of central government money to local government. Equally important, the 'new local magistracy' in England and Wales numbers well in excess of 50 000 compared with under 23 000 elected local councillors.[1]

Taken together the world of non-elected bodies represents a very significant and important pattern of service provision at the local level, although the specific configuration in individual localities varies widely – all will have a DHA but very few a CTC, HAT, or UDC, and others will have a Further Education Corporation, Higher Education Corporation or both. This chapter considers a number of important issues concerning such bodies including their composition and accountability, citizens' views about them, and the patterns of relationship with local authorities.

The governance of local quangos

Public concern with the spread of quangos centres upon the assumption that standards of accountability, integrity, openness and fairness within the public service have been lowered. An initial distinction can be drawn between 'giving an account for actions taken' and 'being held to account for those actions'.[2] Both forms of accountability can refer either to the corporate body or to individuals, but whereas the former depends upon access to information and openness of government, the latter depends upon the existence of sanctions which may be applied if actions taken are incongruent with proper standards. A further distinction may be drawn between political and managerial accountability.[3] The former concerns the accountability of public servants to the people whereas the latter concerns the requirement that agreed tasks are performed according to agreed, largely technical, performance criteria. A final distinction concerns the direction of political accountability which is typically thought of as upwards towards elected bodies such as parliament, but it is equally important to consider accountability downwards to the users of services and the communities from which they come.

Giving an account: openness to the public

The extent of openness and disclosure is variable across and within different types of local quango. Whereas most publish annual reports and accounts there is no general public right to attend meetings, see policy papers, or inspect a register of members' interests. The position is ever-changing, however. The key element in the Department of Health's Code of Accountability launched in April 1994, for example, was that on appointment chairs and members of DHAs, FHSAs and hospital trusts should declare any business interests or other public or voluntary positions held. A review by the government's Public Appointments Unit recommended in January 1995 that there should be easier access to information about appointments ensuring propriety and proper disclosure of interests. Such developments must be seen in the context of concern about the 'sleazy state' and the appointment of the Nolan Committee whose Report made a series of recommendations to ensure probity and openness in public life. The Report concluded *inter alia* that all candidates be required to declare any significant political interests and also consolidated existing examples of good practice into a standard of best practice for openness governing access to information, meetings, and publication of annual reports and accounts.[4]

Appointments and dismissals

Members of the boards of local quangos are either government-appointed or 'self-appointed' by other board members. In practice the sheer numbers of government-appointed positions leads to a situation such as that in the health sector where most members of local NHS bodies are appointed by the Regional Health Authority (RHA) on the basis of advice from other stakeholders such as the chair of the DHA.[5] In this sense many bodies resemble self-reproducing oligarchies which operate alongside government within a tacitly agreed framework which determines the criteria of eligibility for membership. The self-appointed character of some bodies such as grant maintained schools is even clearer, for here a group of appointed 'first governors' have been given a built-in majority on the new bodies and hence the power to subsequently determine their own membership. The use of social networks to recruit to these bodies is not confined to chairs and members, for Chief Executives, Principals and Headteachers also play an important role. In the absence of any formal democratic procedure the use of social networks is inevitable and this is how the majority of housing association committee members and volunteers in social care have been recruited.[6] Margaret Hodge has also spoken of housing association committees as self-perpetuating oligarchies and of 'hunting through my personal phone book to find replacements' after resignations of committee members.[7]

Terms of office vary from three to seven years and provision exists in most instances for the body to remove any ordinary member 'unable or unfit to discharge functions of a member'. The system is largely self-reproducing but the Secretary of State retains powers of last resort in most instances. Thus in the NHS the normal procedure is not to renew contracts and provide no letter of explanation rather than outright dismissal, even in cases of notorious failure such as in

West Midlands Health Authority. One consequence of this recruit-ment process is that business interests tend to dominate, even where they have not been given a majority position by statute. This severely undermines the representativeness of such bodies because they are neither electorally accountable nor do they reflect the class, race, gender, or age profile of the locality. Organisations such as hospital trusts and Higher and Further Education Corporations are companies which have been created by statute and, unregulated by the Companies Acts, constitute virtually a new legal species of corporation[8] For Bastin this implies that a person who has been disqualified from being the director of a registered company can still be a governor of one of these corporations.[9] Moreover several of these bodies are also 'exempted charities' and whilst in theory they are subject to charity law they are not subject to regulation by the Charity Commission.

The system proposed for NHS appointments in April 1995 included measures to achieve the widest range of candidates, to ensure boards reflected population balance both nationally and locally, and an equal opportunities policy. Although the Nolan Report concluded that the ultimate responsibility for appointments should remain with ministers it also made a series of recommenda-tions to improve the system of appointments including that all appointments should be on merit and that boards reflect a range of skills and backgrounds.[10]

Upwards accountability: political and managerial

Weir and Hall identify five main forms of managerial accountability within local quangos, namely performance indicators, the Citizen's Charter, the Ombudsman, public audit and monitoring officers.[11] What is clear from their survey is the weakness of managerial accountability within quangos compared with local government. It could be argued that whereas local government is subject to constant scrutiny and tightly regulated, local quangos have a much freer hand to operate as they wish and are more loosely controlled. However, although there have been some well publicised instances of bad practice within quangos the Public Accounts Committee pointed out that the majority of instances of failure 'far from occurring in quangos or agencies, were found in the "old-style" government departments'.[12] A survey of attitudes of board members of the new NHS bodies found that those with a voluntary sector background had the strictest attitudes towards probity whilst health authority members 'whose previous experience had predominantly been in the NHS had more permissive attitudes' than either voluntary or business-sector incomers.[13]

Perhaps more important, the evidence suggests that the autonomy of local quangos is highly circumscribed and that they 'possess scarcely any independent room for manoeuvre . . . they have specifically been created, or adapted, to act as dependent agencies within parameters of policy and resources set by government'.[14] The transfer of responsibility for a range of functions from local government to local quangos pointed all pathways of political accountability upwards towards Whitehall. The government itself, however, is a direct locus of accountability only in the last resort and increasingly 'steers at a distance'. Virtually all local quangos are dependent upon funding and subject to monitoring by a second tier of arms-length bodies such as Education Funding Councils which have helped to insulate government from an administrative and accountability overload. As Halpin *et al.* argue, this kind of steering 'has the additional advantage for the government of enabling it to avoid responsibility for anything that goes wrong as policies are implemented while taking most of the credit when they succeed'.[15] For Davis and Stewart, 'public accountability, if it exists at all, is through a long and uncertain line . . . to the Minister who appointed them, or who appointed the people who appointed them'.[16]

Personal accountability of members

Members of local quangos may be paid executives or either paid or voluntary non-executive members. The executive member is a recent phenomenon which corresponds to the creation of NHS boards in the image of the private sector company board.[17] Although the chief executive or principal is an ex-officio board member on most other local quangos, only within the NHS has the notion of involving senior managers on the board as executive members been developed. Clearly this potentially causes problems for non-executive members as to some extent they become the only 'outsiders' on the board. As Ferlie *et al.* note, 'one key question may be: will these non-executives act as effective 'whistle blowers' in the event of scandalous behaviour or mismanagement taking place? Or are they too close to the inside?'[18] Unlike local councillors, non-executive members are not subject to surcharge. The question of liability has caused considerable debate within the housing association movement since they have been encouraged to take on private loans for development purposes. As Kearns notes, 'there is uncertainty, until it is tested, as to the limit of individual committee members' liabilities in the event of loan default'.[19]

Accountability downwards

The weakening of the role of the local authority *vis-à-vis* local quangos is well documented but it is less clear whether local quangos have weaker forms of democratic accountability to staff, service users and local communities than elected local authorities. On the issue of formal representation the pattern is again varied. Within the NHS there is no direct representation of users or local communities on the boards. Trust boards must include two 'community members' but like all others these are appointed rather than elected. Despite the rhetoric that non-executive members of NHS boards are close to their community and therefore able to act as guardians of local needs, evidence suggests that one in four Trust members live outside the area they serve. Local input into health care decisions is channelled mainly through the Community Health Councils (CHCs), to which local authorities still have a statutory right of appointment. However, although CHCs can attend meetings of health authorities and can place items on agendas they no longer have the right to speak at meetings, and their remit is even more limited with respect to trusts which individually can decide whether to open their meetings to the public and/or CHCs. In practice individual health authorities and trusts determine their interactions with the local community, including CHC and local authorities. Health authorities are expected to involve CHCs in consultation on their purchasing plans and several authorities have developed new forms of community consultation. Many trusts have also recognised the need to improve relations with local communities and have gone beyond the minimum legal requirements. Some have established community forums, others have regular meetings with CHCs, and others have developed charters guaranteeing CHC rights. However, some trusts do not see a relationship with the CHC as appropriate, arguing that their proper relationship should be with purchasers. Approaches to participation and consultation within the NHS have always been weak and continue to be so. For example Ferlie *et al.* note that 'notions of downward accountability seemed undeveloped in our study, and there were few concrete mechanisms to underpin any such ideas'.[20]

In further and higher education the decline of staff and student representation has coincided with the strengthened position of 'independent' members. Corporations are permitted to nominate up to two staff and one student representative but one survey found that by 1993 10 per cent of all Further Education Colleges had voted to exclude staff members altogether. Graystone also found that all categories of governor other than business interest and principal had been reduced in number.[21] The diminished role of the academic board in further and higher education has heralded a departure from collegial models of decision-taking towards more hierarchical forms.[22] The furore provoked by the actions of governing bodies at Huddersfield, Portsmouth and other new universities led the Public Accounts Committee to investigate the accountability of higher education institutions where generally the dominant model of consultation is the consumerist approach. As part of the Citizens Charter colleges are expected to conduct consumer satisfaction surveys on an annual basis. Many colleges also have community liaison officers but again their primary role seems to be that of marketing the college rather than consulting with local community groups.

In the schools sector the concept of parent power has been construed primarily in terms of the consumerist model of increased parental choice. The 1988 Education Reform Act increased the influence of parent governors and obliged governing bodies to hold an open annual general meeting. However grant-maintained status removes local authority representation from the governing body and invests power in a group of non-elected, self-perpetuating, first governors. Research on grant-maintained schools has noted high levels of governor involvement but no accompanying increase in parental involvement. Some suggest that those schools which have opted-out were already those with high levels of parental involvement,[23] whereas others note that parent awareness of school governors in grant-maintained schools is lower than in local education authority (LEA) equivalents and argue that grant maintained status is 'more of a headteachers' than a parents charter'.[24]

Mechanisms for involving and consulting tenants of housing associations are also relatively undeveloped. Although the Housing Corporation has tried to increase tenant participation, tenants groups within housing associations remain comparatively rare. Kearns, moreover, argues that accountability is still primarily construed by the Housing Corporation in an upwards and managerialist fashion.[25] Charity law has also frustrated attempts to increase tenant representation on housing association management committees because it prohibits those who receive benefits from an organisation from being trustees of that organisation (a sizeable minority of housing associations are registered charities). Formally housing associations are accountable to their shareholding members but Kearns has revealed that the average shareholding membership of English housing associations is just 64 and that in half of all associations the management committee is more than half the size of the membership to whom it is notionally accountable. The extent of accountability is problematic, therefore, because 'housing associations are membership organisations without many members'.[26] The efficiency of the Housing Association in fulfilling its regulatory role has been questioned and there have been calls for the Audit Commission to be given a monitoring role and for the committees of housing associations to be directly elected.

TECs, as the local non-elected body most directly modelled on the basis of the private company, have one of the least developed concepts of downward accountability. According to Peck their 'business-dominated boards and private company status marginalised the local authorities, the trade unions and the voluntary sector and placed a block on local democratic control'.[27] Community involvement typically has been superficial and consultation has often assumed the form of self-publicity. The degree of genuine local consultation and accountability is minimal and often tokenistic. TEC boards' performance is uneven in the extent of their incorporation of non-business interests. Although some, such as the East London TEC, tried to develop good working relationships with local organisations and effective mechanisms of community consultation, these have been the exception rather than the rule. Unfortunately such attempts are restricted by institutional constraints; for example, requests by several TECs to be allowed to have extended boards to reflect strong local partnerships between business and the local authority were rejected by the National Training Task Force (NTTF).[28] Variety of practice is even more noticeable with UDCs partly because of the circumstances in which they were formed. Some, such as the early London Docklands

Development Committee, remained essentially secretive and staffed by business interests but others such as Sheffield worked very closely in partnership with the local authority.

It is not just that these bodies are non-elected but that the systems of managerial accountability which regulate them are weaker than those which operate in local government. Patterns of downwards accountability to service users and their communities are often non-existent but the system of upwards political accountability and control is very strong. The paths of accountability all ultimately lead to Whitehall and the vast majority of these bodies have relatively little autonomy. They are tied to government not just by systems of patronage but by purse strings, and this has led to some disillusion and turnover among members of the new bodies because the hype about bringing change and enterprise to the public sector has proved incongruent with the reality of cash constraint and centralised control.

Relations with local authorities and communities

Citizens' views

Local quangos interact on a daily basis with both elected local authorities and local communities. Much of the available evidence suggests that there is widespread public ignorance of the pattern of service delivery at the local level.[29] An ICM survey in March 1994 found strong support for the elective principle at the local level but that this did not necessarily imply support for elected local authorities. For example, whereas 65 per cent of respondents agreed that local councils should run rented housing, the corresponding figures for schools and hospitals were only 38 and 27 per cent respectively and Dunleavy and Weir have argued that 'this is not the convincing majority needed to push back the frontiers of quangoland'.[30]

The need to develop local democracy, therefore, is not seen simply as the need to defend local government. Citizens clearly hope for a greater variety of locally elected bodies in the future, some single-purpose and some multi-purpose, some involving elected councillors and some not. It is clear, however, that there is virtually no support for the concept of the self-appointed committee which is precisely the basis of Further Education Corporations, housing associations and most other local quangos. People are perhaps more concerned to receive a good quality of service than with who delivers that service but they are also concerned about falling standards and increased charges. People may be inclined to opt for an organisation with more resources at its disposal than a local authority equivalent, even if in principle they are opposed to the idea that the service should be run by a non-elected body.

Marginalisation

Elected local authorities have increasingly been marginalised by the reforms to the system of service delivery and their relationship with local quangos has been fractious in many cases. However, the extension of local democracy may actually involve the redistribution of functions from locally elected councillors to other kinds of groups not constituted through elections. The removal of functions from local authority control does not automatically result in a less democratic form of local governance. Nevertheless, although local government in Britain has never been a paragon of democratic virtue, the dominant perspective on the expansion of quangos is that the process has attenuated local democracy. Resources and functions previously vested in local authorities have increasingly been transferred to unelected, often self-appointing, and unaccountable bodies. Weir and Hall, for example, characterise the recent reforms as involving the 'deliberate curtailment of representative government at the local level and the transfer of functions and services to non-elected EGOs'.[31] Central to this perspective is the assertion that the process has been driven by the ideological totems of new right thinking. So the remedy for bureaucratic, inefficient and unresponsive local authority service provision lies in the extension of managerialism and market forces into service delivery systems. However, in a situation where the issue is 'not whether those who run our public services are elected, but whether they are producer-responsive or consumer-responsive' local government is in danger of being sidelined.[32]

There is no doubt that the formal powers of local authorities have been considerably reduced by the cumulative effect of the reforms in health, education, housing, urban development and training. The pattern of marginalisation, however, is uneven. On the surface it seems that the reduction of local authority influence has been significantly greater where they have been the traditional service providers – in education, housing, and urban development – than in the health service and employment training for which local authorities have never had prime responsibility. It is also possible that, in the short term, health authorities and TECs are able to sustain a sounder view of the value of good relations with local authorities than other local quangos who see themselves as having thrown off the shackles of local authority control.

Formal and informal relationships

Health   In the health sector the fact that local authorities have lost the right to appoint members to DHAs has raised fears that this would make it more difficult to secure collaboration between local councils and health authorities.[33] However, one health authority chair has commented that 'as the health business needs to have a close relationship with the local authority and in particular with social services, so we have a local councillor'.[34] NHS trust boards must include at least two members appointed from the 'local community' and these, as with non-executive members of health authorities, may be local councillors.

Some developments, however, have strengthened the role of local authorities in the health sphere, notably their designation as the lead agency for the provision of community care. The intention that local authorities should assume an enabling role in resource allocation with provision left largely to the private and voluntary sectors, and with budgets devolved as close to the user as possible, is predicated on close co-operation with local health authorities. Local authorities and health authorities also co-operate through the mechanism of Joint Consultative Committees which disburse 'joint finance' to develop new and innovatory day, domiciliary and respite care projects. Moreover a role for local authorities in the purchase of health care has become an issue for debate and some form of joint health and social care commissioning may eventually emerge.[35]

Thus although it might appear that the influence of local authorities in health care has been diminished as a result of the NHS reforms, the situation in reality is much more complex. Some local authorities have developed formal and informal patterns of consultation with health authorities and trusts which go beyond the minimum statutory requirements. It is the quality and intensity of the relationship which is important, not the formal statutory position. Indeed many local authorities may have better developed relations with the reformed health authorities than their predecessors where the formal right of local authorities to appoint members masked the poor attendance record of local councillors.

Education   The important difference between the health and education sectors is that the latter is a traditional sphere of local authority control. The reforms in education have created a system where local authority provision of public education co-exists with that provided by a range of new non-elected institutions such as grant-maintained schools and Further Education Corporations and this has inevitably shaped the relationships between local authorities and local quangos. Elected representatives have no statutory right to membership of most of the non-elected bodies in education. The central consideration in determining the composition of Further and Higher Education Corporations, grant-maintained schools and CTC has been to introduce expertise in business into the management of the education sector and there is no specific provision for local authority representation. Kingshurst CTC, for example, includes representatives from local industry and commerce but none from the local authority – indeed none of the governors live in the school's catchment area.[36] In grant-maintained schools and Further Education Corporations, local councillors will be appointed to governing bodies, and most colleges, for example, have a local authority co-opted representative. In one grant-maintained school in the West Midlands all the outgoing LEA governors were invited to stay on but whilst the Conservative accepted the three opposition councillors withdrew.[37]

Since incorporation, Further Education Corporation ties with local authorities have been significantly reduced although there is still some resource dependency. One of the central determining factors of the relationship is that 'many colleges are now in real competition with the LEA rather than part of the same educational family'.[38] Although the specific evidence is sketchy it does seem difficult to engender co-operation and cordial relations between competitors such as LEAs and grant-maintained schools and Further Education Corporations.

Housing   Local authorities retain a prime responsibility for meeting local housing needs and have historically operated alongside the alternative service providers, principally housing associations. As a result the relationship between local authorities and housing asso-

ciations is better developed and less subject to tension. With
dwindling housing stock as a result of the right-to-buy programme,
and a falling central government budget allocation, local authorities
have looked increasingly to housing associations 'to assist them in
meeting their statutory responsibilities . . . the two sectors have over
a period of time developed a close working relationship'.[39] There is
also close co-operation through Social Housing Agreements between local authorities and housing associations which set out
mutual expectations and 'specify the assistance which each will be
prepared to give the other. In most cases, local authorities will be
able to offer cheap land or other development assistance in return
for the provision by associations of accommodation relevant to the
local authorities' perceived need.'[40] Decisions regarding the distribution of public funds at a local level are also 'now taken within a
coordinated framework, reflecting close cooperation between authorities, the [Housing] Corporation and housing associations in preparing local programmes'.[41] In addition at least 21 local authorities
have transferred their entire housing stock to housing associations
under the Housing Act 1985. Although few HATs have been
established there is provision for some local authority input into
the appointment of members, five of whom are appointed by the
Secretary of State on the nomination of the local authority. However, the local authority nominees are expected to include residents
as well as councillors and once again all members sit as individuals.
Birmingham City Council was proactive in the creation of the Castle
Vale HAT and the Council has two representatives on the board of
twelve, including a minority party councillor.[42]

Urban Development Corporations   UDCs predominantly have been
viewed as a market-oriented attack on local authorities' powers over
urban development. Once again boards of directors are drawn
primarily from the private sector and although councillors may sit
on a board they are not usually seen in terms of a democratic input
into its activities. Much of the evidence for the 'unresponsive to local
needs' thesis is based on the experience of the London Docklands
Development Corporation, whereas the UDC experience as a whole
has been characterised by variety and some provincial UDCs have
been more accommodating to the interests of local communities.[43]
Thus some local authorities such as Bristol objected to the 'imposition' of UDCs and became alienated, while others welcomed them
or reached an accommodation. Later UDCs recognised that 'pro-

gress can be easier with the cooperation of local actors, agencies and the wider range of community interests'.[44] Half of the board of Heartlands and Plymouth UDCs and one-quarter of Black Country are drawn from local authorities; Heartlands has also established a Community Trust to facilitate consultation with the local community.[45] Some UDCs such as Sheffield 'actively forge relations with local authorities, developing new joint committees and committee cycles, and entering into partnership agreements while utilizing shared budgets, strategies which fly in the face of government exhortations concerning the apparent inertia of the local state'.[46] Moreover, the 'local embeddedness of the UDCs, forging links variously with local politicians, community groups, and local civil servants, is both unavoidable and a necessary condition for the successful formation and implementation of UDC policy and strategy'.[47] Birmingham City Council has established very good links with Heartlands UDC and has been able to influence regeneration strategy because of the successful maintenance of a close working relationship. The UDC operates on the basis of consent and the chair of the UDC Planning Board is also chair of the City Council Planning Committee and there is an agency agreement between the UDC and the City Council to manage the planning process. In other words there are close organic ties between the UDC and the local authority.[48]

Training and Enterprise Councils Relations between TECs and local authorities are shaped by the extent of coterminosity of geographical boundaries which can affect patterns of negotiation and co-ordination. Although 93 per cent of TECs in non-metropolitan counties and 76 per cent of those in metropolitan districts outside London have only one local authority to deal with, not one London TEC is coterminous, dealing with, on average, 3.7 local authorities; indeed East London TEC has six local authorities to deal with.[49] TECs are intended to be responsive to local circumstances but their creation has diminished formal local authority representation in the training sector. Only one-third of TEC board members are selected from the public sector and voluntary bodies and in 1992 only 8.6 per cent of all directors represented local authorities; of respondents to an AMA (Association of Metropolitan Authorities) questionnaire, only 17.2 per cent of chief executives had a local authority background.[50] Of 312 non-private directors, only 43 (14 per cent) were drawn from local education authorities.[51]

Private employers not local authorities have sole responsibility for the delivery of training programmes but nevertheless strong local partnerships were envisaged to help achieve overall coherence.[52] Evans, however, sees the creation of TECs as an integral part of the new right's assault on the local state and argues that this effectively removed 'any remaining strategic responsibilities which the LEAs had to promote vocational education and training in their areas'.[53] For Peck, on the other hand, some individual TECs at local level realised that some accommodation to local, non-business interests was necessary.[54] Thomas also concludes that relationships between TECs and local authorities were generally satisfactory. All TECs in the AMA survey had representatives of local authorities on their boards and sub-groups, usually officers rather than councillors, and several local authorities had seconded staff to their TEC. Local authorities have also developed a variety of formal and informal mechanisms for consultation and reporting, such as liaison commit-tees. Of the AMA respondents 61.9 per cent had regular meetings with TECs. On the other hand the survey also found that 14 councils had no established procedure for handling TEC issues and some local authorities were critical of the limited and cursory nature of consultation.[55] TECs were often regarded as unresponsive to local needs: for example, several authorities felt that TECs had failed adequately to provide for the needs of disadvantaged groups.[56]

Although some TECs such as Birmingham and Sheffield have developed partnership arrangements with their local authorities, many local authorities see TECs as potential competitors in the field of local economic regeneration and development.[57] This is clearly one area where local authorities must overcome their distrust of TECs and play a strategic co-ordinating role. If they do not, then they may find that TECs have stepped into the breach – indeed Leicestershire TEC has already 'taken the lead in preparing a strategy that is based on a business rather than a public sector perception of the area's economic needs'.[58] Local authorities will increasingly need to work in co-operation with TECs and other development agencies in competing for government funding. Mur-ray Stewart has identified the emergence of a new 'era of collective partnership' between levels of government and between the public and private sector.[59] A new 'corporatist localism' seeks to involve a variety of local interests in the development of local vision, priorities and bids for resources. Moreover, with the creation of the Single Regeneration Budget the Department of the Environment wanted to 'stimulate proposals from a wide range of local players from the business, voluntary, education and other sectors working in partnership . . . these partnerships are likely to be formed by the local authorities and TECs working in unison to bring together the relevant parties'.[60]

Variety and complexity

The overall pattern of relations between local authorities and local quangos is one of variety and complexity. In practice, relationships between each species of quango and local authorities can fall anywhere on a continuum between co-existence and conflict, depending on the specific configuration of political, social, economic, historical and geographic conditions. In the composition of boards there has been a clear trend away from functional representation towards individual membership. However, the formal position in terms of statutory rights obscures the reality on the ground. Local councillors are not precluded from serving on boards in an individual capacity and obviously many of them do. Although individual councillors cannot be said to be representative of local authorities, informal contacts are likely to result in local authorities being better informed of the activities of the local quangos than would otherwise be the case. Local authority influence can therefore be exercised through informal networks and channels of communication. Indeed it may well be through such channels that more effective influence is exercised, not through a statutory right to appoint representatives to boards.

Conclusion: supplicants, advocates, partners or conductors?

The days of what Clarke and Stewart call the 'unitary authority' are over.[61] The automatic assumption that if something needed doing then the local authority should do it has been subjected to increasing challenge. Today the local authority is faced with a mass of different agencies through which it must work to achieve its own purposes. Relations between local authorities and specific local quangos will vary from one service area to another, but what of the authority's corporate response towards the field of agencies as a whole? One of the dilemmas facing local authorities at this corporate level concerns the balance to be struck between being an advocate of the community on the one hand and forming partnerships with non-elected bodies on the other. The local authority has a legitimate right to be critical of the actions of quangos, to remind the electorate of the local democratic deficit and to throw light upon some of the political and commercial networks through which appointees to such bodies are recruited. Some local authorities such as Kirklees, Watford, Bristol and Nottingham have set up registers of local quangos or have conducted local scrutinies of their membership and activities. Yet at the same time the local authority has to work with many of these bodies in delivering joint programmes, working up bids to central government and elaborating a coherent, strategic vision for the locality. This is a difficult balance to maintain, yet it must be maintained if the local authority is to retain its political role whilst 'getting on with the business'.

Local quangos do not form a homogenous mass. Variety does exist in terms of legal status, composition of governing bodies, mechanisms of accountability, and relationships to local users, disadvantaged groups and local authorities. The point is that a local quango cannot function in isolation. It needs the knowledge and contacts of local community organisations, council officers and politicians to enact its plans. Local authorities can exploit this dependence in an attempt to bring together the fragmented system of service and programme delivery in its area. Faced with a mass of agencies through which it must work some have suggested that in the future the key role for the local authority is to manage this network.[62] There is much to be said for this approach; indeed the business world itself typically operates through networks rather than contracts or hierarchical control. But the problem is that in any given local area the networks which oil the process of recruitment on to the local TEC, Further Education College or housing association are usually highly opaque. The injection of business interests and systems of political patronage into the non-elected public sphere presents a barrier to the typical local authority's capacity to network with them; moreover the relationship between the two tends to mutual distrust. The majority of these bodies also have relatively little autonomy having been specifically set up to deliver the programmes and policies of central, not local, government. Ideally, the local authority of the future may become a conductor orchestrating a mass of performers in a common endeavour, but in today's world the danger lies in believing oneself to be the conductor when in reality one is simply a minor player.

Notes and references

1. Weir, S. and Hall, W. (1994) *Ego Trip: Extra-Governmental Organisations in the UK and their Accountability*, Democratic Audit, University of Essex & Charter 88 Trust, pp. 8–10.
2. Stewart, J. (1992) *Accountability to the Public*, European Policy Forum.
3. Day, P. and Klein, R. (1987) *Accountabilities*, London: Tavistock Publications.
4. *First Report of the Committee on Standards in Public Life, volume 1*, Cm 2850 I, London: HMSO, 1995, ch. 4.
5. Ashburner, L. and Cairncross, L. (1993) 'Membership of the "New Style" Health Authorities: Continuity or Change?', *Public Administration*, vol. 71, pp. 357–75.
6. See Humble, S. (1982) *Voluntary Action in the 1980's*, Berkhamstead: The Volunteer Centre; Kearns A (1991) *Active Citizenship and Accountability: The case of the British Housing Association Movement*, University of Glasgow: Housing Associations Research Unit: Discussion Paper 2.
7. *The Guardian*, 26 October 1994.
8. See Long, R. and Salter, B. (1994) 'Confusion and Control', *Health Service Journal*, 5 May 1994.
9. Bastin, N. (1990),'The Composition of Governing Bodies of Higher Education Corporations', *Higher Education Quarterly*, vol. 44, no. 3.
10. *First Report of the Committee on Standards in Public Life, volume 1*, Cm 2850 I, London: HMSO, 1995, ch. 4.
11. Weir and Hall, *Ego Trip*, pp. 22–7.
12. 'The Conduct of Proper Business', (1994) *Public Money and Management*, vol. 14, no. 2, pp. 4–6.
13. West, M. and Sheaff, R. (1994) 'Back to Basics', *Health Service Journal*, 24 February.
14. Weir and Hall, *Ego Trip*, p. 15.
15. Halpin, D., Power, S. and Fitz, J. (1993) 'Opting into State Control? Headteachers and the Paradoxes of Grant-Maintained Status', *International Studies in the Sociology of Education*, vol. 3, no. 1, p. 14.
16. Davis, H. and Stewart, J. (1994) *The Growth of Government by Appointment: Implications for Local Democracy*, Luton: Local Government Management Board, p. 8.
17. Ashburner and Cairncross 'Membership of the 'New Style', Health Authorities', p. 359.
18. Ferlie, E., Ashburner, L. and Fitzgerald, L. (1993) 'Board Teams – Roles and Relationships', *Research in Action Paper 10*, Bristol: NHS Training Directorate.
19. Kearns *Active Citizenship and Accountability*, p. 31.
20. Ferlie, E., Ashburner, L. and Fitzgerald, L. (1995) 'Corporate Governance and the Public Sector: Some Issues and Evidence from the NHS', *Public Administration*, vol. 73, p. 390.

21. Graystone, J. (1992) 'Relations with Governors, Academic Boards and the LEA', in Turner, C. (ed.) *Guide to College Management*, London: Longman.
22. Robertson, D. (1993) 'Establishing Strategic Direction in Higher Education Institutions', *Public Money and Management*, vol. 13, no. 3, pp. 45–51.
23. Bush, T., Coleman, M. and Glover, D. (1993) *Managing Autonomous Schools*, London: Paul Chapman, p. 173; Bush, T., Coleman, M. and Glover, D. (1993) 'Researching Autonomous Schools: A Survey of the First 100 GM Schools', *Educational Research*, vol. 35, no. 2, p. 121.
24. Power, S., Halpin, D. and Fitz, J. (1994) 'Underpinning Choice and Diversity? The Grant Maintained Schools Policy in Context', in Tomlinson, S. (ed.) *Alternative Education Policies*, London: IPPR/ Rivers Oram Press.
25. Kearns, A. *Active Citizenship and Accountability*, p. 48.
26. Kearns, A. (1994) *Going by the Board: The Unknown Facts About Housing Association Membership and Management Committees in England*, Centre for Housing Research and Urban Studies, Occasional Paper no. 10, University of Glasgow.
27. Peck, J. (1993) 'The Trouble with TECs . . . a Critique of the Training and Enterprise Councils Initiative', *Policy and Politics*, vol. 21, no. 4, p. 289.
28. Peck, 'The Trouble with TECs. . .', p. 294.
29. See Widdicombe Committee (1986) *Research Volume 3 – The Local Government Elector*, Cmnd 9800, London: HMSO, p. 30.
30. *Local Government Chronicle*, 29 April 1994, p. 12.
31. Weir and Hall, *Ego Trip*, p. 15.
32. W. Waldegrave as quoted by Stoker in Chapter 9.
33. House of Commons Social Services Committee (1988–89) *Resourcing the National Health Service: The Government's Plans for the Future of the NHS*, HC214-III, London: HMSO, p. 52.
34. Painter, C., Isaac-Henry K and Chalcroft T. (1994) *Appointed Agencies and Public Accountability: Proactive Strategies for Local Government*, Report on behalf of the West Midlands Joint Committee of District Councils and the Institute of Public Policy and Management, University of Central England Business School, p. 11.
35. AMA (1994) *The Future Role of Local Authorities in the Provision of Health Services*, London: Association of Metropolitan Authorities.
36. Painter *et al. Appointed Agencies and Public Accountability*, p. 17.
37. Painter *et al. Appointed Agencies and Public Accountability*, p. 35.
38. Blackmore, R. (1994) 'Chill Winds After April', *College Management Today*, May.
39. House of Commons Environment Committee (1992–93) *The Housing Corporation*, HC 466-I/II, London: HMSO, p. xviii.
40. House of Commons Environment Committee, *The Housing Corporation*, p. xix.
41. Department of the Environment (1994) *Annual Report 1994*, Cm 2507, London: HMSO, p. 89.
42. Painter *et al. Appointed Agencies and Public Accountability*, p. 16.

43. See Imrie, R. and Thomas, T. (eds) (1990) *British Urban Policy and the Urban Development Corporations*; Lawless P. (1990) *Economic and Physical Restructuring of the City: The Case of the English Urban Development Corporation*, Centre for Regional Economic and Social Research, Working Paper no. 9, Sheffield City Polytechnic.

44. Imrie and Thomas, 'Urban Policy and the Urban Development Corporations', p. 18.

45. Painter *et al. Appointed Agencies and Public Accountability*, pp. 15–16 and 28.

46. Imrie and Thomas, 'Urban Policy and the Urban Development Corporations', p. 5.

47. Imrie and Thomas, 'Urban Policy and the Urban Development Corporations', p. 5.

48. Painter *et al. Appointed Agencies and Public Accountability*, p. 26.

49. Bennett, R.J., Wicks, P.J. and McCoshan, A (1994) *Local Empowerment and Business Services: Britain's Experiment with Training and Enterprise Councils*, London: UCL Press, pp. 76–80.

50. Thomas, I. (1994) 'The Relationship between Local Authorities and TECs in Metropolitan Areas', *Local Government Studies*, vol. 20, no. 2, pp. 264–7.

51. *HC Deb*, 26 July 1993, c679–80.

52. Department of Employment, (1988) *Employment for the 1990s*, Cm 540, London: HMSO, p. 41.

53. Evans, B. (1992) *The Politics of the Training Market: From Manpower Services Commission to Training and Enterprise Councils*, London: Routledge, p. 121.

54. Peck, 'The Trouble with TECs. . .', p. 291.

55. Thomas, 'The Relationship between Local Authorities and TECs. . .', p. 271.

56. See Thomas, 'The Relationship between Local Authorities and TECs. . .'.

57. Thomas, 'The Relationship between Local Authorities and TECs. . .', pp. 283–5.

58. Thomas, 'The Relationship between Local Authorities and TECs. . .', p. 293.

59. Stewart, M. (1994) 'Between Whitehall and Townhall: The Realignment of Urban Regeneration Policy in England', *Policy and Politics*, vol. 22, no. 4, p. 134.

60. Department of the Environment as quoted in Stewart 'Between Whitehall and Townhall', pp. 143–4.

61. Clarke, M. and Stewart, J. (1994) 'The Local Authority and the New Community Governance', *Regional Studies*, vol. 28, no. 2, pp. 201–7.

62. Clarke and Stewart, 'The Local Authority and the new Community Governance', pp. 205–6; Stewart, M. and Taylor, M. (1993) *Local Government Community Leadership: The Strategic Role of the Local Authority*, Luton, Local Government Management Board.

9 Reforming the New Magistracy

John Stewart

Introduction

The range of public appointed bodies operating at local level has been documented in a number of studies.[1] Public organisations with appointed boards are distinguished from local authorities in two significant ways. Firstly, they are specific function authorities as opposed to the multi-functional local authorities. Secondly, they have appointed boards (or have a majority who are appointed) as opposed to the elected local authorities.

Appointed boards are not, however, a homogeneous group. The extent of that difference is in part dependent on the range of bodies included and there is considerable disagreement about which public organisations should be included as appointed bodies. In discussions of this issue, government spokespersons tend to focus on the number of non-departmental public bodies as recorded in the annual publication, *Public Bodies*.[2] 'Non-departmental public bodies' was the term coined by Sir Leo Pliatsky as an alternative to the popular and still widely used 'quango'.[3] In its application the majority of appointed bodies at local level are excluded: some, like health authorities, because they are departmental public bodies; some, like many of the educational bodies, because they operate at local level; and some because they are private companies like Training and Enterprise Councils, or because they are voluntary bodies like Housing Associations. It is arguable whether some of the latter bodies should be included as public bodies, but the use of the over-narrow definition of non-departmental public bodies would effectively exclude consideration of most of the appointed bodies operating at local level. This chapter, therefore, will ignore the definition of non-departmental bodies and will concentrate on a range of appointed boards which are constituted at local level to exercise public functions.

Consequently, this chapter discusses the issues and concerns raised by Greer and Hoggett in the previous chapter (Chapter 8), and builds upon this to suggest ways in which local quangos could be made more accountable. It raises the issue of the public accountability of these bodies and whether that issue should be resolved through local democratic control. It shows that the bodies concerned differ in role and structure and argues that the issue of local democratic control has to be decided on a case-by-case basis. Both the issue of local democratic control and whether that should be achieved through an extension of the responsibility of local authorities are necessarily matters of judgement, but those judgements can be guided, and criteria by which judgement could be guided are put forward in this chapter. Depending on those judgements the relationship between local authorities and the present responsibilities of appointed bodies can take different forms varying from direct or indirect control to powers and rights to enhance influence. The alternatives are outlined. Where direct control is decided upon a series of issues to be faced are discussed. Even where it is judged that local democratic control is inappropriate there remains a case for reforms to enhance public scrutiny, and some of the possibilities are discussed.

The issue of public accountability

The existence of appointed bodies at local level raises issues of public accountability. The concern is that those who exercise public power or spend public money should be answerable to those on whose behalf they exercise it. Attempts have been made to suggest that this is not necessarily an issue. William Waldegrave has argued that accountability to the individual customer can meet the requirements of public accountability.[4] It is difficult, however, to see how accountability to the individual customer can meet the requirements of accountability for policy, particularly where it involves, as it often will and has to, the denial of a service in the form required by the individual. In public services there can and should be responsiveness to the customer, but within the limits set by public policy and the allocation of public resources. Accountability to the individual customer cannot replace the need for collective accountability for that policy and that use of resources.

Ken Young has argued that accountability can be met by a sense of social responsibility (or responsibility for one another) in those appointed; a notion of stewardship.[5] But there are grave dangers in actions taken with a sense of social responsibility dependent upon individuals' own judgement alone. Stewardship requires that those who exercise power should account for their actions and be held to account. Councillors probably differ very little from appointees in their sense of social responsibility. Where they differ, however, is that they can be held to account for what they do in the name of that social responsibility, by those on whose behalf they act.

It will of course be argued, as it was by Waldegrave, that the framework of public accountability remains based on democratic control exercised by Parliament.[6] Indeed, he goes as far as to argue that the traditional framework of public accountability remains unchanged. Issues arise about the adequacy of that democratic control and hence of that framework of public accountability. One specific issue relates to the lack of public procedures for appointment or scrutiny of appointments and of public registers of appointments. Another issue relates to the inadequate 'auxiliary procedures for accountability'[7] governing these bodies when compared with local authorities – for example the limited access of the public to information or to meetings, or the absence of provision for surcharge. These are, however, not fundamental objections, since they can be reformed while leaving the basic structure of accountability unchanged. There must, however, be grave doubts about the limited capacity of the already strained doctrine of ministerial responsibility to bear the burden of accountability for the actions of the wide range of appointed bodies operating at local level.

The critical issue is, however, whether in any event public accountability at national level is appropriate for appointed bodies at local level. It is not merely that accountability for public services has in the past been spread between national and local level, reducing the burden on ministerial responsibility. It is rather whether, if the appointed bodies are making decisions on behalf of local people, they should be accountable to local people for those decisions through appropriate forms of democratic control. In exploring this issue it has to be recognised that appointed bodies operating at local level differ in many ways and that the approach adopted to ensure local democratic control could vary from body to body.

Distinction and difference in the complex of appointed bodies

Clearly, appointed bodies differ in their functions. The main bodies operating at local level are concerned with health, with education, with training and economic development and with urban regeneration. Depending on their function their role and relationship to local communities can vary. Functional differences apart, there are distinctions between whether the body is itself responsible for delivering a service or for planning, controlling or in other ways securing the delivery of the service. This corresponds to a degree with the distinction between purchaser and provider. Thus the district health authority is a purchaser while health service trusts are providers. The Training and Enterprise Council is a provider in so far as it acts as a contractor to central government, but is also a purchaser in so far as it contracts out work to other organisations. There is a difference in role between those bodies which are responsible for a function covering a geographical area, such as the Training and Enterprise Council or the District Health Authority, and those which are responsible for a separate institution such as a grant-maintained school, a Further Education College and certain health service trusts. This can affect the nature of appointment with, in the latter case, people associated with the particular institution being appointed – in the case of grant-maintained schools, some members of the boards of governors will be elected by parents.

The relationship of appointed bodies to central government can also vary substantially. In the health authorities there is what can be described as a hierarchical relationship through the Health Service Management Executive to the Department for Health. By contrast, Training and Enterprise Councils (TECs) have a contractual relationship with the Department for Education and Employment. Grant-maintained schools and Colleges of Further Education receive their finances from National Funding Agencies and are subject to controls by the Department for Education and Employment, but cannot be described as being in either a hierarchical or a contractual relationship with central government. Related to these differences of relationship is the extent of discretion available at local level, which depends on both the relationship with central government and the legislation governing the appointed body. The status of these bodies varies considerably – in itself a cause of the difficulties of definition. A distinction can be drawn between public bodies – although in a variety of forms – and bodies constituted as private companies such as the Training and Enterprise Councils or as voluntary bodies such as housing associations.

The appointed bodies differ in the extent to which they are subject to what Weir and Hall describe as 'auxiliary provisions' designed to ensure accountability.[8] This phrase covers many of the provisions which apply to local authorities. Some do not apply to these bodies at all, such as surcharge or the requirement to appoint monitoring officers, although the requirement to appoint accounting officers in certain bodies may be held to be equivalent. These bodies also differ in whether they are subject to the jurisdiction of ombudsmen, whether they come within the remit of either the National Audit Office or the Audit Commission and in the provisions governing access of the public to meetings and to information. Thus, while district health authorities are required to hold their main meetings in public, health service trusts are only required to hold one meeting in public each year, while urban development corporations can and mostly do hold all their meetings in private.

Finally, appointed bodies differ in the method of appointment. Broadly there are four groups: where appointments are made by a Government minister (for example, Urban Development Corporations); where appointments are made by an intermediate body such as the regional health authority (for example, certain members of the district health authorities); where the bodies themselves make the appointment (for example, TECs, Colleges of Further Education); or where local authorities make the appointment (for example, Joint Boards in metropolitan areas or local authority companies). Many of the bodies combine different methods of appointment. District Health Authorities for example have their chairs appointed by the Secretary of State and their non-executive members appointed by the Regional Health Authority, who in turn appoint the executive members. This analysis highlights a series of differences between these bodies. They can be divided between differences in role and differences in structure. Differences in role include the function of the organisation, whether it has a service specifier or purchaser role, and whether it has responsibility for an institution or an area. Differences in structure include the status of the organisation, its relationship to central government, its degree of discretion, the rules governing its accountability and the method of appointment employed. The issue raised is whether the structure of the organisation ensures adequate public accountability in relation to its role. In particular it is an issue of whether the role requires a structure which ensures local democratic control, and if so what form that should take.

Criteria for judgement on local democratic control

The extent to which local democratic control is required to ensure public accountability and the form it should take, will necessarily vary between organisations. Because of the differences highlighted, there will be a need for a government committed to reform to undertake a case-by-case analysis. The role of this section is to suggest criteria that should guide that analysis. It is not possible or desirable to produce criteria that will automatically determine whether local democratic control is required: that is necessarily a matter of judgement. The purpose of the criteria developed here is to set out the issues to be considered in making that judgement.

The criterion of local choice

The main criterion should be the extent of the responsibility for determining local policy. Where an appointed body has, and should have, a significant responsibility for determining local policy (or put another way, the significance of local choice) – albeit within a framework of national policy – then it should be subject to some form of local democratic control. The case becomes stronger where those choices involve values rather than technical considerations although it is necessary to recognise that in many issues values and technical considerations are intertwined. The application of the criterion necessarily involves judgement of the significance of local choice.

The significance of local choice is not reduced by the existence of a national framework within which local bodies act. Local authorities themselves operate within a national framework of legislation and regulation for which ministers are accountable to Parliament, while local authorities are accountable to the electorate for their decisions within that framework. Where an appointed body is merely administrating national policy, it would be inappropriate for it to be accountable at local level – although it is not clear why a layer of appointees is required in such circumstances.

Applying the criterion of local choice is a matter of judgement. Judgement can be assisted by such questions as: Does the body have, or should it have, a resource allocation function between different priorities? Does the body have, or should it have, responsibility for setting local policy within a national framework? Thus, on these issues the district health authority would clearly be regarded as having a significant local choice. The Audit Commission has written about the commissioning role of the district health authority (DHA) which is its central responsibility:

> The ultimate aim of commissioning is to improve the health of the population while increasing users' satisfaction with health services. Put fashionably, it is to achieve 'health gain'. Such a broad aim encompasses many specific outcomes, both for individuals and populations. Examples are: increased life expectancy for 70-year-old's, reduction in avoidable deaths in those aged under 60, or improvement in the quality of life to sufferers from chronic diseases such as rheumatoid arthritis. Such objectives are unlikely to conflict with each other directly, but they will always be in competition for limited resources. It is therefore desirable that each DHA debate and clarify its underlying values so that its purchasing plans . . . reflect agreed strategic priorities. This process will be contentious and difficult, and it is doubtful whether the NHS is professionally, managerially or politically ready for it. But in the long run such clarity will be essential if real headway is to be made with the broad aims.[9]

The emphasis is on the DHA debating and clarifying values rather than on technical issues. As an institution constituted for local choice, the criterion would suggest the need for local democratic control of the DHA.

Criteria for separateness

It is assumed that local democratic control should be achieved through direct election. This can be through giving responsibility to a representative body by direct elections or by making the functions the responsibility of the local authority. The argument for direct elections is that it would focus attention on the body concerned and on its responsibility, allowing the local electorate a choice clearly related to that body. The argument against would be that it might be impossible to arouse interest in a separate election if held on a different day from local elections, or to distinguish it, if held on the same day. In addition it would maintain, or even enhance, the fragmentation of local governance.

The criteria that should govern the choice on the form of democratic control are therefore:

- the extent to which direct elections would open up possibilities for participation for different interests and groups
- whether a separate election is likely to arouse sufficient interest – the criterion of electoral viability, recognising that turnout is a problem
- the extent to which the responsibilities involved are related to other community services, and in particular to those of local authorities – the criterion of inter-relationships.

Thus, while the responsibilities of district health authorities could be judged to be more than sufficient to justify a separate election, the inter-relationship between health services and other community services has also to be taken into account. It is not merely the problematic relationship with social services that is involved but the potential of a closer relationship between health and other community services, both in the promotion of good health and in the regeneration of urban communities, if they were the responsibility of a single representative body.

One alternative to direct election is indirect election in which the local authority appoints some of its members to another body such as a joint board, which is in its own way a method of appointment and should perhaps be considered as such. As a method of appointment it has its own problems of accountability since there is evidence based on research in metropolitan counties that in many instances 'joint board members are not held accountable by districts, nor it would appear by anyone else'.[10] The need to consider indirect election does, however, arise where the area over which local choice is considered appropriate does not correspond to that of any existing local authority and where a separate election is not considered viable or justified. The most important examples of indirect election are the joint boards created as a result of the abolition of the metropolitan authorities and the Greater London Council. Where such joint boards are created the means by which they are held accountable by local authorities should be kept under review.

The appropriate constituency

Separate issues arise about appointed bodies responsible for institutions, such as hospital trusts, grant-maintained schools or colleges of further education – the so-called self-governing institutions. If democratic control at local level is sought then this can be achieved either by direct elections to the institution or by responsibility to the local authority. Direct democratic control can be achieved for grant-maintained schools by, for example, an extension of parental elections to constitute the Board of Governors. It may be more difficult to identify a separate constituency in the case of Colleges of Further Education or hospitals and indeed community health trusts. The issue for self-governing institutions is who is the 'self'. Is it staff, parents, patients, pupils, or the community at large? It may be necessary to consider multiple constituencies. A key criterion that has to be considered, therefore, is whether there is an identifiable constituency as a basis for elections.

Division of responsibility

There can be other instances where it may be argued that the appropriate constituency is not the electorate at large but is, for example, local commerce and industry in the case of TECs. If that is a valid case it suggests that TECs should be appointed in a way that is more representative of that constituency, either through building up membership arrangements or through linking with the Chamber of Commerce. The issue as to the appropriate constituency turns on whether the work of TECs is of wider interest than that of those of commerce and industry. Thus, the criterion of the public interest is the extent to which interests are at stake beyond those immediately concerned. The public interest could be argued to be at stake in public expenditure and in the nature of the local economy. Whether that criterion is best realised through national or local control depends upon the criterion of local choice.

In considering the alternative of making self-governing institutions the responsibility of the local authority, a distinction can be drawn between issues which are of wider community concern and those which are of concern only to the institution. This distinction is relevant both to grant-maintained schools and bodies for which it may be impossible to identify an appropriate constituency. Institutions have a responsibility to those who use their services, which can be recognised in the constitution of their governing bodies, if that is practicable. They can have a wider responsibility to the local community which extends beyond their immediate users. This responsibility can involve the planning of provision, assurance of quality and specification of the role of the institution. The issue raised is whether a self-governing institution can or should stand alone, or whether there are issues which concern the wider community and, if so, at what level those issues should be dealt with. One example of such an issue is the planning of the provision of schools, which is an issue that cannot be resolved by a particular institution, but which could be argued to be an appropriate matter for local choice. At present the planning of education provision is shared between the Funding Agency and the local authority, where the percentage opted out is between 10 per cent and 70 per cent. Hence, the criteria to be applied should be are there issues which cannot or should not be resolved within a self-governing institution – that is, the criterion of the public interest – and are these issues which can and should be resolved at local level – that is the criterion of local choice again.

These considerations suggest the possibility of a relationship between local authorities and self-governing institutions in which the local authority has the responsibility for setting the framework within which the self-governing institution acts. This could be achieved for example by exercising the commissioning responsibilities of the district health authority in the field of health and by giving the local authority certain defined responsibilities over grant-maintained schools.

We have proposed five criteria to determine both whether local democratic control is required and by what means it should be achieved. The key criteria in determining local democratic control are the criterion of local choice and the criterion of the public interest. The key criteria in determining the means are the criterion of electoral viability, the criterion of the appropriate constituency, and the criterion of inter-relationships. As already emphasised, these criteria are not such that they can be applied automatically. Judgement is required – thus the public interest can be sought but it can rarely be finally resolved. The criteria are guidelines as to whether judgement is required. They are designed to structure debate and discussion – not to predetermine it.

In applying these criteria, it may well be that they are judged to lead to different conclusions in respect of functions currently exercised by a particular type of appointed body. It is not the case, however, that all the functions should be treated in the same way. Thus it has been suggested by the Association of Metropolitan Authorities in their discussion document on health that national accountability might be appropriate for 25–50 regional specialist centres of excellence, while developing the case for a local authority to assume the commissioning role of the district health authority.[11]

Two other issues arise. The first is if democratic control is to be achieved through the local authority, where that responsibility should lie in the two-tier system. It will depend on the application of the same criteria and in particular the criteria of local choice, or in this case the appropriate level of local choice (with an initial presumption that it will relate to the current level of operation), and of the inter-relationship with the present functions of the tiers. On these criteria one would, for example, expect the functions of the district health authority to be allocated to the county level in a two-tier system – although the district council might have a role in appointing members of health service trusts. Similar issues would arise if there were a regional tier of government. Although that remains a hypothetical question, the same criteria would be applied. It would be important to safeguard against the danger that in the search for regional functions, responsibilities currently exercised appropriately at local level were unnecessarily drawn up to regional level, in order to justify a regional tier of government.

The second issue is the need for specialist expertise. It is argued that where such expertise is required on the board of a body, appointments are required, since the electoral process cannot be relied upon to deliver the appropriate expertise. It could be argued that if expertise is required it is more appropriate to secure it in the officer structure. But in any event the issue of the organisation of expertise depends on the relationship between the elected body and the organisation, which can take many different forms. It is that issue that will be dealt with in the next section.

Local government and appointed bodies: a variety of relationships

If the responsibilities of a local authority are extended to include the functions of certain of the appointed bodies (or indeed if a new separately selected body is created) it should not be assumed that the relationship between the authority and the function need be modelled on that traditionally governing its working. Thus it need not be assumed that a local authority would discharge those functions directly through a traditional committee system. There may be a need for experiment to test out alternative approaches – for one of the strengths of local government is the diversity it makes possible. Local authorities have learnt to operate in different ways. They have learnt under the impact of compulsory competitive tendering that the client role can be separated from the contractor role and that the contractor role need not be controlled directly through a hierarchy but rather through a contract. In Passenger Transport Authorities, the executive role of the passenger transport executive is separated from the policy role of the authorities. In City Challenge Boards and in a variety of other ways, local authorities have learnt to work in partnership with other bodies. The Report of the Joint Working Party on Internal Management[12] has opened up alternatives to the traditional committee system. Many different ways of working have already been established and are possible in the future.

A distinction can be drawn between four forms of relationship between a local authority and the responsibilities of appointed bodies. Two forms involve the local authority taking over the responsibilities of these bodies but distinguishes between direct and indirect control. The other two forms involve the local authority being given either power or rights in relation to appointed bodies without taking over responsibilities. Within these latter forms a further distinction can be drawn between giving the local authority powers over the body and rights which fall short of powers, but which can enhance influence.

Direct control

This will be achieved through the normal workings of the authority by the functions being undertaken within the departments of the authority or within departments newly created for that purpose. Where the committee system operates, the responsibility for the function will be given to an appropriate committee. The report of the Working Party on Internal Management[13] opens up other possible forms of councillor control, such as the use of co-option to bring into the work of the council particular expertise or interests. At present such co-opted members cannot be given voting rights, but that is not necessarily appropriate for such roles. Co-option opens up the possibility of combining election with local appointment in new forms of direct control.

Indirect control

This will be achieved through a combination of elements, including: a separate organisation; appointments to the body made in whole or in part by the local authority; and a policy framework or contract set by the local authority for the body. Such an approach could be adopted where it is considered desirable to give an organisation clear executive responsibility within an overall accountability to the local authority. In one sense this could lead to local authority appointed bodies – the argument for such an arrangement as opposed to national appointed bodies would be the immediacy of the accountability.

The choice between these two approaches will depend upon, firstly, the extent to which it is possible to separate policy-making from implementation, enabling the preparation of adequate contracts or policy frameworks, and secondly, the extent to which implementation can properly be regarded as a matter of expertise or management which raises no significant value issues beyond those specified in the framework. The argument for indirect control will be strengthened where there is a call for a relatively independent status for the organisation because of the need for separate expertise or the representation of other interests. One example could be TECs, whose functions could be made the responsibility of the local authority, but which could operate within a framework set by the authority through a Training and Enterprise Agency appointed by the authority to be representative of commercial, industrial and other interests.

Even where it is decided that the appointed body should not be subject to direct local democratic control it may be considered desirable to give the local authority certain powers or rights in relation to the body concerned. This would arise when the judgement is made that the main accountability should be at national level but there remains a need to ensure a degree of local accountability. It could also arise with self-governing institutions where it is determined that they should be subject to certain limited powers of the local authority or of the public at large. A distinction can be drawn between powers that can be used to control, to an extent, the activities of the body, and rights to enhance the influence of the local authority or of the public at large.

Powers

The local authority could be given certain powers over appointed boards, requiring them to exercise their responsibility in a particular way. One such example could be extending the local authorities' power of planning provision in education to grant-maintained schools (irrespective of the extent of opting out) and to colleges of further education. The local authority could be given powers to require the replacement of a particular appointed board – the use of that power possibly being made the subject of a local referendum. Alternatively such a referendum could be called by a specified percentage of the electorate.

Rights

The local authority could be given rights that would enhance its capacity to monitor the activities of appointed bodies in its area – indeed such rights could be associated with a formal duty to monitor such bodies. Such rights could include the right to information, the right to explanation and the right to require representatives of appointed bodies to appear before scrutiny committees of the local authority. Generally, the rights of the public to attend meetings, of access of information and to information on the membership of these bodies could be enhanced. In some instances it may be considered appropriate to give the local authority the right to appoint a specified number of members of appointed boards as a means of enhancing its influence on the body. This should be seen as a means of enhancing influence, not of ensuring democratic control. The councillor sitting on an appointed body cannot be seen as ensuring democratic accountability. The functions of the body cannot be regarded as the responsibility of the local authority nor can councillors in a minority control the body. Often such arrangements are proposed as a compromise. It is a compromise which can lead to confusion because it cannot provide democratic accountability. It can be a means of enhancing a local authority's influence but nothing more than that. Even that influence will not be enhanced unless it is accepted that such a councillor represents the interests of the authority and should be guided by those interests rather than being regarded as merely another member of the appointed board.

Transfer of responsibilities

Transfer to local democratic control raises many issues. It will involve, as we have seen, consideration of the form in which that control is exercised. Even where the control is exercised through direct control by an authority, it will involve very significant organisational change in the authority. The addition of the functions of the district health authority would, for example, have a major effect on the financial position of the authority and the budgetary process. This raises a number of issues that would have to be dealt with in such a transfer.

Finance

Unless local authorities or a new separately elected body were to be given new taxation powers, the new responsibilities will have to be financed from central government grant transferred in effect from the appointed body to the new authority. The issue would arise whether, if transferred to a local authority, the grant should be ring-fenced and whether the local authority could add to it. Over-rigid ring-fencing would restrict the development of the benefits of transfer, since the local authority would be restricted in its capacity to review the overall use of resources in, for example, community care. While some ring-fencing might be necessary as a transitional arrangement, it could be argued that if the case for transfer of responsibilities to local authorities is accepted, then once established the expenditure should be regarded as a normal part of a local authority's budget. Such transfers would increase the gearing effect brought about by a high dependence on government grant, and enhance the case for additional local taxation powers.

Central government control

Transfer of responsibilities to a local authority or to a new elected body does not mean that central government relaxes all control over the body. In most services there are national as well as local interests. It is a mistake to assume a choice has to be made between the two. In most services this is achieved by local authorities operating within a framework of legislation, inspection and regulation. Central accountability for that framework can be combined with local accountability for action taken within it. In a transfer of responsibility, consideration will have to be given to that framework of legislation, inspection and regulation.

Joint action

In some fields the authorities to which responsibilities are transferred may operate over more limited areas than the appointed bodies they replace. In those instances consideration will have to be given to the extent of joint action required and the structures and processes to support it.

Strengthening local government

If public accountability and democratic control is to be achieved through local authorities, it should not be assumed that all is well with the accountability of local authorities. A programme of transferring responsibilities to local authorities should be accompanied by a programme of strengthening the accountability of local authorities and deepening democratic control.

Transitional arrangements

The transfer of responsibilities to local authorities would require legislation. It would be possible to envisage steps that could be taken without legislation by, for example, ensuring that the appointed boards consisted of councillors nominated by local authorities. This would not be a satisfactory long-term solution, since it would not clarify where responsibility lay. It would, however, permit experiments as a basis for learning prior to legislation.

Alternatives to democratic control

Even where local democratic control is considered inappropriate, the evaluation of policy and performance at local level can be enhanced by opening up these bodies to scrutiny by local authorities and local people. Several potential measures are relevant. Firstly, codes of practice governing these bodies could be introduced. These could include such measures as: laying down requirements to hold meetings in public; giving the public rights of access to information; creating statutory obligations about consultation; detailing provisions governing public declarations of interest and restrictions on involvement in business; stating rights of appeal to ombudsmen; providing for scrutiny by externally appointed auditors making public their reports; and the publication of reports by inspectors. Secondly, clear public procedures governing appointments, external scrutiny at both local and national level and public registers of appointments held both at national and local level, giving relevant details of appointees, could be developed. Thirdly, local authorities could actively support individuals and groups who wish to raise issues about the work of appointed boards.

While the emphasis has been laid on opening up these bodies to scrutiny, it would also be possible to consider giving the local authority or the public at large rights to require reappointment of the body concerned if backed by a local referendum. It would introduce an element of contestability into the working of these bodies and their relationship with the public, providing a means of expressing their evaluation of its policies and performance. Such rights should only be used as last resorts. Local authorities need to work with other agencies. Scrutiny should not be seen therefore merely as a way of criticising such bodies, but of deepening understanding. Partnership and scrutiny will not always sit easily together, although partnership can sustain scrutiny and many appointed bodies would welcome the chance to submit their performance to consideration by elected councillors and through them to the public beyond. Many appointed bodies are anxious to enhance their accountability to local people, as concern has grown about their legitimacy.

Conclusion

There is a growing recognition that the development of an alternative system of local government by appointment raises issues of public accountability. The stage has now been reached when it is necessary to move beyond statements of the issue to a discussion of how the issue can be resolved. There is no one answer because there is no one type of body. Choices have to be made both on where accountability should lie and on the form it should take. There is a need for a period of debate and discussion. Criteria can be stated as a basis for that debate and discussion but in the end a judgement has to be made. In developing proposals for the reform of government by appointment a variety of forms of democratic control have to be considered, going beyond the assumption that the only alternative to the present is direct control by a local authority through its traditional ways of working. The approach adopted can and should vary as the nature of the responsibilities involved itself varies.

Notes and references

1. See Stoker, G. (1991) *The Politics of Local Government*, London: Macmillan; Davis, H. and Stewart, J. (1993) *The Growth of Government by Appointment*, Luton: Local Government Management Board; Gray, C. (1994) *Government Beyond the Centre*, London: Macmillan; Weir, S. and Hall, W. (1994) *Ego Trip: Extra-Governmental Organisations in the United Kingdom and their Accountability*, Democratic Audit and Charter 88.
2. For example, Cabinet Office (1994) *Public Bodies 1993*, London: HMSO.
3. Pliatsky, L. (1980) *Report on Non-Departmental Bodies* Cmnd 7797, London: HMSO.
4. Waldegrave, W. (1993) *The Reality of Reform and Accountability in Today's Public Service*, London: Public Finance Foundation.
5. Young, K. (1994) *Rethinking Accountability: An Issues Paper*, QMW Public Policy Seminar, 28 April 1994.
6. Waldegrave, *The Reality of Reform*.
7. Weir and Hall, *Ego Trip*.
8. Ibid.
9. Audit Commission (1993) *Their Health, Your Business: The New Role of the District Health Authority*, p. 6.
10. Leach, S., Davis, H., Game, C. and Skelcher, C. (1991) *After Abolition: The Operation of the Post-1986 Metropolitan Government System*, Birmingham: INLOGOV.
11. AMA (1994) *Local Authorities and the Health Service*, London: Association of Metropolitan Authorities.
12. Working Party on the Internal Management of Local Authorities (1993) *Community Leadership and Representation: Unlocking the Potential*, London: HMSO.
13. Ibid.

10 Redefining Local Democracy

Gerry Stoker

Introduction

This chapter is concerned with potential solutions to the crisis of local government and democracy. It takes inspiration from Phillips's argument (see Chapter 2) which establishes that democracy matters and that local democracy has many positive attractions. Democracy matters as a safety net against tyranny or corruption. Opportunities for political participation also matter because they help reduce inequalities in the distribution of power and encourage a responsiveness to individual and collective needs. Local government and democracy is especially attractive because it involves a decentralisation of power and the opportunity to use local knowledge to meet local needs. Above all, local democracy can rest its claim on being the most accessible avenue for political participation. It is in local politics that people feel most competent and are most immediately engaged.

In the first section of this chapter it is argued that a particular 'solution-set' has dominated thinking in Britain about local government for much of the last thirty years. The problem is seen as how to deliver with efficiency a range of public services and the solution defines the role of local government as a service provider. There have been disputes about how that role is to be undertaken. But for many officials in both local and central government, and politicians of all parties at all levels, local government has been seen as essentially about providing services. Politics – the development and expression of voice and weighing of community objectives – is downplayed.

The height of the anti-politics vision is reached, as Phillips notes, in the celebration of the market as the better way of empowering people to make their preferences known. This has been accompanied by the growth of a managerialist style of thought that claims to learn lessons from the private sector about how to run public services. It can readily be conceded that market-based reforms have brought some benefits to local service provision. What is challenged is the view that such procedures are adequate in themselves to the task of governance. The first section of the chapter, then, argues that we need to confront established and entrenched patterns of thought and offer a wider vision of the virtues of politics within local public life.

The second section takes the argument a stage further by outlining the values that should underlie 'good' local governance. This discussion draws on traditional insights from liberalism as well as more unconventional contributions from communitarian and green perspectives. Local governance should be open so that people are recognised as having the right and opportunity to act in local public life. There should be a capacity for deliberation about the key issues confronting a community both on the part of civic leaders and 'ordinary' citizens. Finally the system requires a capacity to act. It should enable institutions and actors from public, private and voluntary sectors to blend their resources and skills to achieve common purposes.

A brief concluding section addresses the issue of how to develop a reform strategy. The task of persuasion needs to reach out not only to those in central government but also to those within local authorities and various appointed local bodies. A crucial task is how to stimulate a process of experimentation and learning so that new forms of democratic politics can be seen in practice.

Beyond service delivery: in praise of politics

Local government in post-war Britain came to be seen as a series of separate services required by national legislation. Related to this understanding are the particular features of the British system which stand out when comparisons with other countries are made.[1] First there is the exceptionally large size of the basic units of local government in Britain. The reorganisations of the 1960s and 1970s in Britain were justified by the need for large-scale units for effective service delivery. As a result, the average population size of local authorities in England stands at 127 000, compared with 30 000 in Sweden, the next largest system. Second, the British system is characterised by the number and prominence of professional or technocratic officers. The employment of these officers rests on their claim to special expertise and knowledge in relation to the delivery of particular services.

In seeking to justify the existence of local government in Britain a review[2] of the core arguments concluded in 1970 that it was through its capacity for efficiency in service delivery that the best case for local government could be made. This general line of reasoning also emerges in the various major official reports of recent years on local government – Redcliffe-Maud, Widdicombe. Values such as participation and responsiveness were seen as handmaidens to the end of better service delivery. The Widdicombe Committee, for example, argued: 'Local government is government by local communities rather than of local communities. It is a means by which local communities may take decisions affecting the delivery of public services in their area.'[3]

Resting the defence of local government on its role as an agency for delivering services made it vulnerable to the public choice critique which came to the fore in the late 1970s. Local government, so the argument went, is dominated by producer interests, so lacks real incentives to be efficient either in terms of saving public money or in being responsive to consumer needs. The introduction of market or quasi-market mechanisms provides a more effective way of achieving efficiency. Competition between producers and choice for the consumer were to be the crucial weapons of reform.

The emphasis on service delivery also provides the context in which a managerialist vision of central–local relations and the organisation of public services has been able to come to the fore. The issue is how to manage Public Services (UK) plc, and the answer learnt supposedly from private business is management by contract. Central government sets the broad guidelines of what is needed and what can be afforded. It then devolves responsibility by way of contract-style relations to a range of other agencies, including local authorities, to meet those needs. These agencies, in turn, operate internally and externally through contracts. Customers, too, will have contracts giving them strengthened rights to redress for unsatisfactory service – plus, increasingly, the right to go elsewhere.

This model, as Mather notes, leaves 'the elected status of local government somewhat behind' and the onus 'on the elected politician to show that they are necessary to this service provision'.[4] A similar message emerges from Waldegrave's defence of recent management reforms. Output in terms of better quality service delivery is the challenge. 'The key point in this argument is not whether those who run our public service are elected, but whether they are producer-responsive or consumer-responsive'.[5]

The rhetoric of the market, managerialism and consumerism which is so rampant in Britain attracts some interest in other western democracies but it is a qualified interest. The reason, as Blair[6] explains, in the case of other European countries is that they do not follow the tendency in Britain 'to view local government almost exclusively as an instrument for the delivery of services – or at least for making arrangements for the delivery of services'. Rather their judgement is coloured by a view of local government 'as what the (English) name implies: the first level of government in the community'. In the light of such a perspective local government becomes an agency of political activity.

This wide-ranging political view of local government also dominates thinking in North America. In the United States the original Jeffersonian commitment to direct democracy and individual participation has given way to a more group-orientated pluralist view. This view is characterised by Wolman[7] in the following way:

Local democracy consists of the expression of and conflict among diverse views and values held by contending groups attempting to shape local government decisions to meet their ends, with all important groups having the ability to gain access to and exercise some degree of influence over decision makers. Local government's role is thus with . . . the authoritative allocation of values or in . . . classic language, 'who get what, when and how?'

The concern with reform measures and efficient government has only partially checked this view of local government as an arena for resolving political conflict.

The view of local government as involving something more than service delivery involves a pragmatic acceptance of the inevitability and a positive affirmation of the desirability of politics. Blair's view of how other European democracies perceive local government can be compared with Anderson's[8] definition of politics:

In essence, we act politically whenever we make decisions on behalf of other people and not for ourselves alone. Politics means planning and organising common projects, setting rules and standards that define the relationships of people to one another, and allocating resources among rival human needs and purposes.

As Bailey[9] notes, this is a view of politics as 'an orderly competition'. It can break down into 'a fight' – a coup or a revolution – but
the focus here is on routine, day-to-day, relatively orderly politics.
However this is not to suggest that this is a politics of the mundane.
What is political is defined by the participants. As Heller[10] argues:

> The 'political' becomes actually political if men and women so
> desire that it should be discussed, contested, decided in the public
> domain . . . No-one and nothing is excluded in principle.

Politics involves collective decision-making.
    The contract model does not completely deny politics but seeks to
confine it to the specification of services. Politics is reduced to the
making of choices about what level of services to provide. Central
government sets the broad framework. Local agencies adapt services
to local needs. However, it is unrealistic to assume that political
activity can be constrained in this way. The process of delivering
services is itself prone to political dimensions. The market-orien-
tated contract model falls into the trap of assuming a clear distinction can be drawn between 'ends' and 'means'. Moreover it assumes
that politics is confined to issues of service delivery. Politics exists
whenever and wherever people decide it does. It arises when issues
are contested and resolved through a process of collective decision-
making.
    Politics cannot be constrained if it is accepted that there are
different interests each with some resources within a system. Within
a governmental system diversity of interests and resources create the
pre-conditions for politics. Politics is inevitable in a divided yet
interdependent society. As Crick[11] argues:

> Politics is simply the activity by which government is made
> possible when differing interests in an area to be governed grow
> powerful enough to need to be conciliated . . . Politics allows
> various types of power within a community to find some reason-
> able level of mutual tolerance and support.

Market advocates and managerialists may try to confine politics or
wish it away but they will fail. Worst of all they may drive politics
underground to a series of 'shadowy' exchanges between clients,
producers, regulators and auditors. The solution is not to deny
politics but to recognise its potential benefits, and bring it out into
the open.

Politics is a social activity which takes people beyond the individualism of the market.[12] It involves discussion and debate. It
involves more than self-interest at a minimum because it encourages
a realistic construction of self-interest based on an appreciation of
how relationships with others should proceed. It allows different
interests to be reconciled. Equally it allows each interest some
reassurance of mutual tolerance and support. It can create a sense
of community yet it allows scope for diversity. It ensures that justice
is seen to be done. Politics practised in this manner treats people in
the round rather the narrow vision of rational utility maximisers
favoured by market models.

Politics is attractive because it provides a mechanism for coping
with ambiguity, uncertainty and dealing with the unexpected. As
Crick argues, the 'political virtues – of prudence, of conciliation, of
compromise, of variety, of adaptability, of liveliness' stand against
the search for 'certainty in government'.[13] The 'government by
contract' model expresses a managerial search for certainty that
can never be fully realised. It is necessary to have a degree of
flexibility within the process of social co-ordination. Politics provides that flexibility. It is suited to coping with ambiguity, crises and
uncertainty.

Politics can be beneficial when it helps create the capacity to work
towards shared purposes. At its most abstract it is about furthering
the welfare and assuring the survival of a body of citizens. Politics in
this sense is about the production rather than simply the distribution
of benefits. If the 'great' issues such as the economy, the environment, and crime are to be tackled, processes of integration and
networking are necessary to bring together a range of diverse actors.
Politics offers the mechanism for blending together the capacity of
various governmental and non-governmental actors. This is not to
invoke a romantic image of equal citizens agreeing to work with one
another. It is to see politics as having a capacity through a mixture
of positive and negative incentives to obtain a capacity to act within
a social system. What is involved is the 'social production' of power:
'it is something created by bringing co-operating actors together, not
as equal claimants, but often as unequal contributors to a shared set
of purposes'.[14]

Politics is defended here as a mechanism for the orderly regulation
of competition and as a means of integrating human activity to help
cope with unexpected change and to achieve common purposes. The
political activity involved is not restricted to party politics or those

who choose politics as a vocation. It is a vision of politics that includes all those who choose to enter the public domain of discussion and decision even if only for a brief moment.[15] Political behaviour, as defended here, does involve elements of manipulation and the pursuit of self-interest. Yet it also contains a concern for others, a toleration of the views of others and a commitment to certain rules of behaviour. Markets rely on the pursuit of self-interest but in the context of 'moral' behaviour such as honesty, fair-dealing and a respect of the law.[16] Politics, as presented here, requires a recognition of the capacity for human behaviour to move beyond a narrow instrumental satisfaction of individual preferences. It requires not the abolition of selfishness but rather that individuals will behave reasonably in conditions of social co-operation and co-ordination.[17] Finally politics does, as promoted here, involve compromise and ambiguity. This does not deny the value of beliefs or commitment. As Crick[18] explains: 'Political activity is important not because there are no absolute ideals or things worth doing for themselves, but because, in ordinary human judgement, there are many of these things.' Politics 'is a way of ruling in divided societies without undue violence'.[19]

Local government should not be defined by its task of service delivery; rather it should be valued as a site for political activity. This lesson emerges strongly from the approach and outlook of other western democracies. Politics is to be valued as a mechanism for social co-ordination for, at least, three reasons. First it enables people to co-operate and make choices on the basis of something beyond the individualism of market contracts. It treats people and encourages them to treat others with a recognition of the full roundness of human qualities and experience. Second, political decision-making is flexible so it can cope with uncertainty, ambiguity and unexpected change more effectively than formalised market contracts. Finally, politics can move beyond a distribution of benefits – a rationing function also offered by quasi-markets – to establish a process of social production in which interests are brought together to achieve common purposes.

The core characteristics of a sytem of good local governance

Government is the term conventionally used to refer to a formal institutional structure with authoritative decision-making powers.

Local authorities constitute local government in that they have decision-making responsibilities for their territories. Other agencies such as Training and Enterprise Councils or NHS Trusts have defined responsibilities and also make a contribution to the welfare of their localities. They are part of the governmental apparatus. To be concerned with local governance means considering the role of all these agencies but it also reflects a recognition of the system of political and social-economic relations in which the agencies operate. Governance implies a concern with both the internal power relations of the governmental system and the wider distribution of power held by external societal interests. Our concern should be with governance and the meaning of good governance within a locality. Only in this way can the role and purpose of local government be clarified.

The virtues of an active local politics and decision-making have been established in the abstract. This section develops this vision by clarifying the core characteristics of a system of good local governance. Three elements are identified. A system of local governance should have a capacity for openness, deliberation and integrated action. These are not the only relevant values but they deserve the highest priority. They are necessary if not sufficient to the establishment of a system of good local governance.

Openness

In a democratic system the participation of all is not required – rather its defining characteristic is its openness to all. As Phillips in her chapter points out, it is possible to make a fetish out of participatory democracy. Many people prefer to spend their time on non-political activities, or they face social and economic constraints that limit their time for political activity. Indeed the very ease of participation at the local level gives a particular value to local democracy. To argue for a local government system which is a focus for politics builds on the inherent strengths of the locality. Yet it is not necessary to imagine an active citizenry interested in politics and little else. The crucial value for good governance is that the system is open, has low barriers to the expression of dissent and limits the disadvantages of the poorly organised and resourced.

This broadly defined concern with openness finds many echoes in a long tradition of liberal argument which in its many guises shares the belief that 'we promote people's interests by letting them choose for themselves what sort of life they want to lead'.[20] To this end, liberalism's thrust has been 'to create a sovereign democratic state, a diversity of power centres and a world marked by openness, controversy and plurality'.[21] Equally, as Phillips notes, opponents and critical supporters of liberalism have recognised the limits that material and other conditions place on the exercise of democracy. Moreover, the various instruments of democracy have been subject to critical assessments of their strengths and weaknesses. In arguing for an open local governance it is possible to draw inspiration for the liberal advocacy of democracy and at the same time recognise the need to meet some of the challenges and difficulties that have been identified.

Much thinking about local government is based around the virtues of representative democracy. The Widdicombe Committee saw the desirability of politics but viewed it largely in terms of party competition:

> At its best politics is the essential currency of representative democracy. It provides an organisational basis through which citizens can achieve the type of government and the type of services they want without themselves needing to partake directly in the process of government. If the political party for whom they vote fails to deliver, that party can be held accountable through the ballot box at the next election.[22]

There are, however, grounds for doubting how effectively traditional representative democracy operates at the local level. It has become a mechanism for granting legitimacy to decision-takers rather than a strong mechanism for governmental accountability to citizens.

The problems with the current representative system can be summarised under three headings.[23] *It is too crude.* It covers some but not all agencies of local governance. Too many bodies are appointed rather than elected. *It is too exclusive.* The officeholders that emerge from the system are drawn from too limited a spectrum of society. *It is too uncertain.* The checks on officeholders are not strong or sensitive enough. Minority interests can be ignored, and in general public influence over decision-making is too limited.

Party competition, for elected office on a first-past-the-post basis, does not exhaust the limits of democratic practice. The challenge is how to extend citizen control without making excessive demands on people's time and in a way that provides access to all social interests. The answer of nineteenth-century liberalism was representative democracy. As we move into the twenty-first century it is necessary to move beyond the watered-down practice of representative democracy that dominates the system of local governance. The scale, complexity and diversity of the system requires us to delve much more deeply into the richness of democratic forms and options. Adapting the scheme offered by Phillips, an open system of local governance would provide space for each of the three procedures of democratic decision-making: electing representatives, voting directly on issues, participation in meetings.

There are many attractions to representative democracy and many options for enhancing its effectiveness. The vote casts a long shadow and to a degree encourages elected representatives to make policies that satisfy citizens. It provides a low-cost mechanism for citizens to hold governmental agencies to account. Voting should be extended to some of the array of appointed bodies that operate in the system of local governance, especially those with a broad strategic and planning responsibility for a locality. Experiments with different systems of voting should be encouraged including various forms of proportional representation. Local elections which return one party to power constantly on the basis of less than a majority of votes cast are difficult to justify. Systems of plural voting might be developed to allow citizens to emphasise their choices and preferences. Various mechanisms for enhancing turnout could be the subject of experiment. The dynamics and processes of representation could be enhanced within the council chamber. More radical reforms could see the election of a separate executive as a focus for local accountability.

There should be scope for introducing opportunities for direct voting and other forms of direct participation (such as local phone-in lines, electronic networks, video-interfaces).[24] Direct voting could take the form of either council-run referenda or citizen-initiated ballots. Some local authorities in Britain have experimented with referenda. Strathclyde Regional Council in March 1994 obtained over a 70 per cent turn-out for its referendum on the issue of water privatisation. Such council-run referenda can be criticised on the grounds that they are called to win approval for a policy position already supported by the council and are called at the discretion of the council in circumstances that it judges favourable.

Much more challenging although not practised in Britain is the citizen-initiated ballot. This form of direct democratic device is, however, widely employed in other western democracies especially at a local level in the United States.[25] Such 'initiatives', as they are called, may be binding or advisory. They require a certain number of signatures of petitioning local citizens for an issue to be placed on a ballot and trigger a vote. At times the local council may respond with a counter-measure of its own on which people can vote. The range of topics covered by such ballots is considerable. Road building, fluoridation, environmental measures and land-use planning matters have all been addressed. There are a number of issues to be considered in the case of binding citizen ballots: the role of pressure group funding of advertisements, the impact on minority interests, the oversimplification of complex issues. However it is difficult to deny the freshness that direct democracy approaches could bring to local democracy. Survey evidence indicates a substantial degree of public support and interest in such innovations.[26]

The final form of democratic procedure sees the involvement of sections of the public in 'face-to-face' meetings. As Phillips notes, such procedures are attractive because of the depth and intensity of involvement that they offer. They may also encourage a move away from a narrow concern with competitive self-interest towards a broader promotion of consensual areas of common concern. She goes on to note that such face-to-face meetings have their drawbacks. Some individuals are more willing and able to participate than others. Meetings can create a sense of false consensus, masking substantial minority interests and opinions. For these reasons Phillips argues for a cautious approach to using face-to-face meetings, restricting their use to the debate of less divisive issues or confining their role to consultation rather than final decision.

The concerns expressed by Phillips about face-to-face meetings can be overcome to a degree and should not, as Phillips herself notes, be used to dismiss the contribution made by such procedures to the openness of local governance. A range of options have been tried in practice, including:

- public meetings organised to encourage debate and discussion of a particular issue
- neighbourhood forums

- co-option of representatives on to local authority committees or governing bodies.
- user panels

In the case of the last option, experience with carers and frail older people[27] suggests that such panels can provide a way of giving voice to groups that in many instances are excluded from decision-making processes. Whilst not being elected or a statistically valid sample of the population the participants can claim 'typical representativeness':

> The legitimacy of the views expressed was seen to lie in the personal experience of a group of carers who shared that experience with many others in similar positions. That sense of legitimacy was enhanced by the openness which developed during the course of panel meetings.[28]

The value of face-to-face meetings in adding to the depth and variety of learning mechanisms for decision-making should not be underestimated.

A core value of good local governance should be openness. As Held argues:

> What is at issue is the provision of a *rightful share* in the process of 'government'. [I]t requires that people be recognised as having the right and opportunity to act in public life. However, it is one thing to recognise that right, quite another to say it follows that everyone must, irrespective of choice, actually participate in public life.[29]

Citizens may well decide on reasonable grounds not to avail themselves of the opportunities to participate, believing that their interests are already well protected or not threatened. The value of openness does not require or assume large-scale and continuous direct participation. It rests its case on the richness of democratic practice and the options for extending participation that are available. These options should operate without making overwhelming time demands and in a way that enhances the broad social representativeness of those involved.

Deliberation

People are recognised as having the right and the opportunity to take part in local public life. Many of their interventions may be specific to the consumption of a particular service. Those interventions should be expected to be short-term, of low cost to the individual and bring forth a rapid response from the appropriate service organisation. They are likely to deal with a matter of direct material interest to the person. This is not to say that the outcome of the exchange will always lead to 'customer' satisfaction – resource and policy constraints may intervene – but the process should be straightforward and relatively low in its demand of time and effort. Such a 'customer' orientation is now rightly regarded as a commonplace virtue within public service organisations, although, of course, there is always room for improvement in practice. To see local government as a site for political activity, however, requires opportunities also for a deeper, more sustained level of public intervention and debate. Good local governance requires opportunities for deliberation.

This concern with deliberation can be seen as a strong theme in communitarian visions of the virtues of local government and democracy. The trouble with liberalism, so some communitarian critics argue, is that it only encourages a 'thin democracy' based around self-interested bargaining.[30] From a communitarian perspective what is required instead is a 'politics of the common good' in which neighbours look for common solutions to their problems. Judgement requires 'the sharing of experiences and the give and take of collective deliberation'.[31] Political institutions must be designed to enable citizens to relate to each other as deliberators or reason-givers and not as bargainers engaged in exchange. Local political institutions with their accessibility and closeness to communities would seem well-equipped in principle for this task.

Deliberation should be central to the decision-making of political leaders. The Widdicombe Committee[32] recognised the need for 'deliberative' committees within local authorities and contrasted them with the formal 'decision taking' committees. Rules of procedure, pro-rata membership and openness to the public are expected in the latter case. Deliberative committees are seen, on the other hand, as more informal opportunities for policy formulation where politicians can review options in confidence before presenting their final choice for public decision. In practice, many local authorities have an array of working parties and panels for policy deliberation and formulation alongside formal decision-taking committees. Why is it appropriate that such panels should always operate in confidence? An element of behind-closed-doors reflection plainly is essential to politics but the spirit of deliberation as championed here argues for a more public process of debate, review and questioning.

In other western democracies there is a stronger interest in creating forums which enable political leaders to debate issues in public – select committees, scrutiny reviews, commissions, blue-ribbon forums. Building on the limited experience of similar initiatives in Britain, political leaders could be encouraged to move their deliberations about policy development into public forums, inviting a range of interested participants to give evidence or present options. Public discussion in such a deliberative manner provides a sounder basis for civic leadership than behind-closed-doors policy development.

What may also need to be considered is whether different institutional forms of political organisation would create a greater capacity for civic leadership. The issue of the elected mayor again comes to attention. Another option might be to organise elections so that some councillors are elected on the existing 'ward' basis but others are chosen to serve 'city-wide'. It is this latter group that might be expected to have a greater role in civic leadership. Of course it is possible to take a further step and suggest that civic leaders will be drawn in from beyond the elected politicians of a locality. The private sector, appointed bodies, voluntary organisations, the churches and community groups could all provide civic leaders. What is required as Donnison comments, is 'a group of people who have a lasting commitment to their "place" – be it village, town or country. They have a vision of its future, and a capacity to work with each other, with the private sector, with community groups and with higher levels of government to bring that future about.'[33]

Civic leadership does, however, need a commitment to deliberative politics to check the tendency for it to collapse into the creation of a narrow regime of public and private actors fulfilling their own agenda and their own self-interest with little regard to the wider concerns of the community. There are many examples of such processes within US experience.[34]

The spirit of deliberation drawn from communitarian ideas requires that some consideration is given to drawing in a broader spectrum of the public into deliberative settings. Public meetings, young or elderly people forums, and neighbourhood assemblies could provide appropriate instruments. Each of these instruments suffers from a number of drawbacks in terms of the spread and range of response they are likely to obtain from citizens. Multi-choice referenda provide another option. As Elkin explains:

> Referenda items can be written so that citizens must pick from among several responses, each of which both lays out a reason for picking that response and denotes intensity of feeling. The important point about the referenda is that citizens are induced to think about the reasons for their votes.[35]

A further option is to adapt the jury system for consideration of policy issues. In Germany, experiments have been undertaken in which a sample of inhabitants have been drawn together and exempted from their normal work.[36] They have been asked to make recommendations about planning and design issues with full access to expert advice, data and administrative support.[37] The great attraction of the last two options is that those who are not normally activists are likely to be drawn into deliberative processes.

A capacity to act

J. S. Mill saw a radical distinction between controlling government and actually doing it. Representative democracy provided the mechanism for control. Bureaucracy with its professionalism and expertise was seen as central to the tasks of carrying out government. It was important for representative politicians not to take to themselves the task of administration or detailed legislative drafting. 'Mill valued both democracy and skilled government and believed firmly that each was the condition of the other: neither was attainable alone. And to achieve a balance between them was, he thought, one of the most difficult, complicated and central questions in the art of government.'[38]

Mill was surely right to emphasise that a good governance system requires both mechanisms of control and mechanisms for effective action. Openness and deliberation are to be valued but they lose their lustre in a system that lacks the capacity for effective action. Good local governance requires the capacity to act. It also requires something beyond classic bureaucratic organisation.

Bureaucracy and professional expertise will continue, as Mill suggested, to be central to good local governance. The management context may vary and the particular organisational forms may change but a large part of the daily work of government is going to be undertaken by full-time professionals, administrators and other employees. From the point of view of the citizen there are many attractions in letting these people get on with their complex variety of tasks. The issue is rather how to check the classic faults that emerge in all organisational systems of service delivery: insensitivity, rigidity and lack of responsiveness. Many 'customers' will be satisfied but mechanisms are necessary to allow those that are dissatisfied to make themselves known. In the classic formulation of Hirschman,[39] many users will display 'loyalty' but others will need access to the instruments of 'exit' and 'voice'. Sound management and political guidance, learning from the threat of 'exit' and the experience of 'voice', in turn may limit the requirement to exercise these instruments for the citizen. A good system of local governance may well be one where many people do not exercise the option of exit or voice because they are satisfied with the system of collecting rubbish, the management of their houses, or the running of their schools.

Yet in the vision of local governance developed here the capacity to act is about more than meeting service delivery objectives, important as they are. If the 'great' issues of poverty, economic renewal, unemployment, environmental decay and crime – for example – are to be tackled what is required is a capacity to act which goes beyond the traditional role of state bureaucracies. What is also required is the blending of the resources of government with those of non-governmental actors. Some users of the term 'enabling'[40] also see this as important task. In the USA the talk is of government being 'reinvented'[41] and having a catalytic role. The interdependence of governmental and non-governmental forces in meeting economic and social challenges focuses attention upon the problem of co-operation and co-ordination both within government and between government and non-governmental actors.

The potential of local government to provide scope for integrated action to tackle complex social and economic problems is considerable. This finds particularly strong expression in the arguments of the Green movement. Ward[42] notes that Greens recognise that environmental problems require national and even international action. Yet they see considerable scope for local action. The argument behind the Green slogan 'Act locally think globally' is that the key to successful resolution of global environmental problems is to change individuals' everyday behaviour and consumption patterns, something best done through local initiatives and intercommunal processes. To focus on global or national dimensions leaves people feeling powerless and uninvolved. Local action provides a worthwhile benefit in itself and a broader capacity to act.

The paradox of 'globalisation' and its impact on economic and social issues is that it enhances the argument for integrated local action. As the national state finds its powers trimmed by the growing interdependence among states and the rise of supranational bodies, so the local and regional tier can be seen as a vital arena of intervention. Why? Because it is at a local level that the chances of an effective blend of governmental and non-governmental forces emerging are enhanced. Whether it is over economic growth strategies[43] or issues of social justice[44] the local arena of action has much to offer.

Good local governance, then, should provide a capacity for integrated action. It is worth distinguishing the nature of the co-ordination that is desired.[45] One response to the problem of co-ordination would then be to set up an agency to impose order and coerce others to go along with its policy goals. Co-ordination in this sense becomes a form of power. People are co-ordinated by being told what to do within a hierarchical frame of reference – or, to use the jargon of organisational analysis, the solution is vertical integration. A second response to the case for co-ordination is to ask for machinery which, in effect, grants a veto to all those with a stake in the matter. Co-ordination becomes the search for consent which given a context of conflict and disagreement can become a recipe for inaction.

The search for co-ordination does not necessarily imply coercion by a higher authority or an endless search for consensus. An alternative approach would be co-ordination through networks. Co-operation is obtained, and subsequently sustained, through the establishment of relations premised on solidarity, loyalty, trust and reciprocity rather than through hierarchy. Under the network model, organisations learn to co-operate by recognising their mutual dependency; through discussion, negotiation and open communication; and by the development of shared knowledge and experience. The outcome of successful networking is a long-term commitment to one another and shared goals.

We are a long way from understanding how to build such effective long-term partnership.[46] Le Gales and Mawson[47] draw some interesting comparisons between the much-praised City Challenge initiative in Britain and the Contract de Ville procedure developed in France. Both schemes share a concern to improve co-ordination and create greater partnership between government, private and voluntary sectors. Yet in their style of working fundamental differences begin to emerge. The British approach is essentially short-term whilst the French have a longer-term perspective. The competition for funding in City Challenge which is not a feature of the French system, leads to short time horizons 'for putting together partnerships raising doubts, in some cases, as to their underlying strength'. The Treasury-driven concern to justify public spending also leads in the British case 'to the requirement to produce evidence of relatively short term pay offs'. The French in contrast have concentrated on the need to build up effective working relationships over a number of years. The emphasis in evaluation is 'more on the achievement of organisational/process outcomes designed to achieve greater co-ordination and cohesion of public policy'.

The capacity to provide an integrated approach to social and economic issues rests on partners that are trying to assemble long-running relationships rather than secure for themselves access to immediate spoils. It is a politics of social production. Local authorities, because of the depth of their local knowledge, the range of potential instruments available to them and, above all, because of their relative permanence, provide a solid base for developing the long-term commitment associated with networked, integrated action. They need access to resources to oil the wheels of co-operation. They need staff, perhaps, given new insights by extensive programmes of short-term attachments and secondments. They need to operate in the context of an open and deliberative local governance. The capacity for integrated action so central to modern local governance needs active and involved local authorities. To quote the Department of the Environment in what some might regard as a slightly unusual frame of mind early in 1994:

Local government's ability to innovate, to anticipate problems, to provide local leadership and processes for involving other groups, represents an important contribution towards the development of strategies for sustainability which reflect local needs and priorities.[48]

This argument developed in the context of environmental policy might well be seen to apply in other spheres.

Conclusions

This chapter has not provided a detailed design of the structural, functional and constitutional procedures of a future local government. A slightly easier task than describing and justifying what such institutions should look like has been attempted. What is offered is a view about what ideally local government should be able to accomplish.[49] Local government should be promoted because of its capacity to undertake the political tasks of regulating competition, making choices and integrating human activity to cope with unexpected change and to achieve common purposes. A system of 'good' local governance should display the values of openness, deliberation and a capacity to act.

If the arguments presented in this chapter are to be taken forward a viable reform strategy needs to be developed. Such a reform strategy would be driven by the qualities of experimentation and learning because of the uncertainty about what are appropriate institutions and methods for achieving good local governance. An experimental strategy also enables reforms to be demonstrated in practice, helping to persuade the reluctant and unsure that they may have attractions. Ideally a reform strategy should have some capacity to challenge those who stubbornly resist change. If an experiment proves successful then central government should have the capacity in some instances to generalise that reform to make it apply within all localities.

Notes and references

1. See Batley, R. and Stoker, G. (eds) (1991) *Local Government in Europe*, London: Macmillan.
2. Sharpe, L. J. (1970) 'Theories and values of local government', *Political Studies*, vol. 18, pp. 154–74.
3. Widdicombe Committee, *The Conduct of Local Authority Business*, Report of the Committee of Inquiry into the Conduct of Local Authority Business, Cmnd 9797, London: HMSO, 1986, p. 52.

4. Mather, G. (1989) 'Thatcherism and Local Government: An Evalua-tion', in Stewart, J. and Stoker, G. (eds), *The Future of Local Government*, London: Macmillan, p. 234.
5. Waldegrave, W. (1993) *The Reality of Reform and Accountability in Today's Public Service*, London: Public Finance Foundation, p. 13.
6. Blair, P. (1991) 'Trends in Local Autonomy and Democracy: Reflec-tions from a European Perspective', in Batley, R. and Stoker, G. (eds), *Local Government in Europe*, London: Macmillan, pp. 47, 49.
7. Wolman, H. (1995) 'Local Government Institutions and Democratic Governance', in Judge, D., Stoker, G. and Wolman, H. (eds), *Theories of Urban Politics*, London: Sage, p. 137.
8. Anderson, C. (1977) *Statecraft: An Introduction to Political Choice and Judgement*, New York: Wiley, p. vii.
9. Bailey, F. G. (1977) *Stratagems and Spoils. A Social Anthropology of Politics*, Oxford: Blackwell, p. 2.
10. Heller, A. (1991) 'The Concept of the Political Revisited', in Held, D. (ed.), *Political Theory Today* Cambridge: Polity, pp. 340.
11. Crick, B. (1993) *In Defence of Politics*, 4th edn, London: Penguin, p. 30.
12. Ibid, p. 25.
13. Ibid.
14. Stone, C. (1993) 'Urban Regimes and the Capacity to Govern', *Journal of Urban Affairs*, vol. 15, p. 8.
15. See Heller, 'The Concept of the Political Revisited', p. 341.
16. A point made by Hirst, P. (1994) *Associative Democracy*, Cambridge: Polity, p. 64.
17. These issues are dealt with at much greater length and depth elsewhere. See, for example, Hollis, M. (forthcoming) 'Friends, Romans and Consumers'.
18. Crick, *In Defence of Politics*, p. 154.
19. Ibid, p. 141.
20. Kymlicka, W. (1990) *Contemporary Political Philosophy*, Oxford: Clarendon, p. 199.
21. Held, D. (1987) *Models of Democracy*, Cambridge: Polity, p. 274.
22. Widdicombe Committee, *The Conduct of Local Authority Business*, p. 60.
23. This list draws on the paper presented by David Beetham at an ESRC Local Governance Conference, Strathclyde University, May 1993.
24. McNulty, D. (1995) *Referenda and Citizens', Ballots*, London: CLD; and Percy-Smith, J. (1995) *Digital Democracy: Information and Com-munication Technologies in Local Politics*, London: CLD.
25. See Caves, R. (1992) *Land Use Planning: The Ballot Box Revolution*, Newbury Park, California: Sage.
26. See the results of a survey reported by P. Dunleavy and S. Weir in *Local Government Chronicle*, 29 April 1994, p. 12. The results showed strong support for innovations including local phone-in lines, local referenda run by the council and citizen-initiated referenda. Respec-tively 69, 78 and 61 per cent of the sample thought such innovations

were 'a good idea', and 64, 53 and 49 per cent indicated they would use such instruments if they were available.

27. See Barnes, M., Cormie, J. and Crichton, M. (1994) *Seeking Representative Views from Frail Older People*, Kirkcaldy: Age Concern Scotland; Wistow, G. and Barnes, M. (1993) 'User Involvement in Community Care: Origins, Purposes and Applications', *Public Administration*, vol. 71, pp. 279–99.

28. Barnes *et al.*, *Seeking Representative Views*, p. 12.

29. Held, *Models of Democracy*, pp. 291–2.

30. Barber, B. (1984) *Strong Democracy: Participatory Politics For a New Age*, California: University of California Press. Key communitarian theorists include Sandel and Taylor. For a review see Kymlicka, *Contemporary Political Philosophy*, ch. 6.

31. Kymlicka, *Contemporary Political Philosophy*, p. 220.

32. Widdicombe Committee, *The Conduct of Local Authority Business*, pp. 77–84.

33. Donnison, D. (1994) *Act Local: Social Justice from the Bottom Up*, London: IPPR, pp. 15–16.

34. See Elkin, S. (1987) *City and Regime in the American Republic*, Chicago: University of Chicago Press.

35. Elkin, *City and Regime in the American Republic*, p. 173.

36. Grunow, D. (1991) 'Customer-Orientated Service Delivery in German Local Administration', in Batley and Stoker (eds), *Local Government in Europe*, London: Macmillan, p. 81.

37. For a broader argument about the virtues of bringing together representative samples of the public to engage in policy-making see Burnheim, J. (1985) *Is Democracy Possible?*, Cambridge: Polity.

38. Held, *Models of Democracy*, p. 95.

39. Hirschman, A. (1970) *Exit, Voice and Loyalty: Responses to Decline in Firms, Organisations and States*, Cambridge, Mass: Harvard University Press.

40. For a review of these arguments, see Cochrane, A. (1993) *Whatever Happened to Local Government?*, Buckingham: Open University Press, ch. 4.

41. Osborne, D. and Gaebler, T. (1992) *Reinventing Government*, Reading, Mass: Addison-Wesley.

42. Ward, H. (1993) 'Green Arguments for Local Democracy', Paper for the ESRC Local Governance Programme Conference, 20–21 May 1993, University of Strathclyde.

43. See, for example, Stoker, G. and Young, S. (1993) *Cities in the 1990s*, London: Longman, ch. 3.

44. Donnison 'A Local Perspective on Social Justice'.

45. The following section draws on Stoker and Young, *Cities in the 1990s*, pp. 9–10.

46. Mackintosh, M. (1992) 'Partnership: Issues of Policy and Negotiation', *Local Economy*, vol. 7, no. 3, pp. 210–24.

47. Le Gales, P. and Mawson, J. (1994) *Management Innovations in Urban Policy. Lessons from France*, Luton: Local Government Management Board, p. 97.

48. Department of the Environment (1994) *Sustainable Development: The UK Strategy*, CM 2426, London: HMSO, p. 200.
49. The idea of this style of reasoning is taken from Offe, C. and Preuss, U. (1991) 'Democratic Institutions and Moral Resources', in Held, D. (ed.), *Political Theory Today*, Cambridge: Polity, p. 170.

11 A Power of General Competence for Local Government?

Hilary Kitchin

Introduction

Local authorities in Britain have a different status from that given to local government in many other European countries. Here, the powers and duties, or *vires*, of local authorities are found in statute, and any activity outside the statutory framework would be unlawful. The responsibilities of local government have been established by parliament, and have been interpreted, and constrained, by the courts. The doctrine of *ultra vires*, originally a tool to interpret the extent of company powers, has developed in relation to local authorities so as to make the extent of local authority powers uncertain in many ways.

Without a binding constitutional statement of the role and status of local government, local authorities had operated until the early 1980s as part of an established order. It was assumed that local councils were free to set the rate of local taxes, and had considerable discretion over the provision of services. This position was unaffected by cuts in central government grant to local authorities from 1977.

In Britain, no special legal status has been recognised for local authorities acting for the general well-being of their areas. Local authorities' freedom to develop their own policy objectives, and their ability to act within a local democratic framework, has been undercut by an intensification of central government control and reduction in power since 1980. From 1980 onwards 'The government has seen local authorities as little more than agencies: thus there is no assumption that local authorities can act unless they can quote legal justification or limit their 'free expenditure' to a low statutory level.'[1] The Conservative government's attitude to central government is illustrated by its refusal to sign the Charter of Local

Self-Government published by the Council of Europe, which had been signed by seventeen member countries and ratified by eight by 1989.

Those in local government and elsewhere who are projecting a programme for greater democratic and operational freedom for local government in Britain have turned to the experience of other countries in Europe for positive examples of local autonomy. The concept of a power of general competence, enabling councils at the level closest to communities to regulate and administer local affairs, has particular resonance for those immediately concerned with local democracy.

Margaret Hodge and Wendy Thompson write that 'At present we think local authorities exist to exercise a specified range of functions rather than to govern local communities. The power of general competence is not simply an add-on but derives from and expresses the role of local government as the community governing itself. A power of general competence could release a local capacity for innovation and initiative.'[2] Politicians such as Margaret Hodge argue that a general power would be exercised within a framework of law and accountability. However there is no consensus on what such a power would mean within the British legal, financial, and democratic structures. In a real sense the proposal for a power of general competence indicates that a new constitutional settlement for local government is needed. Certainly the experiences of the last fifteen years indicate that a major re-evaluation of the relationships between central and local government, on a political and administrative level, is essential.

European comparisons

Those European countries where local government has greater competence differ from Britain in having written constitutions. Such constitutions guarantee a system of local government or administration and give it a secure position within the national system.[3] Ironically, European authorities have found themselves more bound by centrally imposed regulations than their counterparts in Britain, although this balance has altered to some extent in recent years, in part due to major decentralising programmes implemented by certain European governments during the 1980s, and in part due to new British legislation.

In *France*, local authorities exercise a power of general competence to make and implement decisions on behalf of local people; a right to act in whatever way fulfils collective needs. General competence means that many local authority activities are not defined by law, although use of powers varies considerably according to size; French local authority units are very much smaller than those in Britain. The impact of central control has been extensive, and efforts have been made to decentralise over the last decade.

The *German* constitution is based upon a post-war settlement designed to decentralise and develop local responsibility after the destruction of the Nazi state. A complex web of individual rights was established, an extensive expression of human rights within society, many of which correspond with areas of local government responsibility. The third and most local level of government is guaranteed the right to regulate on its own responsibility all the affairs of the community within the limits set by law, subject to detailed regulation; local authorities are under many pressures to see their role within a national network. Local government in Germany is nevertheless highly regarded, having great influence within the political and administrative structure.

That local authorities 'shall conduct their own affairs' is the principle that underlies *Swedish* local government. This is reflected in local finance. Until the crises of 1991–2 led to emergency measures, central government did not, and was unable to, interfere with the amount raised by way of local income tax. This was made possible by an active concept of common interest, and agreed channels existed for resolution of conflict between central and local authorities on financial questions. Local government plays an important role in the political and economic life of Sweden. The extent of local autonomy has, however, been qualified by the detailed regulation which covers the substantial part of its activities. Despite these restrictions public support for local government is strong.

Local authorities in *Denmark* also have fiscal autonomy; there is no statutory restraint on the amount that may be raised in local taxes, although in practice 90 per cent of local expenditure is mandatory. First and second tiers of local government have a general competence to provide benefits in the interest of local inhabitants beyond those provided by law. Competence is exercised within a framework of restraints that recognises individual rights and limits certain activities, including financial involvement with the private sector. Court interpretations of the role of local government have led to the development of *ultra vires* principles in Danish law.

The future of local government powers in Britain

Knowledge of the status accorded to local government in Europe has increased pressure for a transformation in local democracy in Britain. Developments within the European Community, introducing local politicians in Britain to concepts of subsidiarity and greater autonomy for local government, have also had significant impact. Complex issues arise as a result of local demands for democratisation and for wider powers, increasingly expressed to include a demand for a power of general competence for local government. Even should consensus emerge on the need for positive change, the questions of what changes should be made, and how they should operate in practice, will have to be addressed. One approach is to explore the possibility of change in the form of experiments in local government. The experience of Sweden, Norway, Denmark and Finland in experimenting with new forms of local government administration and differing degrees of local autonomy has transformed not only local government in those countries, but approaches to change in the public sector as a whole. The use of experiment would make it possible to test in practice those concepts of local government autonomy and democracy that we are learning from Europe.

The debate

Discussion about the possibility of a power of general competence for local government in Britain reopened in the late 1980s. This period saw the Conservative government intensify its challenge to local government by imposing restrictions and controls on the functions of local councils, particularly in the provision of basic services. Academics with direct professional working relationships with local government reacted to the government's programme of centralisation and devaluation of local affairs by proposing a revaluation of the role of local authorities. Rather than trying to maintain the position of local government that had prevailed in 1979, they argued 'future government policy must be based on a wider conception of local authorities' role as the basic unit of community government'.[4] Recognising that for local authorities to take on the role of community government it would be necessary to extend their capacity, Stewart and Stoker identified a number of possible future roles for local government. Their proposal also foresaw new patterns of organisation, and the development of closer ties between central and local government. Local authorities would not be limited to being service providers, but would be 'units of community government' which would play a strategic role in enabling communities to meet the problems and needs they face; seek responsiveness in action within collective purpose; and extend and develop an active local democracy. They proposed a Standing Commission on Central–Local Relations to monitor an agreed statement of principles based on the European Charter for Local Self Government.

Following from this Stewart and Clarke[5] have argued for a new approach to local government as a challenge to government policy, and have emphasised 'the need to consider the range of possible roles and so to explore the full potential of local government'. Considering the possibility of a community role for local government, they ask 'should local authorities have a power of general competence?'. They see such a power as valuable as much for its symbolic expression of the community role as for any increased discretion that it might provide. They also acknowledge that general competence would need to operate within a broad regulatory framework, and be complemented by changes in representational role, management, and central–local relations.

Later work by the same authors[6] has explored the experience of European countries. Without suggesting that European solutions should be adopted, they approach the operation of powers of general competence in Europe from a perspective of challenging British assumptions. They illustrate that European powers of competence are to be considered in the context of comparatively smaller units of local government, a concept of community self-government, and different means of providing services. Again, however, the discussion does not place powers of general competence beyond the symbolic. This approach implicitly recognises the questions of limited size and lack of resources experienced in many parts of Europe, but does not take into account those instances where European local authorities do exercise their wider powers. The symbolic significance of a general competence cannot be understated in this argument however: 'it is an expression of the concept of local government underlying the European system', the 'concept of the community governing itself'. As such it provides a lesson for Britain, a means of 'enabling the community to meet its needs and problems in the most effective way'.

This perspective means little in the analysis developed by Malcolm Grant.[7] In Grant's view, since the recommendation of the Redcliffe-Maud report, 'the idea of a power of general competence has . . . developed into a narrower version of a power of general spending competence'. He argues that a power of general competence would be 'so hedged around with limitations on activities that might adversely affect individual rights, that its effect could well [be] to authorise only those activities whose sole adverse effect was on the collective pocket'. Grant recognises that a power of general competence means something more that the discretionary spending which is already within local government's powers (although subject to a low upper limit). Yet the case for more extended powers is in his view weakened by the fact that local authorities do not make significant use of these discretionary powers. Grant concludes that the argument for a power of general competence has been defeated. Yet he recognises the need 'to foster greater diversity and innovation in local government'. Hence, he concludes that 'the impact of a general competence would likely be more symbolic than real' and suggests that a re-examination of the powers of local government within the framework of the *ultra vires* rule would be more effective.

Grant's proposal for the introduction of an experimental programme suggested by those in the Nordic countries aims to induce local authorities to 'come out from behind the *ultra vires* shield', and would involve Parliament in an experiment in local democracy. But, despite his recognition of the need for diversity, Grant's proposal is essentially flawed. His case is that the experiment would test whether there is any real support for change and whether the *ultra vires* rule does present difficulties for local authorities. While he argues that his approach would be 'a means of putting the initiative back in the hands of local authorities' and show confidence in local government, this is undermined by his failure to recognise that the case for change being made extends wider than strictly legal or financial powers, or to recognise that the crippling effect of the *ultra vires* rules is widely understood, despite the view of government to the contrary. His argument also omits – perhaps not surprisingly given that a more thorough understanding of the Nordic experiments is only just emerging – a recognition that change requires impetus and resources beyond an opportunity that is limited to tinkering within a narrow framework.

Yet Grant's argument that the solution for local government frustrations may lie in a re-evaluation of powers cannot be dismissed entirely. Local government in Britain has exercised wide powers, and may be able to do so again given legislative change and guarantees of its status. There is a strong argument that this cannot be the case without a power of general competence, but both approaches are currently being discussed, and in the event of an experimental programme being agreed, both might be tested, and even found to be complementary.

The development of ideas involving a comparison with European experience and initiatives has continued. Philip Blair,[8] looking at the restrictions in terms of resources faced by many countries, in southern Europe, considered that 'it is arguable that British local authorities, with their still relatively broad range of well-defined functions and often substantial degree of discretion, are quite well off even without a general competence'. However, his view that the effect of such a power might well have only symbolic value (although with positive implications) is explored more fully by Batley.[9] Having argued that a distinction should be made between direct *spending functions* and the usually wider range of *responsibilities* exercised by local authorities in Europe, Batley attributes 'the wide spread of responsibilities . . . to the underlying constitutional principle of "general competence" which is prevalent in continental Europe'. While financial constraints and restriction by higher levels may mean that general competence has little more than a symbolic meaning in terms of what local government can actually do, 'it does mean that local government in Scandinavia, Germany and France has been able to retain wide spheres of legitimate responsibility and influence even though often sharing these responsibilities with other communes, elected regional governments or the voluntary sector'. Batley goes on to argue that in contrast 'the British principle of *ultra vires* has led to the statutory allocation of specified spending functions to local government'. While ensuring certain clear and protected spheres of operation, he suggests that it follows that the weakening of local government's direct providing role 'is a profound challenge to the role of local government'. He argues that this has a quite different significance from that of the evolution of shared responsibility in Europe, and concludes that there are three lessons that Britain can learn from Europe: as part of the constitutional status of local government, 'the concept of general competence is important at least symbolically but also as a statement of local government's wider community responsibility, if not always of wide spending functions; the smaller scale of European local government; and the lack of an effective national platform for local government in Britain'.[10]

This debate has laid the groundwork for a discussion which has been continued with increasing vigour. Graham Allen MP has lobbied hard for the constitutional independence of local authorities. He proposes a route that lies between continued restraint and long-term constitutional change within a European constitutional framework. Thus he argues that local government should have 'a right to undertake locally whatever is not prohibited by statute law'.[11] This right would have statutory protection within the constitutional framework of the Parliament Act. From a different perspective, The Alexander report, published by the Legal Risk Review Committee in 1992, following the outcome of the 'interest rate swaps' cases, argued for an end to the *ultra vires* principle. This proposal was rejected by the Audit Commission and disregarded by government. Vernon Bogdanor, writing in the context of the European Charter of Local Self Government, argues that local authorities should be freed to act as genuine representatives of their communities. To this end he proposes that authorities should be given the freedom to experiment within the law, either within a power of general competence, or within an experimental programme.[12] In contrast, Donald Hirsch compares the constraints faced by local government in Britain with the greater sense of autonomy and political legitimacy experienced in other European countries. He notes the shift in Britain away from direct service provision and asks whether a role for local government to look after the interests of the inhabitants of an area can be retained in the context of the 'enabling local authority'. He concludes that to meet the demand for such local representation the retention of at least some discretion in expenditure and 'a stake in running at least some services' is needed.[13]

Meanwhile, assessment of the need for an improvement in the position of local authorities, including a general, or wider, competence, continues amongst the members of local authorities and their representatives.[14] The Association of Metropolitan Authorities has recently canvassed views on a policy paper which ranges across the issues identified since 1988.[15] The Labour Party's recent policy paper on local government[16] includes proposals that councils could be given a new power of community initiative allowing them greater freedom to respond to local needs, providing what they did was not unlawful and did not duplicate the duties of other statutory bodies. It is plain that these discussions are complemented by an internal debate within the Department of the Environment (DoE) from which a proposal for 'Trust Councils' was leaked to the Local Government Chronicle in the summer of 1994.[17] According to these reports the Department has given consideration to a project allowing a select number of councils possible new freedoms and responsibilities, including a power of general competence. This project, developed sufficiently to be discussed in the local government cabinet sub-committee, is reported to have been dropped only because of the anticipation of opposition from the Treasury. The government rejected the possibility of a general power proposed in the debate on the Local Government (Wales) Bill on the 28th April 1994. The debate will continue, and the operation of general powers of competence for local government in the Republic of Ireland (adopted in 1990) will be keenly observed.

Revitalising local government in Britain

A number of broad but key issues will be at stake in a future strategy to revitalise local government in Britain. The driving force of such a strategy, as demonstrated in the current debate, will have to be a recognition of the need to establish positive new authority and status for local government in Britain. Work will need to be done to identify how such powers would be brought into effect, the relevance of a power of general competence, how it would impact upon the application of existing local government powers and duties, and how fundamental the changes would be that such a power would demand in the constitutional relationship between local and central government. Implications for the regulatory framework, local government finance powers, and the operation and management of local authorities would also arise. Reform of local government also presents the opportunity to revitalise the relationship between central and local government, and to augment local community involvement in, and support for, local authorities. Cultural changes can be promoted in local government amongst officers and members. Such a programme could also examine whether there are any functions that can be passed from central to local government either directly or by involving local authorities in their management. There may be other functions carried out locally in which local authorities may play a role. The implications of such a programme would be to give effect to the Charter of Local Self Government, and principles of subsidiarity.

As already stated, the common approach has been to introduce general reforms often without a full understanding of their implications. An alternative strategy to change has been attempted – 'pilot studies' such as the centrally directed local studies on compulsory competitive tendering in estate management, and in the operation of the common funding formula for schools. The actual detail of any reform programme ought to be based upon initiative from local government. An experimental programme would provide a role for individual local authorities, enabling them to apply to take part and develop projects, as well as including roles for their associations, the DoE and others, including the public sector trade unions. It would also allow central government to suggest experimental programmes for which local authorities could be selected as part of the same programme. This would be particularly important in encouraging experiment and promoting a positive role for local government.

A major step in developing a new approach to change was made in the joint report of a working party of the DoE and the local authority associations in July 1993.[18] This recommended an experimental project to explore the possibility of changes in committee structures and the role of councillors that would be based on consultation between the DoE and local government. The concept of trust councils developed by the DoE, according to the *Local Government Chronicle*, takes up the experimental form. Its promotion, albeit not officially admitted, suggests that support for such a programme exists within the department in a way that parallels the first stages of development of the experimental programmes in Scandinavia.

Free commune experiments in Scandinavia

The governments of Sweden, Norway, Denmark and Finland made extensive efforts to counter powerful tendencies towards the centre during the 1980s. Each country introduced similar programmes to reform local administration, and established a programme of experiments releasing selected local councils from specific central controls, facilitating local initiatives. The four independent national programmes have in common the aims of encouraging local autonomy, and of implementing a process of deregulation and decentralisation. The programmes also shared the aim of improving methods of service delivery, although from differing perspectives. In Denmark councils were freed from financial controls on co-operation with the private sector, which led to a major programme to promote new technology and technological change in North Jutland, while relaxation of financial controls in Norway meant that local and central government were able to work more closely together through delegation of local investment in economic development. The Swedish scheme allowed councils to experiment with primary health care, as well as in the fields of education and social services. In Finland local councils have been able to undertake extensive reorganisation of services according to local perceptions of need.

Experiences of the 'free commune experiments' have varied widely, and the evaluation process is by no means complete,[19] but there are identifiable indicators of the value of the programmes. Experimental programmes have in many instances led to major change in national legislation, particularly in education. In Norway, the Ministry of Local Government and Labour review demonstrates that local government wants the opportunity for innovation to be continued and the programme has been extended to other state agencies.[20] Negative commentary typifies individual projects as small, without significant repercussions either locally or nationally, and suggests that local authorities have failed to respond in an innovative way, and that decentralisation has been limited. The national picture may be different.

The governmental white paper presented to the Norwegian parliament recognises that the experiments were not in themselves the only relevant outcome of the experimental programme. Rose refers to the parliament's finding that the effect of individual dispensations 'must rather be seen as an integral and necessary part of a larger wave of change'.[21] More specifically, while recognising that many particular projects and exemptions are small, Baldersheim and Stahlberg, having an overview of research on all the experiments, write, 'taken together, the projects and exemptions amount to a major change in central government attitudes towards local government and in local government practices as well. Organisational reforms have been more numerous and more profound than in any earlier period of modern local government.'[22] Many of the difficulties in implementation of the experimental programmes appear to have arisen from factors such as bureaucratic selection and implementation processes, and conflicts between different interest groups. It is significant that the Norwegian programme has recently introduced the opportunity for developing experiments on a more flexible partnership basis.

A programme for Britain

In recent years two possible approaches to an experimental process have been considered in some detail.

A select committee?

Malcolm Grant, in a proposal later adopted by John Stewart, proposed arrangements for an experimental project in Britain.[23] Selected local authorities would seek local disapplication of law, or the conferment of special powers. This would be by formal application, not, as in Scandinavia, to the government, but to a select committee made up of members of the House of Commons and the House of Lords. Projects would be implemented by a simple order-making procedure administered by the select committee. The proposal would involve quite significant changes to the constitution and powers of select committees.

Applications would undergo a vetting procedure to exclude applications affecting individual rights before being considered by the select committee. Relevant government departments would be invited to make representations to the select committee, and the government would be able to make objections or indicate support. Evidence would also be taken from third parties. When a project was approved the committee's resolution to that effect would be implemented by a negative resolution procedure in Parliament. If financial or third party issues were invoked an affirmative resolution procedure would be necessary. It is proposed that local authorities carrying out experimental projects would be directly accountable to the select committee.

The select committee process is attractive because it provides direct local authority involvement with and accountability to Parliament, but it moderates party political influences on the selection of experimental projects. There can be no question that relationships between local and central government are worthy of review and positive revision, although the value of the form of accountability provided by responsibility to a select committee is a questionable form of democracy. In the context of the experience of the free commune programmes in Nordic countries, however, the select committee approach falls down on a number of key points.

Firstly, if applications are lodged directly with Parliament those that require further development, which are outside the framework, or which are already covered by existing powers will all have to be considered by the select committee. This will prejudice all but the most straightforward of applications by delay, and would mean that applications were considered without the opportunity of being perfected by a process of review and negotiation. Secondly, the possibility of partnership between local and central government will be lost; they will be competing in their representations to the select committee, and will not have the opportunity to fine-tune projects in co-operation. Thirdly, further delay, and yet a further hurdle, is introduced by requiring all applications to be considered by the select committee and go before Parliament. Applications will differ in scope and in terms of exemptions sought. Only those raising issues of substantial public interest need be considered by Parliament; decision on other applications can be delegated by the originating legislation. To do otherwise could only intensify central control and ownership of the projects.

Consideration by Parliament of all applications should not be necessary on the grounds of legitimacy, if the framework of the experimental programme originally set by Parliament is clear. Further, the neutralising of government in the process is unrealistic, and risks undermining ministerial and cabinet commitment, shown to be essential to the success of projects in Scandinavia. A requirement that there be party political consensus on each project (rather than simply on the experimental programme as a whole) will risk, as in Sweden, undermining the ability of local authorities to put forward radical or imaginative projects. Grant concedes that under his scheme local authorities may find themselves having a rough ride in Parliament with controversial schemes. The expense and resources demanded by this process would act as an effective deterrent to innovative proposals.

An advisory panel?

The experimental programme suggested in the DoE report[24] of an experiment with the internal management of councils is, in the light of the lessons to be drawn from Scandinavia, not suitable for the wider programme proposed in this paper. The report recommends that applications would be made to a panel of advisors, which would make recommendations to the Secretary of State, and evaluate working projects. The detailed management of an experimental programme of the scale envisaged in this paper would require considerable resources, beyond that of a team whose members had other, extensive, responsibilities. The main concern would be, however, that the panel would cut out the involvement of departmental staff in the negotiation and development of projects, with the attendant values of projects being further refined and developed on the basis of effective partnership.

Implementing an experimental programme in Britain

The Scandinavian programmes demonstrate that:

- Responsibilities on councils are onerous, and resources are needed locally. In the early stages those authorities with resources and a culture of promoting change will respond to the opportunity, others will be drawn in as experience and broader knowledge develops.
- The financial implications of developing and sustaining programmes must be addressed. There are strict controls upon local authority spending in Britain. An experimental programme may mean extending the financial powers of individual local authorities. Consideration is needed on how this can be done without implications between central and local government on financial issues, if this is a requirement.
- There is a need for centrally based resources, including access to advice and information.

- There will be a need for people with ability to carry forward experiment locally and centrally. This will involve addressing the culture of central–local relations at an interpersonal level.
- The process should involve all interested parties at relevant stages of development, in order to ensure support for and development of projects.

Consequently, a number of lessons can be drawn about the operation of an experimental scheme. Firstly, there is a need for a positive approach within a clear framework which lays down guidance on the basis of which applications will be accepted from selected authorities. This should include the principle that projects be approved unless there are significant grounds for not doing so. This would facilitate the management of the programme, and encourage co-operation between central and local interests. Furthermore, the overall terms of the experiment should be clear, and need further research. For example, David Etherington argues, based on his survey of Denmark, that proposals should not adversely affect employment and consumer rights.[25]

Secondly, there is a need for a framework that provides for the effective negotiation and development of projects. This should include a system which allows proposals to be negotiated and developed in a way that encourages effective projects and excludes those that are outside the terms of reference of the programme or are permissible under existing powers. Moreover, it should also include a strategy to enable the exemption process to resolve sectoral interests. This would need to allow for a consultation process but ensure that the process did not obstruct the development of individual projects.

Thirdly, the scheme should encourage the joint ownership of projects. This would require a system for the adoption of projects that would enable both central and local authorities to have a stake in the experiment, encouraging work on a partnership basis.

Fourthly, it should make provisions for a range of means by which projects that have been accepted are implemented. This may involve changes in legislation – by government amendment to legislation originating the experiment, possibly on a negative resolution procedure unless involving exceptional issues. Others may be dealt with by powers delegated to the minister, who will be accountable to Parliament, and required to report on a regular basis.

These four elements would ensure that those issues that involve significant matters of public policy are debated in Parliament, but that other projects proceed without the need to overcome a further hurdle. It would avoid the need for individual local authorities to develop their own byelaws, an approach which would deter authorities without considerable resources at their disposal.

These criteria suggest that an experiment in the UK would be based on a team at the Department of the Environment with an advocacy role for the experimental programme. A system of selection of authorities for the programme would address issues including the representational nature and the capacity of the authorities concerned. Applications could be made to take part in experiments proposed by the government, for local initiatives involving exemption from national legislation or regulation, or for additional powers. A system of experiment with organisational matters could be expected to run as a separate scheme. Applications, based on local consultation processes involving local interests, including the voluntary sector and businesses, and public sector trade unions, would be made by local authorities to the Department of the Environment. The Department would consult other ministries. It would be expected that Trade and Industry, Health, and Education, would in particular have roles in the development of projects. The Treasury would also expect to be consulted in some instances. The Secretary of State at the DoE would make the final decision, putting forward amending legislation where necessary. The project would be based in the local authority, but be carried forward in co-operation with the DoE and any relevant specialist ministry.

There remains the need to provide for effective accountability, regulation, and evaluation of the programme. A strong case can be made that regulation should be based upon existing forms. Where an experiment includes self-regulation, this would be specified in the project and monitored. The minister would be accountable to Parliament for the operation of the experimental programme. Councils would be answerable to the courts, the Department and to local people by a system of reporting and consultation. It would be essential that a British experimental programme be a learning process, and that evaluation be carried out externally in order for it to be independent of the control of any interest group. An authoritative associated body, to promote the benefits of the experimental programme, encourage experiment, and suggest strategies for improving central–local relations, would be invaluable.

Conclusion

It was possible for the Scandinavian authorities to explore change in the role of local government and in their relationship with central government through experimental programmes. The programmes are seen both locally and centrally to have had positive outcomes, have resulted in permanent legislation, and over a period of time led to greater co-operation and understanding between the two sectors of government. There is pressure for greater autonomy and local democracy in local government in Britain. The argument that local authorities have a power of general competence has advanced considerably, general competence being part of a wider case with a number of interrelated elements:

- for the prevailing centralising tendency to be countered by a programme of decentralisation of decision-making, powers, and functions from the centre to regions and local authorities following the example set by other democracies in Europe
- for local decision-making to be extended to involve people in new ways and at the level at which the decision is implemented; that the principle of subsidiarity be studied with the aim of applying it at every level
- for the role of the local authority in the community to be enhanced to enable councils to reflect local needs and create opportunities
- in order to achieve the above, that the capacity of local authorities to act be extended by the implementation of a power of general competence, which would not be simply a wider spending power, and that this development be accompanied by a review of the existing powers and duties of local government
- implicit in these changes is a need for reconsideration and enhancement of the relationships between local, regional, and central government, and other public agencies and for a national role emerging for local government, which would include the involvement of local figures in the development of national policy.

It is clear from the experience of European countries, and the financial background to the Nordic experimental programmes, that financial reform will be necessary to give local authorities the leverage to play an effective and active role and respond to local conditions.

The United Kingdom's involvement in Europe, and pressure to reverse a trend of increasing centralisation that is counter to that in other advanced democracies, mean that a new constitutional settlement is in prospect. A period of experiment in local government, with positive support from the government of the day, set up with a view to identifying areas of permanent change, could be an alternative to, or an enhancement of, a reform programme based upon untested, and possibly overcautious, ideas.

Notes and references

1. Norton, A. (1994) *International Handbook of Local and Regional Government, A Comparative Analysis of Advanced Democracies*, London: Edward Elgar.
2. Hodge, M. and Thompson, W. (1994) *Beyond the Town Hall – Reinventing Local Government*, Fabian Pamphlet 561.
3. The following comparative analysis draws on Norton (1994) *International Handbook*.
4. Stewart, J. and Stoker, G. (1988) *From Local Administration to Community Government*, Fabian Research Series.
5. Clarke, M. and Stewart, J. (1989) *The Future of Local Government: Issues for Discussion*, Luton: Local Government Training Board.
6. Clarke, M. and Stewart, J. (1990) *The Future of Local Government – Some Lessons from Europe*, Luton: Local Government Training Board.
7. Grant, M. (1990) *The Rehabilitation of Local Government: Vires or Virus?*, paper for Annual Conference of Society of Local Authority Chief Executives, 1990; Grant, M. (1992) *The Case for Diversity in Local Government*, conference paper for INLOGOV and Faculty of Law, University of Birmingham, 1992.
8. Blair, P. (1991) 'Trends in Local Autonomy and Democracy: Reflections from a European Perspective', in Batley, R. and Stoker, G. (eds), *Local Government in Europe: Trends and Developments*, London: Macmillan.
9. Batley, R. (1991) 'Comparisons and Lessons', in Batley and Stoker, ibid.
10. Batley, ibid, pp. 226–7.
11. Allen, G. MP (1993) 'Independent Local Government', *European Policy Forum*, November 1993.
12. Bogdanor, V. (1994) *Local Government and the Constitution*, The Society of Local Authority Chief Executives.
13. Hirsch, D. (1994) *A Positive Role for Local Government: Lessons for Britain from Other Countries*, York: Joseph Rowntree Foundation.
14. The Local Government Information Unit published papers in 1990 and 1991. The local authority associations published a statement of

principles in 1991 which included 'a power of general competence to act on behalf of local communities on all matters not specifically excluded or assigned to any other authority, subject to the primacy always of basic civil rights and parliament'.

15. September 1994.
16. The Labour Party (1995) *Renewing Democracy, Rebuilding Communities*, London: Labour Party.
17. Local Government Chronicle, 8 and 15 July 1994.
18. Department of the Environment (1993) *Community Leadership and Representation: Unlocking the Potential* (Report of the working party on the internal management of local authorities in England) London: HMSO.
19. The Norwegian scheme has been most closely assessed and monitored.
20. Lodden, P. (1992) *The Status of Local Government: Recent Experience in Reform, Restructuring and Reorganisation*, Royal Ministry of Local Government & Labour, Oslo, Norway.
21. Rose, L. (1990) 'Nordic Free-Commune Experiments: Increased Local Autonomy or Continued Central Control?', in King, D. and Pierre, J. (eds), *Challenges to Local Government*, London: Sage, p. 197.
22. Baldersheim, S. and Stahlberg, K. (eds) (1994) *Towards the Self-Regulating Municipality: Free Communes and Administrative Modernization in Scandinavia*, Aldershot: Dartmouth, p. 216.
23. Grant (1990) *The Rehabilitation of Local Government*, and (1992) *The Case for Diversity*; Stewart, J. (1991) *An Experiment in Freedom: The Case for Free Local Authorities In Britain*, London: IPPR.
24. Department of the Environment (1993) *Community Leadership*.
25. Etherington, D. (1994) *Innovation in Urban Government: An Evaluation of the Danish Free Local Government Initiative*, paper for ESRC urban policy evaluation seminar at University of Wales, Cardiff, 1994.

12 What Future for Local Democracy?

Lawrence Pratchett and David Wilson

Introduction

The apparent decline in local democratic practices and the concurrent demise of its primary institutional location – local government – have been recurrent themes throughout this book. The preceding chapters have emphasised factors such as a reducing functional and financial base for elected local government; a Whitehall and Westminster culture that derides all things local; a disaffected and passive citizenship who only participate in local affairs as economic actors; a disillusioned and demoralised workforce that is increasingly self-interested; and an emerging structure of local governance that is fragmented and dispersed, and which is becoming progressively more distanced from the traditional mechanisms of local democracy. But at the same time these chapters have held out some hope for local democracy. They offer remedies and prescriptions for the disease to which they bear witness and make recommendations on how both local democracy in general, and local government in particular, can be resuscitated to form a solid foundation for a vibrant UK democracy beyond the year 2000.

This concluding chapter is divided into three main sections. Firstly, it brings together the various themes that run throughout this book which point to a so-called crisis in local democracy and to the importance of renewing and revitalising the democratic foundations of local government. Secondly, it will consider the proposals which have been put forward by the Commission for Local Democracy (CLD) in the context of these themes, and especially in relation to alternative proposals for enhancing local democracy. Thus, it will explore the underlying assumptions of the Commission's proposals, and offer a critique of its model for the 'rebirth of local democracy'. Finally, it discusses the prospects for local democracy and local government in relation to these proposals and considers the scope for change.

Underlying themes and assumptions

There are several recurring themes and assumptions which are
common to a number of the contributions and which underpin
many of the proposals made by the CLD. These provide a frame of
reference from which a critique of the proposals can be developed.
Three of these themes are particularly relevant here.

The dichotomy of democracy in the UK polity

The chapters in this book have been implicitly concerned with a
dichotomy that is prevalent throughout the UK polity, but which is
particularly conspicuous in relation to local government. This
dichotomy is centred upon a disparity between, on the one hand,
a widespread belief in the desirability and value of democracy as a
fundamental principle in all forms and levels of government, and on
the other, an increasing tendency to demean and subvert the
institutions and processes of democracy in practice. It is essentially
a disparity between rhetoric and reality. The rhetoric claims an
immutable and sacrosanct place for democracy in the institutions of
government, but the reality suggests that traditional democratic
structures and practices are no longer considered to be wholly
relevant, and that emerging replacements are less than democratic
in both their organisation and purpose. This implicit dichotomy
warrants more explicit investigation.

A general belief in the value and desirability of democracy at the
local level is difficult to refute. As Phillips points out (see Chapter 2),
justifications for democracy are a mixture of instrumental (or
prudential) reasons, and an acceptance of the dynamic or developmental value of democratic participation in local politics. Democratic processes guard against tyranny and ensure that divergent
interests are represented in local decisions. At the same time a
healthy local democracy also develops a democratic culture amongst
the population, providing both a training ground and a platform for
democratic participation across the polity. But these are justifications for democracy which have become so deeply entrenched within
UK political culture that they are taken for granted and rarely
questioned. Consequently, 'improving democracy' has become a
legitimating term attached to all types of reform, many of which
do little to enhance either the instrumental or developmental
features of local democracy.[1] As Jenkins[2] demonstrates in his

discussion of twelve different policy areas across central and local government, many of the Thatcherite reforms have led inexorably to a centralisation of power in UK politics and a consequent demise in democracy, despite claims by successive Conservative governments to the contrary. The concern here, however, is that despite increasing academic and media disenchantment with changes that appear to undermine democracy, there is still a widespread popular belief in the intrinsic virtues of the democracy that supposedly forms the foundation of UK government.[3] Nobody would deny the desirability or importance of democracy in government, but few currently seem prepared to uphold its principles.

The other side of this dichotomy, that of the reality of declining democratic practice, is not restricted to a central government assault on particular institutions, but is a much more endemic feature of late-twentieth-century political culture. It is not simply that recent governments have sought to circumscribe or debilitate the democratic autonomy of elected local government, although such efforts have been widely noted.[4] It is also that citizens have tacitly accepted such interventions as necessary reforms to the structure and organisation of government. The consistently low turnout at local elections analysed by Rallings *et al.* (see Chapter 4) illustrates this point effectively. They argue that, amongst other reasons, turnout increases where voters are galvanised by particular issues, the unpopularity of the poll tax in 1990 being a particularly strong example. But other reforms which have struck at the very heart of local democracy, especially those associated with the emergence of local quangos, have not had the same provocative effect; voters have remained largely disinterested in such changes. Turnout has certainly not increased dramatically in recent years despite profound and extensive changes to the ways in which local services are organised and local interests are represented. Democracy may be a highly regarded and laudable concept in principle, but for most voters, it appears, it is considerably less important than a low council tax and efficient service provision. Whilst the latter are being achieved, there is little call for improvements in the former. It is difficult not to conclude, therefore, that whilst most citizens would argue in favour of democratic structures and practices, few are prepared to show an active interest in developing, or even maintaining, democratic forms. Democratic participation, for most, appears to involve a fairly simple choice between lower taxation or improved services, or some combination of the two. Concern with the more recondite issues of democracy is extremely limited. This is an argument that has particular resonance with the rational actor models of public choice theory.[5]

The interdependence of local democracy and local government

The chapters in this book have addressed this dichotomy of local democracy by analysing both the desirability of democracy at the local level and by considering ways in which it can be enhanced. The principal belief throughout the book has been that there is a necessary degree of interdependence between local democracy and the traditional institutions of local government. Hence, Greer and Hoggett (Chapter 8) lament the declining influence of local government in relation to local quangos, but conclude that the opportunity exists for local authorities to become the 'conductors' of fragmented and largely unco-ordinated single-purpose bodies in their localities. Similarly, Stoker (Chapter 10) builds upon Phillips's distinction between prudential and developmental justifications for democracy to argue for the extension of local democracy beyond the confines of the traditional structures of local government whilst retaining a central role for those institutions. This is supported by Kitchin's call (Chapter 11) for a power of general competence for local government which would enable it to take proactive measures to become a focus for all local needs and demands. The message from these chapters is that elected local government remains a fundamental component of any local democracy. In an emerging system of local governance the process of rekindling local democracy involves recognising its interdependence with traditional institutions and developing new structures and working arrangements which build upon this interdependence rather than circumvent it.

This, of course, does not deny the relevance of Bulpitt's criticisms of local government as being the haven of professional interests which demonstrate very little democratic practice.[6] Indeed, many of the chapters in this book have pointed to the ways in which the current politics and organisation of local authorities are anything but democratic. Game and Leach (Chapter 7), for example, have shown how the increasing dominance of the major parties in local government has occurred at the same time as widespread disaffection with political participation through these same parties, leading to a form of local democracy that is becoming dependent upon a limited number of ageing activists. The main channels of contemporary political participation at local level are now through issue-specific pressure groups that are rarely associated with one of the major political parties. Hence, the dominance of increasingly un-representative political parties, they conclude, is one of the major problems facing conventional local government. Similarly, Pratchett and Wingfield (Chapter 6) argue that local government employees feel a declining sense of democratic accountability towards their communities, and an increasing sense of dependence and loyalty towards their immediate colleagues and functions. This implies a distancing of service providers from their customers, not only in terms of organisational structure, but also in terms of employee perceptions and attitudes. The consequence is a declining awareness of, and support for, the democratic purposes of local authorities amongst their own staff.

Overall, therefore, the chapters in this book have evaluated local government in a less than favourable light, especially when judged on democratic criteria. In this respect Bulpitt is right to question whether local government is a necessary component of local democracy in late-twentieth-century Britain. But recognising the short-comings of traditional local government is not, on its own, a justification for abolishing it, especially where the alternatives appear even less democratic. Alongside the message that contemporary local government is failing to deliver its full democratic potential, therefore, previous chapters also infer a need for democratic reforms to be based upon the existing institutions of local democracy, rather than the creation of entirely new institutions. The argument is that whilst a 'clean-slate' approach to local democracy may be superficially appealing, it ignores the complex of social, political, economic and cultural histories which are associated with the institutions of local democracy and local government. These histories provide for an intricate set of informal relationships which form the basis of local democracy, and which cannot be easily disentangled from the formal institutional structures of local government. Replacing the existing formal structures without taking account of the informal institutional relationships would only serve to undermine the existing democratic processes without necessarily improving upon them. Consequently, it is necessary to work within existing institutions, both formal and informal, in order to enhance democracy at local level. The various contributors to this book recognise the interdependence of local democracy and local government, and both the opportunities and constraints which this relationship poses. Hence, they seek neither to abolish local government nor to circumvent it. Rather, they look to a reformed and revitalised local government as the focus of a new and more active form of local democracy, building upon the strengths of existing social, political, economic and cultural contexts.

The need for radical reform

Having acknowledged the need to work within existing institutions, a third theme developed in previous chapters has been the need for radical rather than incremental reform. Whilst this book cautions against abandoning existing institutions, it nonetheless recognises the need for fundamental and extensive change if local democracy is to be revitalised. This need for radical reform stems from a recognition that the complex of institutions and relationships under analysis is apparently in crisis. As argued earlier (see Chapter 1), a sense of crisis and impending catastrophe has been a recurrent them in the study of UK local government throughout the twentieth century. In this context it is difficult to see what is new about the current supposed crisis. Most of the failings of local government have existed for several decades, and significant limitations on local democracy and autonomy have long been recognised as being an inevitable feature of the UK's unitary and largely centralised system of government. What is new about the current context, however, is the unique combination of social, economic and political pressures for greater local democracy which are highlighting the limitations of existing democratic mechanisms and emphasising the latent tensions of local governance. It is this which is creating a sense of crisis in local democracy, and to which the Commission for Local Democracy (CLD) is responding.

Consequently, the contributors are not simply arguing that there is a crisis of declining electoral turnout; of diminishing local government powers; of the rise of the 'new magistracy'; of a disaffected workforce; or of a fragmentation of local governance generally. They are suggesting that it is a more systemic problem of which these various issues are symptomatic: one which increasingly questions the very role and purpose of local democracy and local government in contemporary society. In other words, if there is a problem of local democracy it is not just one of an observable set of phenomena which point to the diminution and marginalisation of local government in the emerging national, European and global context of political and economic relations. It is one which asks more fundamental questions about whether there remains a need for local democracy in the modern polity and what its relationship should be with the economic and political institutions that are evolving outside specific localities, at regional, national and international levels.

Any immediate response to such profound questions must necessarily be bold and radical. The various authors in this book have responded by arguing for local democracy, not simply as a means of securing local control and choice over local issues, nor even just as a check against central tyranny, although these remain important features. Rather, they have placed local democracy, and the institutions of local government, as the cornerstone of a vibrant democracy; one which must be protected and enhanced if democracy is to prevail throughout the polity. Underpinning this argument is the assertion that local government is a vital place of learning for a democratic society. The principles and practice of democracy are learnt, developed and reinforced most effectively in the context of local politics, where participation is relatively easy, and the rewards more immediate. Consequently, if local democracy is allowed to wither and die then the prospects for democratic behaviour elsewhere in the polity look bleak. Radical reform is essential to protect this cornerstone of UK democracy. The challenge for reformers is to find ways of enhancing the democratic potential of existing institutions in order to ensure that this fundamental element of political life is firmly embedded. It is to this challenge which the CLD has endeavoured to respond.

The Commission for Local Democracy: a radical response?

The CLD announced its final recommendations in June 1995 after nearly two years of deliberation. The extent to which their findings can be seen as a radical response is very much conditioned by the way in which the apparent problems of local democracy and local government are defined. A narrow definition of the problem would have led the Commission to an equally narrow prescription. Within such a narrow focus its proposals may well have been radical, but their impact limited. The findings and recommendations of the Commission's final report,[7] however, indicate that its definition was broad enough to encompass the systemic problems that pervade the contemporary institutions of local government and thus it makes recommendations that address the more fundamental challenges facing local democracy. The recommendations are, at once, both conservative and radical in their response to the perceived crisis of local democracy and local government. They are conservative in so far as they work within existing institutions to enhance their democratic potential, and to resuscitate those essential features which have become marginalised by the increasing adoption of managerialism and market mechanisms in the public sector. That is, the CLD does not recommend the abolition of any existing institutions, or the creation of any new ones. The recommendations concentrate upon making existing institutions work better. But the proposals are radical in so far as they recommend fundamental changes in the roles and purposes of the current institutions of local democracy: changes which will affect the very nature of the institutions both internally and externally and which could lead to a much stronger and more vibrant democracy in the future. Central to these proposals is the reaffirmation of local government as the heart of local democratic processes, acting as the catalyst for democracy at the local level and the focus for political activity in localities. The CLD's recommendations, therefore, are radical not only because they fly in the face of current trends, which move politics and democracy away from local government, but also because they involve a much more profound and extensive role for the elements of local government in the polity. Acceptance of many of the Commission's proposals would lead to major changes in the roles and relationships of various actors at both the local and national level, including politicians, officers, party groups, citizens, and other public, voluntary and private agencies. Consequently, it is not so much the scope of the specific changes recommended by the CLD that is radical: indeed, many have been proposed previously. Rather, it is the underlying message and nature of the proposals that is most radical.

The Commission made a total of 43 recommendations grouped under five headings,[8] which ranged from rebuilding the existing institutions of local government, through involving citizens and dealing with the 'quangocracy', to adjusting local boundaries and tiers. It is not necessary to list all the recommendations here but it is useful to consider the proposals in relation to three headings: constitutional change, organisational change, and role change. It is in relation to these three headings that the nature of the proposals can be critically analysed, and the implications of the Commission's proposals for the future of local democracy and local government properly assessed.

Constitutional change

The constitutional change recommended by the CLD involves a range of proposals aimed at reforming the status and position of local government in relation to other public, voluntary and private agencies. Thus, the Commission suggests a variety of measures aimed at giving elected local authorities a much greater degree of discretion and autonomy in the management of local affairs. These recommendations include a call for a power of general competence for local government,[9] similar to that argued for by Kitchin (Chapter 11), and the ratification of the European Charter on Local-Self Government,[10] including the enactment of various pieces of legislation which define a clearer role for local government in this context. In addition, the Commission recommends that local authorities should be given the right to represent their local communities on any issue that they feel is appropriate, and to have particular responsibilities for monitoring and campaigning on behalf of their citizens in relation to other public bodies. This would involve a combination of both specific measures aimed at ensuring that local government participates in, and at times intervenes in, the activities of other agencies, and other more general measures that provide for a capacity to act when they so desired. Amongst the specific measures, the CLD emphasises the need to retain, and in some instances return, responsibility for a number of services to local authorities. Thus, they make specific recommendations on such services as education, police, fire services and highways.[11] Furthermore, they make recommendations about which quangos local authorities should be able to appoint representatives to, such as TECs.[12] Amongst the more general measures are calls to endow local government with the rights to 'monitor and comment on the activities of other local government bodies, including public utility companies operating within their locality'. The Commission also recommends a leadership role for local authorities in economic regeneration initiatives and calls for the relaxation of current constraints on capital receipts to enable local authorities to invest in long-term resources for their area, and to examine alternative forms of local taxation to complement such a process.[13]

These more general proposals do not impose new responsibilities upon local authorities or force them into taking particular actions. But in combination with a power of general competence they would provide a new constitutional autonomy for local authorities, giving them the capacity to identify the most pressing needs of their areas, and also the ability to determine and implement appropriate responses to them, without continual reference to the constraints and sanctions of central government. Constitutionally, therefore, local authorities would be operating in a very different climate from the existing one. The dominance of the doctrine of *ultra vires* would be replaced by a more autonomous and democratic constitutional role for local government: one which would not only provide local authorities with more opportunities, but which would also at the same time constrain and limit the capacity for central government intervention in local affairs. The Commission has, in effect, proposed a very different constitutional basis for central–local relations than that which currently exists.

The CLD's proposals not only aim to alter constitutional relationships in favour of the traditional institutions of elected local government, but also to develop the constitutional significance and legitimacy of other bodies at the local level. Consequently, several of their recommendations propose that other agencies may also be subject to periodic elections, rather than the systems of appointment and representation that currently exist. Most notable of these recommendations are that all health authority members, and a majority of members on police authorities, should be directly elected by local communities.[14] The proposals also include scope to review local authority joint body arrangements, to determine whether any of them are large enough to warrant direct election rather than appointment. The key to this element of the Commission's proposals appears to be that some services are of sufficient importance at the local level to justify direct representation of local communities, but are sufficiently differentiated from the existing institutions of local government to justify maintaining an organisational separation between them. Thus, for example, the CLD rejects the Association of Metropolitan Authorities' proposal that local authorities should take on direct responsibility for the purchasing aspects of health care in their localities.[15] The significance of these proposals, if implemented, is that comparable democratic legitimacy will be endowed upon several institutions at the local level. This would not alter the organisational features of local functions but could have significant implications for the relationships between these organisations.

Organisational change

The Commission's recommendations for organisational change focus upon changing the political structures and processes of local authorities. In so far as they would require legislative amendments to the electoral processes of local government, and the roles, responsibilities and remuneration of elected members, they also involve a degree of constitutional change. But their primary aim is to alter the internal organisation and workings of local government in order to enhance its democratic potential, and consequently these proposals are viewed here as being primarily organisational in nature. Two aspects of the Commission's many recommendations for organisational change are worth highlighting:

Firstly, the Commission recommend that there should be a clear electoral and structural division between the leadership or executive of a council, and its general assembly. It proposes that each council should have a directly elected mayor, and a separately elected assembly, and it makes a number of recommendations on the relative responsibilities and relationships of each.[16] This, of course, is not a new proposal for local government, having been briefly considered by Michael Heseltine on his appointment as Secretary of State for the Environment in 1990, and was subsequently the subject of several Department of the Environment papers.[17] It has also attracted academic interest in recent years, particularly in relation to the US mayoral system.[18] The significance of it in this context, however, is that it is proposed by the CLD as an important means of enhancing democracy in local government, by providing a focus of power which would be 'highly visible and thus highly accountable'.[19] The assumption here is that the mayor would be a more conspicuous and active executive of the council who would be associated with specific policies and who would be better placed to provide direct leadership to achieve these policies. Hence, citizens would identify policies as belonging to individual mayors, and would vote for or against these individuals accordingly. But at the same time the Commission also imposes a number of direct and indirect means of limiting the power of such executives, thus reducing the extent to which such accountability can be achieved. Amongst a number of direct checks upon the leadership it is proposed that the council would retain overall responsibility for the budget and policy plans of the authority.[20] These direct checks on executive power would be complemented by several changes to the electoral format of the council, in particular the introduction of proportional representation, with the explicit expectation that it would be much less likely for a single party to have majority control of the assembly. Consequently, the potential excesses of a directly elected mayor would be balanced and moderated by the need for the executive to continuously reach compromises and consensus with a cross-section of political parties. Whilst providing an important element of democratic balance this compromise by the Commission on a 'weak executive' model limits the extent to which a mayoral system could really become the focus of more active local politics.

Secondly, to complement the proposals for a separate executive, the CLD also makes a number of recommendations for electoral reform. These reforms appear to be directed at two separate problems of contemporary local democracy. Some of the reforms are aimed at increasing electoral turnout. These include varying the timing and venue of elections, altering the term of office for members, and exploring means of increasing voting through improved postal ballots and electronic methods.[21] Other reforms are more concerned with improving the representativeness of elected members in proportion to the votes cast. These include increasing the total number of members on each council, extending the potential candidature (for example, by reducing the age at which individuals can stand for election), and the introduction of a single transferable vote system in larger multi-member wards.[22]

These proposed organisational changes imply very different internal working arrangements for local authorities. The creation of a separately elected, and thereby separately accountable, high-profile executive, would not simply involve a change in the roles of elected members in local authorities. It would also require significant changes in the behaviour of senior officers in those authorities, and particularly in the context of officer/member relationships. These are role and relationship changes which are only hinted at in the CLD's report but which would have significant, and as yet uncertain, implications for both the formal and informal workings of local government.

Similarly, the move towards proportional representation implies a much greater likelihood of hung councils. Whilst this may well have the capacity to make the policy process more democratic in some respects (for example, by preventing one group from dominating the policy agenda), the experience of balanced local government in the UK has been mixed, and has engendered its own political and managerial problems.[23] In particular, this experience suggests a form of local government in which there is the opportunity for much greater political activity, but much less likelihood of innovative or radical policy outcomes. Consequently, whilst these organisational changes may offer increased opportunities to enhance the democratic potential of local authorities, they also pose a number of uncertainties and ambiguities for the functioning of local government which have yet to be addressed.

Role change

Implicit in most of the constitutional and organisational changes proposed by the CLD is a more general change in role for both local government and local democracy. It is a change aimed at enhancing the principles of active citizenship and intensifying political activity within localities. From the Commission's perspective, politics is the most manifest representation of a healthy democratic culture and should be encouraged wherever possible. Many of its recommendations, therefore, focus upon the complementary aims of creating 'the habit of citizenship' and of 'managing for democracy'. Amongst a range of proposals to meet these aims, the CLD advocates making citizenship a core component of the national curriculum,[24] requiring all local authorities to produce an annual 'democracy plan' detailing their proposals for decentralisation and citizen involvement,[25] and establishing various consultative mechanisms such as referenda and staff consultation systems.[26] These proposals serve a dual function. Firstly, they aim to create a culture amongst citizens which desires greater political activity, and is more prepared to engage with other individuals and groups in democratic discourse: proposals such as allowing referenda on any issue to be called by a specified number of citizens encourage such a culture. Secondly, they make the promotion of such a culture a major feature of local government. Their proposals would make local authorities become not only the focus of local politics and democracy, but also the champions of it. A fundamental responsibility and function of local government would be the advancement of democratic practices throughout the community, not only through internal organisation and structure, but also through external promotion and consultation. This will demand

a delicate balance between the need for local authorities to demonstrate stable and consistent policies, and a growing demand for them
to become more responsive to an active citizenship.

In many respects the Commission's proposals for role change are
its most revolutionary. At a superficial level they have great popular
appeal without appearing to lead to any radical changes in the day-
to-day activities of local government or the practice of local
democracy. Beneath the surface, however, their implications are
profound because they aim to influence and change the underlying
attitudes and culture of citizens, to encourage them to become more
politically aware and active, and to make government more responsive. If achieved, this change in political culture has implications not
only for local government, but also for all other public, voluntary
and private organisations. The development of a more democratic
and politically active citizenry implies a fundamental change in the
relationship between the state and its citizens. A role change for
local government in this context has implications that extend far
beyond the institutions which the CLD focused upon.

The prospects for local democracy and local government

The recommendations of the CLD outlined above suggest a very
different set of constitutional and organisational relations for local
democracy and local government, which define profoundly different
roles for both citizens and governments. It is a role for local
government which extends beyond conventional norms of local
authority influence. Indeed, it is a role which extends even beyond
the current themes of local governance and the enabling authority,
by making local authorities the very heart of a reinvigorated
democracy in the UK. Thus, despite being primarily concerned with
reforming existing institutions, the Commission's recommendations
are essentially radical in their impact. The revolutionary nature of
these proposals raises questions about the extent to which the
changes are either desirable or likely in the foreseeable future. These
can be explored by examining both the internal limitations of the
CLD's proposals and the external constraints on their acceptance.

The Commission's proposals attempt to define a comprehensive
and coherent vision for local democracy and local government into
the next century. Although this is a compelling and cogent vision,
various elements of it have attracted criticism from a variety of

sources. To a certain extent this criticism is a measure of the Commission's success: it reflects the fact that the assumptions and interests of these various groups have been challenged sufficiently to provoke a response. This section, however, is less concerned with the criticisms that emerge from challenging these vested interests than it is with the more deep-rooted problems which the proposals may imply for local democracy. At least two criticisms can be levelled at CLD's proposals.

Firstly, there is the issue of the fragmentation of democratic legitimacy which the Commission's recommendations imply. Whilst the CLD concentrates especially upon strengthening the role of local government in a modern democracy, several recommendations also acknowledge a role for alternative democratic procedures in other organisations. In particular, separate direct elections are proposed for health and police authorities. This acknowledgement of the importance of democratic structures in a range of important single-purpose bodies at the local level would undoubtedly serve the Commission's dual purpose of enhancing political interest in these bodies, and making them more responsive to democratic pressures. But, at the same time, these proposals pose something of a dilemma for a reform of local democracy which is so clearly based around the traditional, multi-purpose institution of local government. The creation of separate elections for a number of local bodies would disperse democratic legitimacy across several bodies thereby enabling each organisation to claim a legitimate electoral mandate for pursuing its own policies. Such a fragmentation of democratic legitimacy heralds a number of potential problems. Different organisations may wish to pursue different, even competing, objectives. Where the activities of these organisations overlap (for example, health and local authorities in relation to community care), this may cause significant tensions in the democratic process, especially if the different organisations are controlled by different party groups. These problems would be further compounded where the boundaries of different organisations are not coterminous.

At this point it is important to acknowledge that these separate bodies already exist, and that the CLD's proposals simply seek to make them more democratic. Separate elections to a variety of single and multi-function local bodies is common in other democracies, such as the United States.[27] The point here, however, is that in the current context of the organisational and political culture of UK local governance, a fragmentation of democratic legitimacy could further complicate and confound inter-organisational relations, rather than enhance democratic control of them. This also appears to contradict the Commission's call for a general power of community leadership which encourages local authorities to monitor other local agencies, and to represent the interests of the community on any issue they see fit. Direct elections to these other bodies would lay down strong principles of demarcation between agencies and could severely limit the ability of local authorities to influence the policies of these bodies. Furthermore, once the principle of direct elections to other bodies is established, the professional and functional differentiation of other local government services could easily justify their separation from the existing structure. There is already concern that this is happening with functions such as education and housing. The danger is that this fragmentation could lead to a proliferation of democratic legitimacy at the local level and a dispersal of political power away from local authorities. Far from developing local authorities as the heart of an active local democracy, therefore, this fragmentation could lead to their gradual marginalisation and an increasingly complex and confused set of democratic processes.

A second criticism of the Commission's proposals is that they focus too much on reforming local democracy through local institutions and underplay the role which broader political, economic and social factors have in influencing democratic development. Consequently, the proposals concentrate upon the ways in which specific institutional and organisational reforms can be enacted in order to enhance local institutions. In as far as they go, these proposals have collective appeal. But the content of the proposals is limited because they make very little reference to the parallel changes that will be necessary in other, more national institutions. For example, the Commission calls for a new financial settlement between central and local government,[28] and makes several recommendations concerning the need for continued central government involvement in the equalising of resources, and the removal of hypothecated grant. But whilst it spells out the implications of these reforms for a more autonomous form of *local* government, it largely ignores the parallel consequences for *central* government. To an extent this focus upon local rather than national reforms by the Commission can be justified. After all, a concentration on national issues and changes would have deflected attention away from the importance of localised reforms. The difficulty now facing the CLD's proposals, however, is that local reform without corresponding change in the broader institutions of the state may lead to a number of unexpected outcomes. Thus, there is the possibility that local reform may provide the catalyst for analogous reform in these other institutions. It is equally possible, however, that broader regional and national institutions will provide a powerful source of inertia which will distort and subvert the recommendations of the Commission, and act against the long-term success of democratic reform at the local level. The main thrust of this criticism, therefore, is that the CLD places too much onus upon local authorities to be the proponents of democracy without taking into account the potential for other institutions to frustrate, distort or impede democratic reform. In the long run this may militate against the development of the form of pluralist local democracy advocated by the Commission.

Whilst the recommendations of the CLD provide a comprehensive view of a future for local democracy, these criticisms introduce some important caveats into the generally optimistic tenor of the Commission's final report. The fragmentation of democratic legitimacy could undermine the central thrust of the Commission's reforms by reducing the ability of local authorities to act as community leaders. Even if this vision was entirely coherent and internally consistent, however, the other criticism suggests that there are a number of internal and external factors that will inhibit and constrain their acceptance. As Sir John Banham stated at the launch of the Commission's final report, success is dependent upon overcoming:

> the combination of arrogance, incompetence and inertia that awaits all would-be reformers of our present ways of governing ourselves at the hands of Whitehall and Westminster.[29]

These are problems which are every bit as pressing as the reform of the formal institutions of local democracy.

Conclusion

A major dilemma facing all would-be reformers of government institutions is whether, on the one hand, to seek consensus on reform by making modest proposals that will be easily acceptable to all, or on the other, to make adventurous proposals that will challenge the status quo and bring about more radical change. The problem of adopting a consensual approach to reform, of course, is that whilst proposals may receive widespread support, their content is likely to be so modest and innocuous as to have only a very limited impact upon the institutions that they are attempting to reform. The problem of adopting a more adventurous approach, however, is that proposals are more likely to meet with widespread criticism and opposition, and hence, stand less chance of being accepted and implemented. The CLD have responded to this dilemma by making a set of proposals that appear modest in their content, but which are radical in their impact. Thus, the Commission does not recommend the wholesale dismantling of existing institutions, nor does it seek to establish new ones. Rather, the radical nature of the Commission's proposals lie in its attempts to breath new political and democratic life into the existing institutions of local government. The proposals, therefore, strike a balance within the dilemma by being, at once, both pragmatic about the scope for possible reform, and radical in their ambitions to rekindle local democracy.

The recommendations of the CLD offer a robust future for local democracy. It is a future which differs radically from contemporary constitutional and organisational arrangements for local democracy and one which implies a fundamentally different role for actors and agencies at both local and national level. Most significantly, the Commission's recommendations imply a future for local government which is at the heart of all local politics. Regardless of their functional focus, local authorities would be empowered to become the focus of political activity on all local issues and to champion the cause of democracy as the seed-bed of a more vibrant democratic culture. The basic assertion is that a strong local democracy is the cornerstone of wider democratic processes and that only by reinvigorating the institutions of local democracy and local government can the long-term interests of democracy be protected. This assertion lies at the very foundation of all arguments for local democracy: it is both the justification for desiring a more active local democracy, and an explanation for the types of mechanisms and processes that are essential to such a democracy. The CLD's proposals are not simply concerned with making local decisions more representative of local demands. They are equally concerned with extending politics beyond the confines of the traditional organisations of local government and developing a more democratic culture amongst citizens. Consequently, the Commission offers a future which addresses the dichotomy of democracy by closing the gap between rhetoric and reality. It is not simply a case of making decisions appear more democratic but also of enhancing the underlying ethos of democracy to encourage much wider participation in politics.

The CLD should be seen, therefore, not simply as a radical response to an apparent crisis in local democracy, but also as a significant contributor to the broader debate about the need for local democracy in the UK polity in the light of more deep-rooted and systemic problems in its traditional institutions. It adopts a radical and positive stance in relation to local democracy, arguing for a more dynamic role for the institutions of local government in engendering and championing democratic structures and practices, and the development of democratic institutions which encourage a more active citizenry. The CLD has put forward the case for local democracy, and shown how it could be developed for the next century. Their final report provides an exciting agenda for change.

But achieving the 'rebirth of local democracy' will not be easy. There are a number of powerful vested interests both within and outside of local government who may aspire to the rhetoric of democracy but will not support a diminution of their own role or influence. These interests provide a powerful inertia against any reforms which will reinvigorate local democracy generally, and especially against those which will encourage the devolution of power away from the traditional institutions in which they have status or influence. By working within the existing institutions of local democracy the CLD does enable some of this inertia to be overcome, at least in the short term. But whether the proposals will be able to overcome the longer-term institutional inertia is more questionable. Alongside proposals for the reform and revitalisation of local democracy, therefore, it is also necessary to recognise the likely limitations of such reform.

Resuscitating local democracy is one of the more fundamental challenges facing the UK polity as it reaches the end of the century. The CLD has presented one way of meeting this challenge that offers a radical set of reforms without abolishing those practices and processes which work. The long-term success of the Commission will be judged not by the number of its proposals which are accepted or rejected, but by the extent to which it has managed to engender both a debate on local democracy, and a sustainable development of the underlying democratic culture of the nation. The challenge to both government and citizens is to respond to this vision, either by accepting and modifying these recommendations, or by offering alternatives. The onus is now upon all those who are concerned with local democracy to give the debate the attention it deserves and to ensure that it is not left to quietly fade away.

Notes and references

1. For example, the introduction of the Community Charge, compulsory competition in service provision, the local management of schools, and performance league tables, have all been claimed by their advocates to be enhancing local choice, and therefore, local democracy.
2. Jenkins, S. (1995) *Accountable to None: The Tory Nationalization of Britain*, London: Hamish Hamilton.
2. Cf Held, D. (ed.) (1992) *Prospects for Democracy*, Cambridge: Polity Press; Zolo, D. (1992) *Democracy and Complexity*, Cambridge: Polity Press; Hutton, W. (1995) *The State We're In*, London: Jonathon Cape; Jenkins (1995) *Accountable to None*.
4. See, for example, Loughlin (Chapter 3) and Stewart (Chapter 9) in this book.
5. See, for example, Dunleavy, P. (1991) *Democracy, Bureaucracy and Public Choice*, Hemel Hempstead: Harvester-Wheatsheaf; Dowding, K. (1991) *Rational Choice and Political Power*, Aldershot: Edward Elgar.
6. Bulpitt, J. (1993) Review in *Public Administration*, vol. 71, no. 4, pp. 621–3. See also Chapter 1 of this book.
7. Commission for Local Democracy (1995) *Taking Charge: The Rebirth of Local Democracy*, London: Municipal Journal Books.
8. See Appendix for a full summary of the Commission's proposals.
9. CLD, *Taking Charge*, para. 6.5.
10. CLD, ibid, para. 6.4.
11. CLD, ibid, paras 6.13–6.15.
12. CLD, ibid, para. 7.12.
13. CLD, ibid, paras 6.29 and 6.28 respectively.
14. CLD, ibid, paras 7.7 and 7.8.
15. CLD, ibid, para. 7.6. See also, Association of Metropolitan Authorities (1994) *The Future Role of Local Authorities in the Provision of Health Care: A Discussion Document*, London: AMA.
16. CLD, *Taking Charge*, paras 4.3, 4.6 and 4.12 *inter alia*.
17. See HMSO (1991) *The Internal Management of Local Authorities in England* and HMSO (1993) *Community Leadership and Representation: Unlocking the Potential*.
18. See, for example, Stoker, G. and Wolman, H. (1991) *A Different Way of Doing Business – the Example of the US Mayor*, Luton: Local Government Management Board.
19. CLD, *Taking Charge*, para. 4.15.
20. CLD, ibid, para. 4.9.

21. CLD, ibid, paras 4.7, and 5.17–5.21.
22. CLD, ibid, para. 5.7.
23. See, for example, Leach, S. and Stewart, J. (1992) *The Politics of Hung Authorities*, London: Macmillan; Leach, S. and Pratchett, L. (1996) *The Management of Balanced Authorities*, Luton: Local Government Management Board.
24. CLD, *Taking Charge*, para. 5.44.
25. CLD, ibid, paras 5.30 and 5.33.
26. CLD, ibid, para. 5.41.
27. See, for example, Stoker and Wolman (1991) *A Different Way of Doing Business*.
28. CLD, *Taking Charge*, paras 6.22 and 6.23.
29. Speech by Sir John Banham in response to the Final Report of the Commission for Local Democracy, London, 21 June 1995.

Appendix
Summary of CLD
Recommendations

Building afresh

1 Local authorities should consist of a directly elected Council and a directly elected Leader/Mayor. Both Council and Leader/Mayor should be voted in for a term of three years but the elected Leader may only serve two full terms in office.
2 The Council would be elected on a multi-member ward basis.
3 The specific powers of the Council would be to approve or reject the Executive budget and other proposals; to call referenda; to approve or reject an annual policy plan for the Authority; to approve or reject the annual Democracy Plan for the Authority; to propose individual policies to the Leader/Mayor, scrutinise the Executive and also the work of other local government organisations in its area.
4 The Council would have more members than is currently the case in English and Welsh local authorities.
5 The principal tasks of the Leader/Mayor would thus be to prepare and submit a budget to the Council; to propose an annual policy review to the Council; to respond to Council scrutiny of the Executive; to produce an annual Democracy Plan including decentralisation to parishes, community councils or geographic areas; to employ and oversee the officers and Executive in implementing policies agreed with the Council; to exercise the functions of the local authority; to act as the representative head of the authority in all external events and lobbying.
6 Councillors should be required to declare any pecuniary interest in all discussion of local authority business in their party group meetings.

Involving the citizen

1 Local elections for Councils should be conducted on a system of proportional representation using the single transferable vote in multi-member wards. The elected Leader/Mayor should be chosen by a ballot of all of the citizens in a council area using an alternative vote system.
2 There should be experiments to see if voter turnout could be improved by changing the polling day; bringing the hours of polling for local elections into line with those for general elections; extending the range of venues where polling may take place.

3 Universal postal balloting should be introduced in local elections.
4 Local authorities should be required to finance a full personal canvass for the electoral register every year and should then maintain a rolling register.
5 Research on systems of electronic voting and counting should be undertaken urgently to produce a comprehensive system available to implement the electoral recommendations of the Commission.
6 The age of candidature for election to a local authority should be lowered to 18.
7 Local authorities should be under a duty to prepare local schemes for the remuneration and support of Councillors to enable them to carry out their functions effectively and without unreasonable financial penalty. There should be no national regulation of such schemes.
8 The rules restricting political activity of employees should be relaxed for all except senior officials.
9 Both the Leader/Mayor and the Council should have powers to conduct a referendum of citizen opinion at any time, such referendum to be advisory and a specified number of citizens should be able to call for a referendum on any matter pertaining to the local authority. Questions to be put to the full electorate may also be inserted onto the ballot paper with a limit on the number allowable.
10 Local authorities should be under a duty to produce an annual Democracy Plan for decentralisation and citizen involvement.
11 Local authorities should develop more effective methods of consulting staff in the course of policy formation. The right of staff to complain about organisational failures should be clear.
12 We consider that the recommendations of the Report of the Speaker's Commission on Citizenship (1990) are of particular help in educating young people in the duties of citizenship and propose that citizenship should become part of the core curriculum.

A new autonomy

1 The government should adopt and ratify the European Charter of Local Self-Government and enact the appropriate declaratory provisions in UK legislation to define the role and status of local government in UK law.
2 Local authorities should have a power of general competence to undertake any activities they consider to be in the interests of their area unless specifically prohibited by law.
3 The recent reduction of function and independence of local authorities must be reversed.
4 Local authorities should resume responsibility for planning and funding the local education service, including 16–19 education, the placing of grant-maintained schools in the local system and their funding; and direct the organisation of the careers service and local inspection of schools.

5 The Fire Service should remain under local authority control and we believe the current police authority reforms should be reversed. The Police Service should be locally accountable (but centrally inspected) with its budget a local responsibility.

6 Highway agencies should be restored to local authorities by the Department of Transport and local authorities should retain control of transport and waste disposal undertakings.

7 Local authorities should be given a clear community leadership role with rights to have access to information on, to monitor and to comment on other local government bodies and public agencies operating locally, and with a right to represent the interests of the local community in any manner they think appropriate.

8 There should be a new settlement establishing the financial relationship between central government and local authorities.

9 Government grant should not be hypothecated in any way. It should be used to equalise needs and resources.

10 The dependence of local authorities on central government grant should be reduced, the right to set the 'business-rate' should be restored to local authorities.

11 The 'capping' of local authority expenditure should be ended but not controls on their borrowing.

12 Local authorities should be able to examine other forms of local taxation.

13 Restrictions on the use of capital receipts and land transactions should be related to allow authorities freedom to invest their own resources in assets for the long-term benefit of their area.

The quangocracy

1 All health authority members should be directly elected locally, and their executive directors should not be members of the health authority.

2 Members of police authorities, currently appointed by local councils, should be replaced by directly elected representatives who should be in a majority on each police authority.

3 Local authorities should have the right to appoint representatives to TECs but not in a majority.

4 Local authority joint bodies should be reviewed as a duty by the constituent local authorities to identify those which operate on a scale and an area to justify direct election to them, rather than appointment.

5 Local authorities should make explicit the way in which they make appointments to bodies to which they are entitled to do so.

6 The appointment process (for appointed public bodies) should be explicit; there should be an explicit rule as to probity of conduct; there should be open meetings, and access to information; there should be a public audit process.

Boundaries and tiers

1 A specified number of electors should be able to petition their local authority requiring them to conduct consultation on specific proposals to give that area separate representation.

2 The formal electoral process should be made available for these subordinate elections, to reinforce their legitimacy and secure their probity.

3 Legal restrictions on the development within local authorities of decentralised structures should be removed.

4. The law should be changed to permit the 'parishing' of the metropolitan and London borough council areas.

5. Regional assemblies would be made up of the elected leaders of local authorities in the area.

6. London should have a directly elected Mayor who would chair a council of Mayors from the London boroughs.

Index